SINGLE FILE

SINGLE FILE

HOW TO LIVE HAPPILY FOREVER AFTER WITH OR WITHOUT PRINCE CHARMING

SUSAN DEITZ
with Anne Cassidy

A
Joan
Kahn
BOOK

ST. MARTIN'S PRESS/NEW YORK

Design by Richard Oriolo

Library of Congress Cataloging-in-Publication Data

Deitz, Susan.
    Single file.

    "A Joan Kahn book."
    1. Single women—United States—Life skills guides.
I. Cassidy, Anne. II. Title.
HQ800.2.D45 1989   305.4'890652   88-36236
ISBN 0-312-02981-0

First Edition
10 9 8 7 6 5 4 3 2 1

DEDICATION

To Morris,
for recognizing and nurturing my potential so lovingly.

To Scott,
for his faith and his spirituality and his lovingness.

To my Mother and my Brother,
for being solidly there with love.

To Merryl, Linda, and Sandy,
for sharing their father.

To Manny, Irving, Dick, and Helen,
whose souls are part of this book.

To Ivor,
my Michelangelo.

CONTENTS

INTRODUCTION

The book you hold in your hands is not the usual paragraph after paragraph of unrelenting data about single women; it contains not one case history—that's a promise. Instead, it is full of practical exercises—not toe-touches and sit-ups, but mind-expanders and soul-strengtheners.

Wherever you are reading this—in a bookstore, at a friend's house, or in the privacy of your bedroom—chances are that you are also in a waiting room, in limbo, waiting for your "real" life to begin. If you think anything like many of the 37 million women in this country who are not currently married, you have decided to put most of the important decisions of your life on ice until you are a married woman. Or at least until The Man comes along. Either scenario keeps you in the waiting room. It's not all bad sitting there, though, patiently biding your time and spinning out your fantasies; the surroundings feel familiar, you don't stress out solving your problems, and everyone who knows you is accustomed to seeing you as a lady-in-waiting.

But you're beginning to get a vague uneasiness in the pit of your stomach, a half-sense that you've also shelved some excitement and fun in your rush to the status quo. You don't get out much these days; your routine is wearing a rut between home and the office, broken only by a few ho-hum men thrown in once and a while, dates whose anticipation only ends in disappointment. You can even see a trace of bitterness creeping into those laugh lines around your mouth. The lack of good men is not at all humorous. In fact, you're discovering there's very little to laugh about.

I put it to you that the real downer you're experiencing is not directly linked to the man shortage, but is at bottom a dissatisfaction with yourself. You're not getting from life what you feel you deserve, and there is a germ of an idea that it could be because you're not putting in enough. Because you're in a half-dream existence of waiting. Still, that wisp of insight comes and goes; when it leaves, its replacement is fear. If you build a stimulating life now, while you are single, will you become unfit for love and marriage? Will men be scared off by your independence? Will you become a stranger to yourself?

You're not meeting anyone who even makes you think about love, so these are moot questions right now. But you're also not doing all you can with the time and space that being unpartnered gives you. And more and more that's beginning to bother you.

If you are identifying with what I'm saying, great! *Single File* will not only prove to you that you have the stamina to build a life for yourself, but it will put you on the path toward that end.

Although there's plenty of room for your personal style and tastes (after all, this book is about individuality), each project (we call them exercises) is laid out as an easily followed progression. Whether it is a financial plan, the Old Girls' Network, or a friendlier view of men, the product of each exercise becomes another satellite in your personal cosmos.

Stop and think how it could be to live out your potential; whatever you imagine today is possible in the future. By making your dreams into goals, they become attainable, and this book provides the practical step-by-step alchemy to achieve that magic.

As your self-development grows, you'll feel more eager to get out of bed in the morning because life will be more fun. If that kind of singleness appeals to you, you're in for an adventure. Taking part in this book's exercises—and the independent spirit behind them—will without doubt expand the possibilities you attract and prove that when individuals develop and exercise their personal power, they put most of life's options on their side. Best of all, as you find your own center, the core of your being, you will discover an inner peace that makes room for spirituality. There's a lot of that, too, in these pages, food for the soul. Life's options mean very little without that inner nourishment.

I learned that the hard way. Widowhood was forced on me when my husband of eight years suddenly died. He left our son Scott, age four, and an underdeveloped wife who had been overprotected all her life. For three years, I coped with a semblance of a routine, treading water from day to day, my view of the future fuzzy at best. As a young widow and single mother (although the term hadn't been coined in the late 1960s), getting by was all I could expect.

The few dates that well-meaning friends passed along were a total waste of time and energy. My son and I were living two against the world, but I resisted the urge to tumble into a ho-hum marriage—even though Scott needed a father and our bank account needed a transfusion. Some instinct somewhere told me I needed time.

It took a chance remark from a friend to crystallize that intuition. When I asked my friend Adele the secret of her own strong fifteen-year marriage, her answer was swift and certain: "I don't allow myself to become dependent on my husband," she said. "Whenever I find myself starting to cling—and that happens more than I care to admit—I take myself out to dinner or to a movie. Alone. I do my *single-person exercise* and feel a lot better for it."

Her words made me realize that independence was not a gift from heaven or a genetic blessing, but a hard-won skill, one I could acquire by flexing my own "singleness muscles." All of a sudden I knew that, partnered or not, it was possible for me to control my life. Since that time, I have seen that strengthening each "muscle" of my self-reliance builds a totality. Step by step, the strengths combine to form an independent woman. And as that process is taking place, mindset shifts and attitudes do, too, adding up to a sum that is larger than any of its parts. Independence is more than an attitude or an action—it is a way of *being*.

As I began to build on that insight in my life, finally getting a handle on setting priorities and on the preciousness of time, I discovered that my friends were asking me how I managed to keep my life together. And I felt a growing sense that I might have found solutions others could use. In those days, before the single world swelled to its current 77 million (43 percent of the population!), its lifestyle was virtually without guidelines. (Singleness had never been taken seriously, but was regarded as a way of life strictly for oddballs and losers.)

From the idea of helping other widows grew an advice column for the unmarried. Developing the column took over four years, and there were moments when I was discouraged enough to consider giving up my dream. But my son was a live-in guru (at age ten!) and a believer. I can still hear his "Keep on trucking, Mom." That column, also titled "Single File," is now in its fourteenth year of national syndication and reaches over 10 million readers, a readership that is extremely thoughtful, decent, loyal. And the more I give to the single community, the more I learn. Students in my classes at the New School in New York City (where I was part-time professor) taught me as much as the listeners to the radio show I conceived, developed, and hosted on station WMCA in New York. One group was in the classroom, soaking up my curriculum on "The Art of Living Single"; the other connected with me through the soundwaves. I can honestly say that when I speak publicly, appear on a panel, or give an interview for TV or radio, the feedback is more valuable to me than my presentation. I already know what I know; I want to know what you are thinking. My probing has taken different forms: In the early 1980s I conducted a survey on single sexuality. The project utilized 6,000 questionnaires and covered thirty-eight states. The findings affirmed many of my hunches, but I learned a lot, too. (More survey facts in Chapter Eight.)

While the column continues to thrive, I have also become the single-living expert in a computer-oriented home-shopping service offered jointly by Sears and IBM. Twice weekly I receive electronic mail from subscribers around the country, asking my opinion on the issues of their singleness. Each person receives my personal response within three days. So, you see, I have my adventures, too—although being with you right now is my mountaintop.

This is not my first book. In 1971, I worked with the founder of Revlon, Charles Revson, and from the experience of being an unmarried woman in the glitzy world of cosmetics came *Valency Girl* (coauthored with Robin Moore, Ballantine Books, 1976). But this book is a different breed. Here I've given my all, and the result is a synthesis of my obsession with single living.

I know the exercises in this book work, because I've lived them. My experiences brought me from confusion and passivity to the security of knowing that I can make my dreams a reality, whittling down the negatives and building on the positives of single living. I have lived my message so I can bring it to you with total conviction: *You* alone can make your life the way *you* want it to be.

You need to know that, as you create your own niche in these postfeminist and post-sexual-revolution times. Moreover, you need to know specific ways to build your life to *your* advantage. And *this* is the time to do it, now while your singleness makes you more mobile and less accountable, with full mastery over your resources. That is the opportunity inherent in being single. And it's the reason for *Single File*.

Like any exercise book, this one works best when you don't just read it but actually do the exercises. Take notes in the margin, turn down page corners, and tuck in slips of paper scribbled with ideas, the fruit of middle-of-the-night brainstorms. Don't feel compelled to do every exercise; start with the ones that attract you and set aside the ones that don't sit right or feel inappropriate. (You may feel ready for them weeks after finishing the last chapter, so keep the book handy.) Above all, know that by the last chapter you will be on friendly terms with your singleness, secured by a safety net of resources and insights that brings peace of mind ... today and all the days of your life, single or married.

To get started, dive into the following exercises and see how good it feels to concentrate on yourself in a positive way. Complete this statement as you choose. Part of it may appear simplistic at first, but my hunch is that you'll spend more time on it than on many of the others. You will probably rewrite it more than once. Better use a pencil.

I am single because (fill in) _____

_____

_____.

Another way to inventory your feelings about being single is these simple agree/disagree statements. Check the appropriate column.

	AGREE	DISAGREE
Being single means being alone and lonely.		
Single women have a tougher time than single men.		
Men don't want the same things from a relationship as women do.		
All women should marry and have children.		

	AGREE	DISAGREE
A woman is incomplete without a man.		✓
Being single means being second-class in society.	✓	
An interesting, full single life leads to lifelong singleness.		✓
Men do not like independent women.		
Independence means selfishness.		
Independence means isolation.		
Independence means loss of femininity.		
My family is embarrassed that I am single.	✓	
I am a half-member of my family because I am single.		✓
I am a half-member of my community because I am single.		✓
I am a half-member of my church because I am single.		
I am a half-member of the world because I am single.		
Self-reliance keeps people (men) away.		
Being financially secure keeps people (men) away.		
People are either born independent or not; nothing can be done about it.		

	AGREE	DISAGREE
Going places alone is the last resort —it makes me look (and feel) like a reject.		
Everyone desirable is married.		
Marriage and children are the ultimate fulfillment for every woman.		
Being single is not normal.		
Being married is better than being single.		
Being older means being undesirable, rigid, out of touch, rejected, powerless.		
Being single is an interim condition that should be ended as quickly as possible.		
The object of the single life is to find a man and get married.		
True happiness is to be found only in marriage.		
Any man is better than no man.		
I don't have to save money; a man will give me financial security.		
I'm only working until I marry; I don't take my job seriously.		
Men want only young, unwrinkled, carefree companions.		
Women should wait for a man to make the first move—in everything.		
Women who are assertive and strong turn men off.		

	AGREE	DISAGREE

Women and men cannot be friends;
they're too dissimilar.

Love should start with fireworks;
otherwise, it cannot develop.

Friendship between the sexes is
boring and the opposite of real love.

Now, pause for a moment. Respond to the following questions with the first answer that comes to mind. (First thought, best thought.) Write your answers on a separate sheet of paper. You'll enjoy going back and looking at these early answers later on, when you're well into the rest of the book.

FREE-ASSOCIATION STATEMENTS

1. *When I tell people I am single, I feel—*
2. *When I tell people I am single, they must think—*
3. *I like being single (better/worse) now than I did a year ago because—*
4. *Single women have more fun because—*
   Single women have less fun because—
5. *The most important reason to get married is—*
6. *If I knew for sure that I would live the rest of my life single, I would—*

(Answer if you have no children):

I would/would not consider becoming an unmarried mother because—

(Complete the next two only if you have children):

*The best part about being a single parent is—
*The worst part about being a single parent is—

If I could change one aspect of my life, it would be—

The one thing I've most wanted to do but don't because I am single is—

When my single friends and I get together, we talk about—

My friends are mostly single/married/a good mix of both because—

If I could describe being single in one word, it would be—

After a short break, look again at your responses. Try to see them as a unit; notice how well they mesh with what is actually happening in your life. That is no accident. The truth is, beliefs shape expectations; chances are, what you expect is what you will get. But ideas can be changed; they *are* open to influence. And just by doing these two simple exercises, you have lifted yourself out of stale thinking patterns and considered another way of looking at the issues in your life. By opening your mind just for a short time, you have started an adventure that will change the way you feel about yourself (and your life) forever. That's another promise, from me to you.

Where your personal changes take you is your choice. Just remember that your courage and persistence will be central to making this book work. My words may make an impression, but it is your actions that will bring them to life. *You* will animate every page. And to help, you have a friend here, every step of the way.

ONE

ALCHEMY:
FROM PARTIAL TO
PRIMARY

This is it. You've been thinking about changing for a while now, wondering how it would feel to live for yourself, and not have to wait for The Man Who Isn't There. I know from my column, "Single File," that you are one of the 37 million single women feeling restless and vaguely disappointed. As a group, you walk many different paths: You are divorced, widowed, or never-married; young, middle-aged, or old; well off, comfortable, or just getting by. You live alone or with a roommate; with your parents or your children. You are a high-school graduate or a Ph.D.; a secretary, attorney, or firefighter; a teacher, chemist, or salesclerk. The city you live in may be big or small. But with all your differences you have one thing in common: You want a man in your life; you don't think you can be happy without one. Life is a one-man show—but the right one hasn't shown up yet.

You probably *have* the trappings of independence—

friends, job, apartment—but the parts don't add up to a whole person. Because you can't shake the notion that it takes a man (husband, boyfriend, date) to make life hum; singleness feels cramped, stunted, second-rate. You're a free agent—and yet you're feeling anything but free.

Sometimes, in late-night talks with yourself, there have been flashes of insight. The cool clarity of nocturnal vision brings the realization that all this waiting around might not make sense. You suddenly intuit that you may not marry—again or ever—and even if you do eventually, given the state of your current love life, you are likely to be single a lot longer than you planned back in high school.

But the revelation weakens, you fall back asleep, and in the morning you slip right back into the old thoughts that are such comfortable friends. The familiarity of Life-as-Usual feels reassuring, so you tell yourself that the right man has to be out there somewhere—it's a matter of time, so you'll just wait and keep the rest of life on hold.

Until today. The same inner voice that intrudes into the night's stillness has brought you to this book and its astonishing premise that singleness, far from being a phase to be endured and eliminated, can trigger the sort of personal development that will enrich every succeeding phase of life—whatever your marital status. The total control you have over your life because of your husbandless state can bring you the kind of single life you believe is reserved for celebrities and Hollywood stars. Your sleeplessness has brought you to these practical ways of building your life. And while they are not exactly wake-up exercises, you are in for a delightful awakening.

Here's how it stacks up: You can either run for cover, back into Life-as-Usual (which doesn't have a lot going for it except predictability), or you can try a new way of being single. My hunch is that you're ready for a change, the full-course run; that's why you've read this far. You like having an alternative to the status quo. Life is the creation of choices, each one significant because of the possibilities it brings.

Every word in this book is the distillation of my research and my work in the world of singleness. These are thoughts that have been forming and reforming in my mind for many years, refined by time and experience. Of course, my vision of singleness may not be yours; more than likely, only a portion of it will find its way into your life.

And you will find no forced-feeding here, no dogma. This book is merely a menu of the actions you can take to make your life full and rich and smooth-flowing. There is no one right way for you to live; the "norm" is only what happens to work for you. So, select only the exercises that bring you closer to *your* peace of mind.

This is a book about power: your personal power, and where it can take you if you give it the go-ahead. To do that, you need to accept your singleness as a fact and move from there to make friends with it. That may be a radical approach to single womanhood, but it makes sense. Embracing your current reality—planning it, expanding it, making the most of its possibilities—is merely the next logical step in your friendship with the present.

Don't misunderstand. You won't have to choose between the good life you create and the love of a good man. Far from it. For some reason, there are women who cling to the notion that developing themselves while unmarried is preparation for lifelong singleness. They never get to know who they are, never dig into the opportunities around them. In other words, they do all they can to avoid acknowledging the present reality. Imagine all the potential energy in those ladies-in-waiting, stored and underutilized, as they live and hope for the love that will make them whole and justify their existence. I'm not saying you are one of them, but a small part of you could be. If you hear even the faintest ring of truth, don't be ashamed, but be glad that you're here with me. *I've* been one of those ladies myself. Yet I am writing this book. And, more important, I am living this book every day of my life. If I can do it, you can too.

As for growth versus love, well, the curious thing is that they are not opposed at all. In fact, it's the other way around. The better you know yourself, the closer you can come to a love object. While this book is not about finding love and a man, it does prepare you in an indirect way for relating on a very real and human level to a man, both as friend and lover. As you tap your inner resources doing these exercises, you will find your inner core, some call it your "center." Genuine liking/loving can take place only between two centered, whole people.

Most curious of all, as you'll find, is that expanded lovingness is only a by-product of *Single File*. The main thrust of its principles is to put you on the path to personal growth so that you can in time make your life your own. Your decisions are yours alone; my role is to bring you to a stage where options abound and insight makes decision-making easy.

WHAT THIS BOOK IS SAYING . . .
AND WHAT IT ISN'T SAYING

CLAIM	DISCLAIMER
Being single is an option, an alternative, neither better nor inferior. It is better than being legally tied for life to someone you don't like, however, since it brings freedom.	Being single is better than being married.

CLAIM	DISCLAIMER
Singleness is your current reality, so it makes sense to explore its advantages and make the most of them.	
Since the most effective way to find love is through expanding the number of involvements thus increasing the odds, it is only logical to increase actively the number of options and possibilities in life while remaining very alert for interesting candidates. This game plan makes life more enjoyable and livable in the present, yet at the same time keeps optimism alive. Strange thing, when you make friends with your singleness and move on to other mindsets, you are edging toward readiness to add another person to your life. The serenity and contentment of being fulfilled are strong attractions.	Give up on finding romantic love and resign yourself to being single.

CLAIM	DISCLAIMER
Whether (and when) you leave the single world is up to you. Shaping a delicious life for yourself increases and deepens your contact with the rest of the world and develops your self-confidence and ability to relate to all sorts of people and handle all kinds of situations. As you widen the possibilities in your life, you also increase the chances of finding a man and love. The woman who makes a career of being single (who prefers bars and dances to trips and classes, low-end jobs to career-satisfying work, and looking for Mr. Right to spending Saturday night with a close friend) is more likely to stay on that track than her sister who relegates her marital status to the back burner and chooses to *live* her life.	Building a life now will mean lifelong singleness.

Before going any further, take a millisecond to put your singleness in perspective. A revolution is in progress, quietly changing the underpinnings of our society. Forty-three percent of this country's population, 77 million adult men and women, are single now, compared with 50 million approximately ten years ago.* Yet there are still times when it feels like a coupled world. This book can help mightily, but it can't make those low moments disappear. Perhaps knowing the size of your community will ease the hurts. You are definitely not alone.

As I said, the ideas in *Single File* have been percolating for twenty years—even before my advice column rolled out across the country—but they've taken on a special urgency lately. Frantic letters from single women about the "man shortage" have convinced me that straight talk is needed to counter the alarmist hype. After the Yale-Harvard study found that white, college-educated women were losing many of their marriage options by deferring marriage, *Newsweek* magazine told single women over forty that they stand a better chance of being struck by a terrorist bomb than of getting married!** You don't need that kind of pressure; you need practical steps that will change your life. They are in this book, and they can make you an alchemist. The process isn't easy. But it is exciting, very exciting.

Did you know that the Chinese word for *crisis* is composed of two characters? One represents danger, one opportunity. Sure, there is danger in being an unmarried woman. Sometimes there is panic and depression. But there is also an enormous opportunity that generations of women have longed for, the chance to cultivate lifelong self-reliance.

---

*Study published in *The New York Times*, February 22, 1986, by Dr. Neil G. Bennett, associate professor of Sociology at Yale University, Dr. David E. Bloom, professor of Economics at Harvard University, and Dr. Patricia H. Craig, sociologist at Yale University.
**"The Marriage Crunch," *Newsweek*, June 2, 1986.

MAKING THE MOST OF THIS BOOK

- Feel free to skip around as you work on the exercises. If one doesn't seem to be working, try another. This is a book to be put down and picked up again.

- Work on the exercises with a good friend, if possible.

- Don't compare your efforts with others; this isn't a competition. And besides, "greener-grass" thinking is counterproductive. Measure your achievements, attitudes, and accomplishments by your personal standards. They are all that matter.

- Read each exercise through before beginning.

- Keep pen and paper at your side when you start an exercise. You might even want to keep a journal.

- Don't prettify the disappointing aspects of your life. Admit them, and use the truth to inspire you to better things. Self-deception gets you nowhere and only keeps you firmly rooted in the status quo.

- Finally, read the caution label (below).

CAUTION: The exercises that follow are hazardous to a stick-in-the-mud mindset. Under no circumstances should women resistant to change expect to emerge with attitudes intact. If this warning *does* apply to you, read on. Ironically, once most tradition-bound women start changing, they go even further than their more liberated sisters. Somehow, the contrast between the old and the new spurs them on to more dramatic transformation.

Above all, work to get on good terms with change. It will bring pleasant surprises:

- You'll suddenly find that you're enjoying yourself on dates. You won't be faking a smile or trying too hard to stay focused on the man and the conversation. Instead, you feel closer to him because you're feeling closer to yourself.

- Being without a husband will seem less and less of a drawback. In fact, you'll have moments when you find yourself actually relishing your unencumbered state.

- You'll feel more energy, more curiosity, and an appetite for new places and new people. There are exciting times ahead. I can't wait to see what happens.

CELEBRATE YOUR SINGLENESS

You've done everything else with it: apologized, denied, hated, wished it away. This is where you make a 180-degree turnaround and actually celebrate your current status. Repeat this a few times and feel yourself smile: Maybe it's not so bad to have total control over your money, your time, your energies ... and your choices. Maybe this book is your rite of passage from a conflicted singleness into confidence. If getting from here to there looks impossible, have faith. It's time to break a few traditions and have a little fun. This celebration is a big step in getting there.

- Buy a Rolodex file with medium-size cards in anticipation of starting your own single file. Now that you're with me on this adventure, you might as well be prepared to write down the names and addresses of the people and groups that will become part of your support system (I call it a "safety net") that provides the goods and services to make life run smoothly. Make a note to go to the stationery store first thing tomorrow. This will be your first step in announcing your growing independence—to yourself.

• Start making plans to host a party alone. It could be that this is old stuff to you, but I bet the others were not given in the same wholehearted spirit. This time you're christening the apartment you've always considered "temporary," or *making* an independence announcement—you have made peace with your singleness and now want your friends to enjoy it with you. You may have been a solo host before, but I bet those thoughts were not in the back of your mind when you bought the wine and washed the glasses. On the other hand, you may not feel up to this; if not, put a paper clip on this page and come back later. It will happen. But it won't be fun unless you're ready.

• This part of the festivities may be equally as challenging or maybe not. It's a written announcement and that may be easier to handle. Yes, I'm suggesting that you send a card to friends and relatives (and maybe the men in your life, too) that you are striking out on your own, setting up house for real. Make it silly, or formal (or a combination of both). If you would like linens and china, include a gift solicitation. (Mention the store that carries the patterns you prefer.)

It's time to poke fun at the worn-out limitations placed on single women. You may not have a day named in your honor because of it, but my best guess is that it will raise more than a little dust within your circle. You may even notice that your breaking out of the usual will inspire friends to make their own stand. (*Hint:* This celebration could be contagious.)

TURN THE TABLES—
A ROLE REVERSAL

Now let's make this a family celebration, because the most telling show of your pride will be with your parents. They may feel that their job isn't complete until you're snuggled into marriage. They may feel that you are their little girl and they want to see you cherished, protected—and safe. In their minds, that may not seem possible for a single woman. Turning the tables is a powerful and significant symbol, with long-term ramifications. Taking your parents to dinner is the first of many ways you will celebrate your coming of age with the people who brought you up from cradle to womanhood. They need to know your changing thoughts and be in on your plans for building life *now.* Watch their eyes widen as you tell them about this book and its premise. As you turn the tables on them in different ways, watch how their respect for you grows. They'll see their little girl standing alone— and reaching out in love and understanding to the people who gave her the inner strength to do it.

There's another reason why celebrating singleness involves your parents. Until you resolve your conflicts about them, until you see them as mere mortals and equals, you will only be partially adult and not ready to assume ownership of your life. Throughout this book you'll be dealing with your folks in different ways, and now you know why.

And while you're out with your parents, you can be doing a special kind of homework that requires keen powers of observation and double scoops of finesse.

MARRIEDS—A CLOSE-UP

Over the next few weeks, make it a point to deliberately study your parents and other married friends and family (without making them uncomfortable, of course). Notice how they behave at dinner, for example, or the way they talk with (or at) each other; how they give each other little signals and leave parties at the same time (even if one of them wants to stay). Note the small amount of time they spend listening to each other's opinions, the hours consumed waiting for each other. Now, with just a dash of cynicism, mull over what you have seen. (Considering the nature of this assignment, the notes you take will probably be mental ones. But you might want to write them down when you get home. They will be interesting to reread during our discussion of mutualism, in the final chapter.)

This is not to convince you that singleness is "better," but to help you see that marriage is no bed of roses, either. For example, you might fantasize that marriage means uninterrupted time alone with a husband, but it takes only a little real-life observation to see that the everydayness of living together must include frequent separations. Substituting eyewitness fact for idealized "connubial bliss" can make you appreciate your status more wholeheartedly.

A MOMENTOUS TRIP

The celebration is building momentum. Let's shift gears and move beyond family to the world out there. While you're in this mood, buy or borrow a world map or atlas—unless you have one already. After you've looked it over well, pinpoint ten destinations that intrigue you, some of which you've probably been saving for (ahem!) a man and a honeymoon.

Now, think about each one as a trip you will take soon, on your own. Imagine hiking in Mexico or in Utah's Bryce

Canyon. Think about rafting down the Colorado River, visiting temples in Thailand, or bicycling along Germany's Romantic Road. Consider a tour through Russia, a cruise through the Greek islands. The destination may be a little less exotic, but the event will be equally momentous if it's only a camping trip to a local state park, because you are going there as a single woman.

- At this point, you're still researching a destination. So, find a guidebook and look up villages to visit; scan maps for interesting parks or landmarks along the way. Write for information that will help you narrow your choices. (See Resources at the conclusion of this chapter.) The more you know, the quicker you'll go.

- Once you're knee-deep in travel brochures, pick out one of them and talk it over with some well-traveled friends. Through a travel agent or auto club, check out transportation, hotels, restaurants, and, of course, the costs.

- Think about when you can leave and how long you can be away. Talk to your supervisor about vacation time. Check the calendar and your bank account and estimate the amount of money you can save on a regular basis. Think positive—you can swing it, if you economize in other areas. And for Pete's sake, don't feel foolish about planning a year in advance. Time flies when you're looking forward to an adventure.

- You may decide to ask a friend to come along, but that's up to you. This is going to be *your* trip, so whatever makes it more comfortable is what you should do. Don't imagine you must make your statement by going solo if that doesn't appeal. The great thing is, you're no longer simply *dreaming* about it—you're *doing* something about it. There will probably be butterflies in your stomach, but think of them as growing pains and be proud. This one trip will be proof that your world is not limited and that you alone decide how far you can go in it.

BE GENTLE

Be gentle with yourself as you do these exercises. You've been moving along quickly, propelled by excitement. That's exactly what I had hoped. But don't get so carried away that your enthusiasm burns out. If some part of any one exercise feels too difficult, wait and try again. If you skip a day or two, make up for it (and keep the rhythm) by continuing to think about that section and planning how you will attack it when you feel ready to begin again.

As a woman, I am familiar with the feelings and issues these strategies can bring to the surface, and I will be reminding you to be kind to yourself. As a widow for nearly a decade, with a young son to raise, I learned how it feels when something you try doesn't pan out. This book is not meant to frustrate but to make you aware. When something in it is giving you trouble, stop and do some deep breathing and some body stretches. Pushing ahead when you don't feel ready is counterproductive; far better to wait it out until you're raring to go! Besides, there's no need to hurry. At any given time, you are exactly where you should be on your life journey.

The first exercise requires heavy-duty soul-searching. It will not be pleasant to discover that you haven't made any close friends since high school or that you've been spending so much time at the office that your hobbies have shriveled up one by one. But seeing the facts in black and white—and in your own handwriting—is a good way to assess the good and bad in your life objectively.

Besides, if you don't like some things, isn't it better to discover them now when you can change them—rather than try to "balance" the deficiency by hurling yourself into the wrong relationship? Deep down you know you're far less likely to put all your eggs into one basket if you have a circle of enriching friends and interests. Coming up is a taste of how large that circle can be when you turn your good mind to expanding its borders.

EXERCISE 1:
INCREASE YOUR POSSIBILITIES

Imagine your life as a flower gently unfolding. At this point, the expansion will be through friendships and interests. Interests make the days more fun, yes, but they are also a route to friendships with both sexes. You are at your best—enthusiastic, relaxed, natural—when you are absorbed in something pleasurable. The people you meet through your interests see you as you are—they know the real person.

As you make your lists, don't leave out any item because you feel its "silly" or unfeminine; don't "forget" a friend because he or she is not the proper sex, age, race, or income level. Throw out the *should*s. And trust your instincts.

And please don't think that because you like weaving rag rugs instead of motorcycling, use pottery instead of china, or prefer contemporary houses to Victorian that you and I don't agree on the bigger issues. Style is personal, and certainly is not arguable or up for criticism. Our conditioning and family life have influenced our tastes, but in matters of substance, in the principles we live by, we are in deep and fundamental harmony—or you wouldn't be taking this journey with me.

PART 1: INTERESTS

STEP 1: The objective here is to write down as many of your current interests as you can think of. Allow at least one page for this list. To get started, ask yourself questions:

- *What are my favorite sports?*
  Swimming, hiking, motorcycling, windsurfing, tennis, soccer? Jogging? Golf? Archery?

- *What do I do on the weekends?*
  Rock climbing, reading, needlepoint, hang gliding, woodworking, fly-fishing? Teaching the puppy new tricks? Sleeping?

- *How do I express my creativity?*
  Painting landscapes? Designing a rock garden? Writing poetry? Playing the guitar? Dreaming up new dance steps? Teaching my niece to make a chain from gum wrappers? Building a shed in the backyard?

STEP 2: After you've made that list, imagine all the things you'd *like* to do. Then write them down on a separate page. Again, here are some questions to get you going, but don't feel limited by them. Use them only as a guide.

- *If I had a month free, what would I like to do?*
  Learn how to drive a race car? Or how to ride a horse? Take an intensive foreign-language or public-speaking course? Read every book on investments I can get my hands on?

Remember, this is a wish list—it is not necessarily realistic. You may not have a month to lavish on your favorite activity, but this exercise will make you realize your hunger to get back to it.

STEP 3: Spend a few minutes studying both lists and thinking about your yens. Which list is longer—your current interests or your "wish list"? Is there much overlap? Make notes to yourself, using questions as guidelines:

- How much time do you have available? Are you spending too much time on current activities when you'd rather be developing new interests? Are you beginning to see that you have a limited amount of free time? (Good. Now you'll stop cluttering golden hours with time-wasting people/projects.)

- Do you prefer solitary pursuits or group activities? It's important to understand your own tastes and patterns so you can build around them. But it's just as important to bend when there's good reason. What I mean is, even if you like being alone with your woodworking, join some interest-centered groups to even the score. Time alone is precious, but so is a dear friend. Keep a balance.

- Are you still making choices based on an outdated image of yourself? (A common one: "Oh, I'm no good at sports . . . I was always the last kid chosen for the softball team.") You've changed. So let this exercise motivate you to probe and experiment.

STEP 4: On this same page, list the things you need to do to make List 1 look more like List 2. For instance, phone the local recreation center and ask about an archery league, or call a friend of yours who plays the piano and see if she has time to give you lessons. (You could barter payment by teaching her to sew.) Make one call today, and keep calling until List 1 and List 2 look practically the same.

Is your mind filled with *should*s and *cannot*s and yes, *but*s? Or are you finding more ideas, goals, dreams filtering in? I am convinced that women as a sex are conditioned to live within narrow constraints and women without a man by their sides are burdened with even stricter limitations.

You know, when I surveyed people about their sexuality, most of the formerly married group told me that they had seen a significant freeing-up of their imaginations after leaving their marriages. They felt more compassionate, less harsh in their judgments of their fellow humans, and in general more open in their relationships. All they needed was a jolt, a change of thinking, to expand their mental limits. It could be that this book is your jolt, and that you too are ripe to shed arbitrary thinking. Molting can be a gradual process, and we're in no hurry here. But be watchful for signs of expansion. It's coming.

PART 2: FRIENDSHIP

- Do I choose friends deliberately?

- Do I let people choose me?

- Do I learn a lot from my friends?

- Do I respect their opinions?

- Do I let them change my opinions?

- Do I try to change theirs?

- Do I consider myself richer for having known my friends?

- Do I trust all my friends? Am I always there for them?

- Do I praise my friends?

- Do I frequently find fault with them?

- Do I deliberately try to make a contribution to their lives?

STEP 1: Before you do anything else in this section, ask yourself those questions. This is not a quiz and there is no score; the only point is that you start thinking about friendship and the kinds of friends you have. Sounds elementary, but I promise you that this will be an eye-opener.

- Write down what you have learned about yourself from your answers; those discoveries may come in handy later on.

STEP 2: Next, you'll think about your friends—why you have them and what they do for your well-being. Begin by listing your current friends. Start with the best ones. Next to each name, write a few words describing the way he or she makes you feel. Think about the reasons they are in your life. Is it because you share the same values? Because you both want the same things out of life?

STEP 3: Now list other friends—co-workers, colleagues, childhood chums, sports partners, confidantes. Describe the qualities about each one that keep the friendship healthy. What draws you together? Does this friend make you laugh? Does he or she make you feel full of confidence, witty and charming? Or are you friends out of inertia—because you've been friends for a long time—and for no other reason?

STEP 4: Come up with conclusions. If your best friend makes you feel valuable and special, there's nothing much to say— you'll probably be friends for life. But if there is someone on the list who triggers anxiety or has a consistently "down" opinion of people (and him or herself), rethink the reason for the relationship and whether it is adding anything to your life. If it's not, promise yourself to phase out the acquaintanceship.

STEP 5: For more surprises, make a list of the friends who have passed in and out of your life. Ask yourself the reason they are not part of the present. Was it a quarrel? A move? A subtle change in life direction? Is there any chance/reason for reconciliation? Asterisk the people you'd like to see again. It might be worth a lunch to reexamine the chemistry between you two and put a fresh face on an old friendship. You've both changed, so maybe it's time for another look.

STEP 6: There are other sources of friendship you've probably overlooked in your diggings here. For example:

- *Men.* I bet the number of male friends on your list is small. Why? Do you think of males in too few ways—as only husband, boyfriend, or lover? Women who work alongside men are able to see them as fellow professionals, people, not the "opposite" sex, so they feel more natural about considering them part of their circle of friends. They know that it's a relief to be in male company without the pressure of a date. It's nice to have someone to call when you need the male point of view—without a tinge of gamesmanship. One final inducement to bring a man home for lunch? More than one woman has fallen in love with someone who was "just a friend." Think about it.

- *Ex-lovers, ex-in-laws, or even ex-spouses.* Society is really weird about people who once loved each other. With work and dedication, former lovers/spouses can salvage some degree of respect and affection even after a split. Naturally, the dynamics shift. But if the ending wasn't too traumatic for either person involved, a relaxed, sane friendship can evolve. So the next time a relationship ends, don't trash it impulsively. The good feelings that brought you together need not die with the end of romantic love. The label may change, but that goodness remains as a rich potential for real fellowship. If you were friends in love, you can be friends outside of it. (See Chapter Nine for more about this.)

- *Couples.* You bring fresh air into their world, and they can teach you a thing or two about a love partnership. It wouldn't be prudent to make them your entire social life, but it would be wasteful to avoid couples simply because they are not single and eligible. Of course, they need to feel you are not after a husband or a meal ticket. (You do need to carry your own weight at all times.) But a buoyant personality can be your passport into the coupled world—given a mutuality of interests and friendly feelings. Your challenge is to make overtures in a nonthreatening way—and to accept them when they come from couples you like.

STEP 7: Write down the names of new friends you'd like to make. Draw from your casual acquaintances, friends of friends. And don't wait for these people to come to you. Put them on your list to contact. Don't exclude people who are older or younger than you—or married friends, either. The more varied the mix, the more interesting your life.

STEP 8: If you don't already have an address book, make a note to buy a refillable one tomorrow. It will become tangible evidence of the changes you are making. The number of names will probably increase—but remember that anyone can accumulate meaningless acquaintanceships that drain time and energy and give back little. *You* are going to build quality people into your life.

You'll probably acquire the habit of making six-month updates in the address book, because you are entering a period of rapid growth, and as you see more in yourself, you will ask more of the people you know. Some of them are sure to feel awkward with the changes in you, and you may decide to part company. As much as that may hurt, a weeding-out process is an inevitable by-product of growth.

As you grow and feel better about yourself, you'll find yourself gravitating toward positive, supportive people who feel good about themselves. Augmenters, as I call them, want the best for themselves and so they bring out the best in you.

Their positivism lifts everyone around them. They are the people who walk on the sunny side, who opt for life. So whenever possible, befriend an augmenter. And, for Pete's sake, fall in love with one.

This doesn't mean you shun all the "downers" on your list, but the more aware you become about friends' effects on you, the more initiative you will take to upgrade your existing relationships. Let's say you have a childhood friend, a dear person who also happens to be a chronic complainer. Once you recognize her effect on you, you can mentally pre-

---

FRIENDLY FIRST

Every day, make a conscious effort to initiate at least one conversation with someone you know only slightly, or not at all. You can do it anywhere: in the elevator on the way to the office ("Don't you work on the seventh floor too?"), in the doctor's waiting room ("I'm done with this magazine. Would you like to look at it?"), at the grocery store checkout line ("I see you've bought eggplants, too. Don't they look scrumptious?"), at your child's PTA ("You must be Carey's mother. He tells me you make the best fudge brownies. I'd love the recipe"), or at the health club ("Do you like the instructor in the low-impact aerobics class?"). You don't have to be clever or witty, just open and interested. It's a strategy similar to one you might have used to meet men back in your "unenlightened" days. But now you're using the same techniques to meet all kinds of people—and with different motivation! You take the first step, and you reap the knowledge that this world is a friendly place. And you have the power to make it even friendlier.

pare yourself for her company and its aftereffects. You can
urge her to get help, but you can't allow her to turn you into
a complainer, too. And so you may decide to see her less
frequently, or in a crowd rather than alone. (Becoming so-
lution-oriented, aren't you?)

Life is all about creating choices and then discriminating
between them. The importance of each choice is magnified
because each one brings its own set of possibilities that become part of your life. Because there is no partner to influence
your decisions, you alone own each one of them. You can
see that as burden—or privilege.

I remember being surprised at a friend's birthday party
when she asked us to write the reasons we were her friends,
and to put the messages in a bowl. After we had done that,
she told us she was going to read them whenever she needed
a boost. She felt very close to us, she said; we meant a lot in
her life. In fact, she felt that we were her second family, her
family of friends.

And in many ways, friends can be as dear as blood
relatives—sometimes even more precious, because we can
choose them! It takes time for a friendship to jell, of course,
but mutual responsibility and caring, once kindled, can burn
with a strong flame of kinship.

Am I coming on strong about the value of friends? For
good reason. The qualifications for being a good friend are
exactly the same as those for being a good parent, child, love
partner: giving without being asked, caring unconditionally,
nonjudgmental fellowship, understanding, time, trustworthi-
ness, respect, dependability, loyalty. The labels change, the
dynamics differ, but the essential elements remain the same
in all kinds of relationships.

So it is only logical that practicing the art of friendship,
besides making your relationships with people better and more
satisfying, is also practical preparation for love relationships.

But the more immediate payoff of a close-knit circle of
friends is emotional enrichment. A shared chuckle goes a long

way and makes you realize that romantic love isn't the only source of the warmth that makes life worth living.

Before you begin this next exercise, try a few stretches. Arms and legs, this time, rather than mind and soul! This will loosen the cobwebs and help you muster the concentration the exercise requires. You might want to take the phone off the hook, too.

EXERCISE 2:
TAKE CONTROL

"Whose life is it, anyway?" The answer is obvious, but as a woman you are sure to lose sight of it at times and give away too much of your personal power. Usually to a man. (Maybe you've been doing that so often and so long that you've lost sight of what it's like to be in charge.)

STEP 1:   Remember your first-thought responses about singleness back in the Introduction? Since this is a continuation of that exercise, now is the time to look at them again. (I told you you'd be using these exercises more than once.)

STEP 2:   After you've done that, make two lists (on separate pages). You'll write the advantages of being single on one of them; the disadvantages on another.

STEP 3:   As you make the lists, you'll discover that some of the advantages are ambiguous. Privacy, for instance. It's often an advantage, but you may have been living alone long enough to realize that excessive aloneness can keep you from reaching out. When you come across these double-faced issues (see below), enter them on both lists. Here's an example, a short story with a moral:

HAVING YOUR COOKIES AND EATING THEM, TOO

A reader from Texas, fresh from a divorce, boasted in a letter about his new freedom. The cookies he had eaten in bed while married, a habit that drove his former wife wild, were now his to eat in peace. I wrote back congratulating him on his newly acquired autonomy and asked him to keep in touch. He wrote again about a year later, complaining that he was feeling awful because no one cared about the piles of crumbs! Cookies are like cake, I suppose: You can't have them and eat them too! Or can you? Perhaps it's just that this particular man hadn't yet found his way. (More about intimacy versus independence later.)

STEP 4: Imagine ways to minimize minuses and enhance pluses, and write them down. For example, if you're worried that living by yourself is making you a hermit: (1) Invite friends to visit you for the weekend; (2) don't unplug the telephone anymore (except when you want to be undisturbed); (3) check out shared living possibilities.

Hints:

- If you're feeling lonely, with too much time on your hands, ask a single parent with small children to help you see this disadvantage as an opportunity. (If you're the one with the kids and without the leisure, ask a friend who has no kids to remind you what it's like to be alone when you don't want to be.) In other words, cross the bridges you are building for fresh opinions, alternatives, strategies.

- Use the "twilight" period at night, just before you feel drowsy, to let solutions jell. This is the perfect time to follow stray thoughts into action-oriented solutions. Keep a pad and pencil by your bed at all times. For that matter, keep one in your purse. When you're in a period of intense concentration, new thoughts can come at the most unexpected times.

• Even if you can't turn every negative into a positive immediately, you can come up with partial solutions. Halfway there is not a bad place; it's a lot better than being nowhere at all. Like all advice that sounds simple, this isn't, I know. But I promise that it gets easier with practice.

STEP 5: Now that you're in a searching mood, take a look at the basics in your life: work, socializing, family, interests. Make an entry for each category, and next to each one write ways to improve that part of your environment. For example:

WORK	WAYS TO IMPROVE
My job as a computer programmer	Enroll in night class and work toward an advanced degree
	Advertise for consulting work in professional journal, on computer bulletin board
	Subscribe to computer magazine
	Attend professional conventions, local meetings; enroll in national groups

STEP 6: Now, make notes to yourself of what your lists say to you—a few remarks to yourself. In which areas are you strongest? In which are you dropping the ball? Are you headed in any direction? Is it where you want to go? (You don't have

to do all this at one sitting; break the exercise up into segments if you like. The more often you think about this, the more you'll come up with.)

STEP 7:   Put this information in a folder, labeled. Put it near your Single File Rolodex to be used as a source of strategies for getting ahead. Make notes to yourself about classes and seminars, local and national meetings you hear about; file their catalogues and these notes in the folder. Like your address book, keep it current. As you change, it will change. You'll see this plan in a larger context in the next chapter.

A BIT OF PREACHING!

There is—or should be—one glaring omission in your list of "controllables." You may have discovered it, but I don't want to risk overlooking such a major point. ROMANCE is the omission because it is something that will not materialize on demand. You can't hurry love, as the song goes. And you can't conjure up The Man Who Isn't There, either. Love has its own timetable. But you *can* accelerate your involvement in the world around you, increase the number of people you know and the areas of interest that round out your life.

It's a sad irony that women who are passive in other areas of their lives take action in the one area where they cannot make anything happen. If they put a fraction of the time and energy they invest in looking and waiting for love into developing themselves, they would probably already have come upon the man of their dreams.

This control exercise is key, because it uncovers the range of options you own. Once you have that menu laid out before you, a man-related disappointment will seem less devastating. You'll come to realize that it's tough enough to manage your own life without hoping to control someone else's decisions, too. Other people also have options, and sometimes their decisions are not in your favor. That's their loss! So for now concentrate on cultivating the real possibilities in your life.

But, please understand: The sort of control you are developing has nothing to do with domination or manipulation. The power it brings is beneficial; it can carry you on to fulfillment in life. You see, you are starting to define your personal power, and as you test the degree of influence you possess, you will realize that you can rearrange much of what you formerly accepted as beyond your control. Limits? In reality, there are very few. The largest are in your mind. And at this point, you are beginning to get out of your own way.

So now, treat yourself to an important event. It's not an exercise, but it will become a daily ritual you look forward to. It's one of the simplest things you'll be doing here, but don't be fooled. This ceremony is central to your work here.

A CELEBRATION OF SELF

You can't jump into this magic moment and shut out the world in a snap, though; you'll need a period of winding down.

So pour yourself a glass of juice—or light wine. Get a pad and pencil and take the phone off the hook. (Write a note to yourself to put it back on later.) Sit down in your cushiest chair and start to relax. If you can, put up your feet. As you sip, let your mind stray. See in your mind's eye glimpses of the future as you'd like it to be: new people, interesting places, exciting things happening.

When an idea comes along, catch it by writing it down. You needn't write in sentences, if you feel hurried; a few key words will jog your memory later on when you read what you have written. This is a time for reverie . . . as real as life gets, dreams must always be part of it. So use this time in your day to waken your imagination and let your fantasies take over. It's foolish not to dream high and hold on hard to the dream. Yes, you may never reach the heights, but if you

don't pursue your highest hopes, they are lost to you anyway. Is there any real choice? Whether or not you realize it,
you are already growing. You are becoming more of a person, connecting with new parts within. And proclaiming that
unfolding is a powerful way to solidify your growing selfhood.

So, put this new habit into your daily routine. Each day,
when you awaken, in the stillness of the morning, claim your
place in this world by speaking your name out loud: "I am
_____ . Today is my day, a day to make good for me. I am
building my life."

If speaking out loud feels strange, just think the words.
Or something similar to them. (They're just a takeoff point.)
What is important is to shift your mind into positive gear and
do more than meet the morning halfway. You will grab hold
of it.

If you like, write the words you use and tape them on
the refrigerator or tuck them into the drawer of your night
table—wherever you'll be reminded to say them. Soon, they
will become a part of you. I'm not saying you'll feel their
resonance in your bones the very first time (or even the tenth
time) you speak the affirmation. At first, you'll probably be
too busy concentrating on words to let the meaning sink in.
But one morning, in the middle of a sentence, you will suddenly notice that the words are coming from your heart and
that you feel bigger than any eventuality the day could bring.
In that instant you'll know you chose the right path. You will
feel the stirrings of growth and a vague hint that you're becoming more of a person, more of a primary person—less
dependent on a man or anyone else.

FEELINGS

How do you feel after this first round? Exhilarated—and a
bit tired? I hope it's the *good* sort of weariness that comes
from being totally honest about things you have never

pondered—at least not in such an organized way. Not that you've been lying to yourself; that's far too strong. But through the years you probably have built up coats of gentle self-deception. We all do, as a way to get through the day. Well, this is the place to peel them off—once and for all.

Use the chart below to note your feelings about the exercises in Chapter One. Jot down whatever comes to mind and write the date beside it. And again, be honest. If you felt like you'd rather take out a week's worth of garbage than make a comprehensive list of your past, present, and future friends, say so! You'll notice that there are several columns here. This is because you'll be doing many of the exercises more than once, and it's important to remember the way you felt each time. You'll be surprised by the difference in these feelings that practice makes. And don't worry about any fatigue you may be experiencing. That tiredness will disappear in the stimulation of a new idea, a fresh face, another slant on an old issue. Come. There is more waiting in the next chapter.

HOW DID IT FEEL? (PROGRESS REPORT)

EXERCISE	DATE AND FEELING 1st TIME	DATE AND FEELING 2nd TIME	DATE AND FEELING 3rd TIME
1 Celebrate Your Singleness			
2 Increase Your Possibilities 1–Interests 2–Friendship			
3 Take Control			

TWO

ACCELERATION: LIVING AS-IF

Now you're moving. Step-by-step you're giving up the waiting game, edging closer to the mainstream where you are free to take action. But you're still unsure of this new independent person you're becoming. At times you long for the old ways that, admittedly, kept life suspended but nevertheless felt familiar and comfortable. Conflict like that is natural, understandable; passivity patterns have been layered onto your psyche over many years. They are not going to disappear without a fight. They had a good thing going.

But you've got something much better—the present. Now, while you're picking up speed and heading into even more ambitious challenges, is the ideal time to remind yourself that you are the only person who can turn the present—and its rich potential—into what you want. No marital status can do it, no amount of money can do it. The right dress, the right job, the right salary can't get the job done. No—your fulfillment, the kind that warms the heart and satisfies the soul—can come only from your actions.

But you've been making an art of postponement up to now. And you thought you had good reasons:

EXCUSES FOR DELAYING

1. Men don't like independent women.

2. I can't afford to be on my own.

3. I'm only happy when a man is in love with me.

4. I don't feel like a woman when I'm not with a man.

5. I'm not a whole person until I'm a wife.

6. If I make single life interesting, I'll never get married.

7. Other women will envy me, so I'll have no friends.

8. I'll make a mess of it.

9. I'll have no men to date if I get too successful.

10. I'm not the type.

11. I'm too shy.

12. I'll get wrinkles.

I know how easy it is to fall into soggy thinking. (Even now *I* stumble, but *I* know what's happening and it's easier to pull myself up.) But I also know that a small part of our gumption dies with each fall, so it's crucial to monitor one's own level of self-discipline. Sure, patience is important; growing gradually day by day is not exactly life in the fast lane. And it's also true that no matter how carefully a life is built, none of us has total control over results. Chance, timing, serendipity—all play a part. But I am convinced that fortune favors the prepared mind. For luck to make a significant difference in life, there must first be an overall design. It is no coincidence that good luck rarely visits the life that is jumbled by indecision and fear.

THE AS-IF LIFE:
ANSWER TO THE WHAT-IF
QUESTION

Years ago, during my single-mom-and-widow phase, fear was very much a part of my emotional baggage. A whole family of what-ifs would wake me up in the middle of the night and begin to drone their litany of negative possibilities: What if my child never again had a father? What if I got sick and couldn't take care of him? What if that nice man doesn't call? What if he doesn't like the way I've arranged my life? What if my parents start calling me an old maid behind my back? These were bad enough, but the most awful question of all would sit on my shoulders and refuse to budge: What if I never got married?

During more midnight awakenings than I care to remember, the same composed woman who is writing this was a panicky child. But her sleepless nights gave way to bright new mornings, and during one of them I finally wrestled insecurity to the mat and forced despair to reveal its other side, realism. Yes, one day during my long widowhood, I suddenly realized that the only way to enjoy my life was to accept my single status and then get on with the challenge of living it. Believe me, that insight brought me up sharp; it seemed so radical and yet I knew it was common sense. After I decided to stop running and face my major fear—that I might never marry again—its power over me was for the most part drained. My paralysis left me. I was at last free to build a life for myself because I had decided to live *as if I would always be single.*

That decision, which I am suggesting you also make, *does not mean lifelong singleness.* It didn't in my case, and it won't in yours. It does mean making your life your own, and not waiting an extra beat to begin the process. It does mean structuring the present in an organized, cohesive, long-range time frame. But while this approach is designed for the long haul, please know that it will not keep you unmarried one moment longer than you choose. In fact, the expansion and involvement built into it could actually catapult you out of the single world sooner than later; love seems to have a better chance for survival in a life made livable before its arrival.

I remember the fun of choosing home base for my son and myself. It turned out to be a one-bedroom apartment down the street from my mother, because my work at that time included late hours and I knew she would be the next best thing for Scott. The apartment was tiny (our guest closet consisted of two brass hooks on a wall), and it meant my sleeping on a sofa bed in the room that was our dining room, living room, and work space. But it gave Scott a good-sized room and closet, and best of all, it was in a first-rate building. I had met my top priorities—security and safety—and the location was right, so our housing was taken care of.

My dates were few and far between at that time, and nearness to Scott meant a lot to me. So most nights found me sitting at my typewriter roughing out notes for a not-yet-born column. My career was still vague, but it was definitely in the works. As for finances, there weren't enough for me to be concerned about growth and investing. We just squeaked by and the cash-flow picture was not exactly rosy (part of the reason I'm so interested in yours). But my "people picture" was okay: I had some good friends, male and female, and somehow there was always someone for me in the crunches.

I didn't know it then, but instinctively I was building the cornerstones that form the foundation of the As-If life: appropriate and secure housing, financial planning, a satisfying career, and enriching relationships. Without this book, instinct and judgment were my sole guides. It was strictly trial-and-error, but making decisions my way, to fit the needs of my family, felt good. And it worked out. The pieces of my life fell together as these basic concerns were being addressed.

So I put it to you to use *your* judgment and make these four cornerstones solid in your life so that its foundation is secure. (You'll build it in your personal style, in your own way, of course.) Actually, you have already begun that process. This whole book is a master plan for As-If living, and you've been on its path since page one. We're merely formalizing the approach here. Step-by-step, if you agree, together we will build your security so that by the end of this book your foundation (and those cornerstones) can be in place and functioning.

And in the future, when and if you decide to share your independence and form a love partnership, you'll be able to bring much of your As-If life into the new phase. When I first met Morris, the man who is my husband today, he remarked that I was "like a wife who only needed a husband to finish the picture." He loved the fact that my tiny kingdom was in order and running smoothly, that the household he walked into was settled. So many of the women he had been meeting were camping out, using paper plates and flea-market furniture, and in general exuding an air of neediness as they waited for their knight to come and make their "real" lives begin.

My knight preferred a home that needed him only for the emotional fulfillment he brought. He liked the fact that the rest had been taken care of, and he appreciated the fact that I was building a career and not sitting and waiting for a man to rescue me. (Even now, he's pleased that I balance my own checkbook and read the lease and ask the right questions of a bank officer.) I left that apartment when I remarried (it was wonderful to have a bedroom door once again), but the basics and the principles developed during my As-If phase came along with me into wifehood. See if you agree that the benefits of that life are transferable to couplehood:

- *Continuity.* Life has a plan and your major actions are in line with it.

- *Feelings of confidence and self-esteem* from seeing your capability in action.

- *Independence.* You take charge of your life rather than waiting to give the reins over to another person.

- *Simpler decision-making.* You approach every problem with the same mindset rather than sorting through confusion, doubts, conflicts, and what-ifs to solve each one separately.

- *Life is real and immediate.* Decisions are based on what is, not what could or might be.

- Liberation from unreal limitations.

The As-If answer is there waiting to be discovered inside that dreaded What-If question, but its effectiveness depends solely on you. Before it can reshape your life, you must first accept your current status. That acceptance, which will deepen as you make your exit from the waiting room more and more final, is the make-or-break factor here. Denied, this single space in your life will continue to be a twilight existence where you daydream of wifehood and never fully acknowledge the richness right under your nose. This can be a time of supercreativity—or an endless interim lived halfheartedly.

LOOKING TO THE FUTURE

In a successful corporation, executives anticipate future possibilities and make their plans accordingly. As Chairman of the Board of your life, you have the same challenge. That means looking at the numbers, the ones about women's chances for marriage that made first-page news not long ago. But instead of looking at them in fear, you can see them as they are.

THE POSSIBILITIES:

1. You will marry soon.

2. You will marry later, probably later than you expected.

3. You won't marry at all—or again.

4. You will marry and live to your last day with your husband.

5. You will marry and live with your husband until his last day.

6. You will marry but ultimately get divorced.

THE ODDS:

–A never-married woman of thirty has a 20 percent chance of marrying.

–A never-married woman of forty has a 1 percent chance.

–There are 86.9 single men for every 100 single women.

–According to one rough statistic, 14 percent of those 86.9 men are homosexual.

–Twelve out of 13 American women who marry will eventually become widows.

–Women outlive men by an average of eight years.

–The divorce rate is 50 percent.

–Seventy-five percent of divorced women remarry (83 percent of men remarry).

–There are 9 million "surplus" women in this country.

–There are currently more than 37 million unmarried women in this country.

–There is a burgeoning trend toward lifelong singleness, more prevalent among women.

THE PROBABILITY:

Significant periods of singleness in your life.

ACTION INDICATED:

All but two of the possibilities listed put you back at square one—life on your own. Only one keeps you partnered for life, and the odds of that materializing are slender. Besides, even the one woman out of twelve who stays married to her last day needs to cultivate her autonomy. Even she needs to live As-If. That's right—even if you knew now you'd be married for life, you would still acknowledge that it's important to assume ownership of your life, because in the most fundamental way we are all responsible for ourselves, and in that sense we are all single.

WAITING FOR THE PRESENT

Before you begin the first exercise, an anecdote:

There once was a little girl who always did what was asked of her. One day in school, when she went to ask her teacher a question, the teacher was too busy to answer and told the child to sit down and wait. For the present. All morning the little girl did as she had been told, refusing to leave her seat when the rest of the class splintered into groups to play games. After a while, the mystified teacher asked the girl why she didn't join the rest of the class. "I'm sitting here, waiting for my present," she said.

So much for misunderstandings. And passivity. You know, in your heart of hearts, that life's bounty is only for the doers. Yet there you sit, single woman, keeping life on hold and rationalizing that things like finances and career are not relevant right now. Things like that will be taken care of when a man comes along. Well, he's not here and it's time to stop sitting and waiting for him to present a life to you. You better start opening the present yourself.

EXERCISE 1:
STRATEGIC PLANNING—
THE AS-IF LIFE

You can't get where you want to go by waiting for the present. You have to know where you're headed. Here you'll start off by establishing goals: some immediate, others longer-term, but all of them giving you a clearer idea of what you want from your life.

STEP 1:   Set aside five sheets of paper; one each for the four cornerstones—money, housing, people, and career—plus an extra sheet. Label each page accordingly. Ask yourself the major goal you would like to achieve with each cornerstone, and then write your answer in the first column. Do the following on each of the four sheets. Code each goal with an (I) for immediate (less than six months), (S) for short-term (six months to two years), or (L) for long-term (two years on).

STEP 2:   Under "Plan" write specific steps you will take to reach this goal.

STEP 3:   In the next column, labeled "Change," describe how this new goal will make your life different from what it is today. (Simply seeing it on paper is a step forward and an achievement.)

STEP 4:   Under "Assessment" write down whether in your judgment the change is possible or unrealistic. Note your thoughts about the project—does it mean enough to you to sacrifice other things? Which ones?

STEP 5:   Ask yourself how much you can do on your own? What help do you need? Is that help available? In which specific ways can you make the change occur? Write the answers in the "Make It Happen" column.

STEP 6: What are possible drawbacks? Are they worth the risk? Put these answers in the "Possible Drawbacks" column. Note the example below:

MONEY

GOAL	PLAN	CHANGE
saving for house	save $__ per paycheck	different priorities;
	save $__ in one year	control over my resources; long-range purpose; end of impulsive spending

---

ASSESSMENT

real possibility, but it will take self-control

MAKE IT HAPPEN

learn to cook, keep up correspondence
start enjoying my own company

POSSIBLE DRAWBACKS

reduced number of phone calls
limited number of dinners eaten out

STEP 7: You'll be answering all these questions for each of the four cornerstone areas—money, housing, people, and career. You can make charts for more than one goal in each category. For example, other financial goals might be saving for a new business, paying off credit-card debt, investing in a certificate of deposit. But keep each goal on its own page, and complete a set of goals for each cornerstone.

STEP 8: When you have more than one goal in each area, rank each one according to its importance. (See example below.) When you rank financial goals, for example, you may suddenly realize that if you don't pay off your Visa card and make that a number-one priority, you can go no further! But for your second priority, you'll have to make a judgment: Should you buy a condominium, an old Victorian house, or set up a mail-order business in your home? Whatever you are considering, consider well. Many of these moves require serious funding and are definitely not for everyone. They may be exciting to mull over, but your particular needs may not call for them. Not everyone wants to handle a booming career or her own home. We don't all need a sense of ownership or an executive position. Mortgage payments and long working hours are very real, and they can feel excessively burdensome without overriding dedication. The point of the As-If Life is to solidify and expand life in exactly the ways you prefer—no more, no less. None of the suggestions here is worth a damn if it does not bring you contentment. But the simple act of contemplating a quilt-making business could spark another thought, far from quilting but on target for you. This list can help clarify dreams and priorities. And if you stick with it to the bottom line, you'll emerge with far more information than you did the last time you thought about the future.

STEP 9: On the fifth piece of paper, with charts nearby, write each goal again, this time describing the method you will use and the amount of time it will take to make it a reality. Use the small, doable steps, like the ones in the example below, to reach each long-term goal. Each achievement will spur you on to the next step. The shorter and more precise the steps, the more likely the project will get done. And do dream, because dreams are the sighing of the soul. Listen well. Then turn them into reality by setting goals.

An example:

GOAL 1: Paying off credit-card debt

Steps:

- pay at least $__ month on each one (you set the amount)
- no new credit-card purchases until all debt is paid
- cut up credit cards and start paying by cash or check only

GOAL 2: Saving a sum large enough to pay basic expenses for six months while setting up your own business _____ (you fill in the blank)

Steps:

- as soon as credit cards are paid off, start saving money ($__ per paycheck)
- even before you've saved enough to rent the space, begin making contacts and other preliminary arrangements. (You don't have to have an office before you can have a business. Many successful businesses began in the head and continued for a long time in the home!)

GOAL 3: After an initial investment to start up the business (rental of space/printing of cards/equipment and supplies, etc.), start saving the maximum possible from monthly revenues for a down payment on a house. You can break this down into much smaller steps, too.

GOAL 4:   Finally, when there's enough profit from the business to invest:

- Begin reading *The Wall Street Journal*, *Money* magazine, etc., to familiarize yourself with the financial world; then, as business begins to take off, investments can, too!

Each of these steps could take years, of course, but having a time frame gives you a clear picture of what you are striving for. (See Chapter Six for in-depth scrutiny of finances.)

You should not have finished this exercise in one sitting. If you did, you didn't give enough credence to your dreams. Please go back and start again. You will probably want to do some heavy thinking about your life and what you want from it, so take your time and enjoy the gradual discovery. One of my abiding dreams will be realized when, face to face with your private daydreams, you realize they have no place in real life and you brush them aside to find the real thing. Only at that point will you be able to bring into your life the dimensions that satisfy your deepest needs. Bringing you to that level of satisfaction is the reason for this book.

Again, don't ever feel pushed. You have your private hopes, and they are too sacred even for well-intentioned tampering. What we are offering are alternatives and strategies to reach these hopes—as always, what they are is your decision. But I do want you to keep in mind that the wholeness you are assembling here is an interplay between assertiveness and receptivity. One purpose of these exercises is to guide you toward the balance of the two that keeps you comfortable as you are growing.

A TRAVELER . . .

. . . came to a wise man and asked him about the people in his city. The wise man replied by asking him about the people in the town he had just left.

"The people there were friendly and helpful," the traveler said. "Very nice indeed."

"Then you'll find the people in this town very nice indeed," the wise man said.

A second stranger came to the sage and asked him the same question. Again, the wise man asked the stranger to describe the people in the town he had come from.

"The town I left was full of thieves and scoundrels," he answered, "all of them rogues."

"You'll find the people in this town the same."

EXERCISE 2:
SINGLE AND EXPECTING

Yes, dear fellow traveler, your expectations deeply influence reality. Your greatest strength comes not from what you have or what you say, but from what you believe. Even at this early stage of the book, you can see changes in your belief system. Turn back to your responses in the agree/disagree exercise in the Introduction. Compare them with your new attitudes—and *then* take a look at what's going on in your life. I bet your days are better now (in more ways than one) than in the Pre-Deitz Era. Agree or disagree?

And if that doesn't win you over, you really should take a look at the studies that link optimism with success and pessimism with depression and shyness. Edward E. Jones, a

Princeton University psychologist, concluded that expectations not only affect how we view reality *but also affect the reality itself.* He believes that we alter our social environment through our behavior in it. And our expectations determine how we behave.*

STEP 1:   Write your primary expectations in life. (Try for a minimum of ten and not more than twenty-five.) These are more sweeping then the goals in the last exercise. Don't be embarrassed if they're lofty or humble—becoming the next Sally Ride or a foster parent; patenting a breakthrough invention or turning your home into a bed-and-breakfast; becoming the editor of a major magazine or manager of your division . . .

STEP 2:   Mark the expectations you believe can happen only in the distant future, and next to them note the reasons that make the delay mandatory. (Read them twice, the second time tongue-in-cheek.) You'll begin to realize how thoroughly expectations color life.

STEP 3:   Which of the "distant future" expectations—until now—required that a man be along? Is it learning how to skydive? Trekking in the Himalayas or hiking to the bottom of the Grand Canyon? Having a baby? Starting a florist shop? Mark each of these with an (M).

STEP 4:   Now, before you put down your pen for the day, write down at least one way (preferably more) you can accomplish the (M) goals *without* a man. Try not to give up major dreams; modify them realistically to make them materialize. If not a trip to Hawaii, then maybe a week at a dude ranch. If a baby is uppermost in your mind, but single motherhood a big question mark, look into that option carefully. (*Note:* This is one dream that demands extensive research. Investigate single-parent adoption, speak with women who

*"Interpreting Interpersonal Behavior: The Effects of Expectations," *Science* magazine, January 1986, pp. 41–46.

have decided to parent alone, get to know people in groups like Single Mothers by Choice or Parents Without Partners, and ask your family how they would feel about your becoming a single mother. Then, figure out your finances and your emotional resources: time, patience, selflessness.) This is a life change that can appear glamorous but on deeper examination prove to have too many negatives. So dream this dream with caution, but even if it doesn't work out, don't stop dreaming altogether. (For more on single motherhood, see Resources at the end of the book.)

STEP 5: Now, reread the list; you have an important set of life goals—and plans for making them come true—on paper in front of you. Whichever ones ultimately come to pass, thinking about what you want is a habit well worth adopting.

STEP 6: Take a brief break, refocus, and then take a few minutes to jot down some lesser expectations, the sorts of pleasures you'd like to come your way often. Label this list "Daily Pleasures." Because life can accommodate only a few grandiose goals, it's usually the small ones that bring happiness daily. List at least ten of these on a separate paper.

STEP 7: Figure out ways to make these happen, too. If you love getting letters, for instance, buy some elegant writing paper as an incentive and start catching up on lost correspondence. Be the one to write first. (Or join a correspondence club.) If you want to take bicycle rides, fix up your "klunker" or look into buying a new bike. And if you're getting weary of making lists, take the rest of the day off. Put down this book—make a mental note to pick it up again tomorrow—and go for a walk! That's it; reward yourself. When you give yourself pleasures from time to time, you'll stop waiting for Santa Claus and begin to realize that you can be the source of your own fulfillments. You'll show yourself just how much you can do for you.

And even if this exercise doesn't fully convince you that

you can do almost anything *single*, at least you will have learned to let your imagination soar, widening the limits of your mind and corralling more possibilities into your corner. You'll start thinking, "Why not? I really want to do that, I can afford it, I have the time." You'll get in the habit of testing whether restrictions are real or only in your mind. You already know what you'll conclude most of the time. . . .

EXERCISE 3:
GET INTO ACTION

Single women, usually minor figures in the financial market, too often put bankers on a pedestal. Well, it's time to bring the bankers (and you) down to earth. You are about to enter their world and pick their brains—in your gentle, firm way, of course. And you'll learn a lot—about yourself, about financial people, and above all, about the difference that expertise can make.

You'll learn about housing, too, since a home loan is to be your announced reason for an appointment with a banking official. You may or may not go through with it, depending on your needs, ability, and preference, but at the least you'll have taken a first step toward putting a range of hand-picked professionals and their savvy into your life.

STEP 1: When shopping around for a bank there are four things to look for:

• convenient banking hours and location

• bankers who talk like real people

• high interest rates on savings

• coverage by Federal insurance (either FDIC or FSLIC)

The institution to choose has more than one or two women visible in their executive area and promotes a friendly atmosphere. Avoid any banks (or bankers) who make you feel defensive or unimportant. Remember that; you must feel welcome, valued, respected. Don't settle for anything less than that combination, because the way you feel has much to do with the outcome of the exercise.

STEP 2: When you've decided on the right bank for you, after a preliminary and informal talk with the people there, go home and compile a list of questions to ask at the more formal meeting you will arrange this week with one of its officials. Suggestions:

- What kind of credit record does the bank find acceptable for granting a mortgage?

- What about employment history—how long should I have been with my current employer?

- Can I qualify for any special loan programs, perhaps even Federal grants or "handyman specials," if I buy an old home to renovate?

Some of your concerns may already have been addressed by the bank, so when you're "shopping," ask for printed information on home loan requirements and other relevant brochures. Be sure you read them so that you show up for the meeting well prepared and knowledgeable.

STEP 3: Having made the appointment for a convenient time (some banks have evening hours), call to confirm the day before and be sure to bring the questions, written *and* memorized. Don't be timid about making notes during the meeting. Take time to breathe slowly and deeply a few times before entering the bank. This is a giant step, and you and I know it. Remember, I'll be there in spirit when you start talking.

STEP 4:   This is the time to demythify the world of finance. So relate to the official behind the desk as a fellow human being, a person more informed than you in this field—but no better. Be friendly, not awed. Establish eye contact often. Show yourself to be eager to learn more about banks and the ways they can help build your As-If life.

STEP 5:   Even if you and the official decide that you are not yet ready for a home loan, remain seated and continue asking questions. Explore the possibility of establishing a line of credit by taking out a smallish loan, say, for home improvement. (Paying it back promptly stands you in good stead when you really need cash, a smart move for your financial record, and, perhaps, an especially good one while you are setting goals.) Anyway, talk it over then and there. Ask about opening a savings or money-market account, a checking account that pays interest, a bank credit card, the latest interest rates on CDs. Write the answers, and as you wrap things up, ask for additional relevant printed material you can bring home to read at your leisure.

YOUR SUPPORT SYSTEM BEGINS

During your visit to the bank, request the bank official's business card. Mentally pat yourself on the back (a trick in itself) because this is the premier card for your personal single file. From delicatessen to dial-a-prayer, you're on your way to putting together an extensive (and ever-expanding) collection of resources that will make your daily routine—and the crisis hot spots—easier to handle. (Now, make a card for the travel agency you called to arrange your trip and see if any other current resources of yours come to mind.) You'll thank me for prodding you to do this.

STEP 6:   A few days later, make a follow-up call to the bank official. Express your appreciation for the time, then go on to say that you are looking for an accountant and could he or she refer you to a good one. See what happens. If a name is given, call the person and arrange an appointment. (That second visit will be easier, I guarantee.) Again, go with a list of questions and take notes. Call to say thanks, and at that time ask for the name of a skilled attorney. And so on. Even before you create an Old Girls' Network (our next topic), you'll be building a support system with referrals from your own resources. The number of business cards in your file will increase and you'll see that there is, after all, a floating sea of helpfulness between us all. You're creating a substantive support system (more about it in Chapter Four), which should begin to give you a sense of control and solidity. You may not (yet) possess a dynasty, but by the end of this book you will have at your fingertips a network of people and organizations available for professional help as well as friendship. And in the next exercise, you'll see how to combine these two.

EXERCISE 4:
THE OLD GIRLS' NETWORK

This is your counterpart to the Old Boys' Network, proving you don't have to be old (or male) to cultivate nurturing linkage. Now that most of us are at the stage where we can regard one another as sisters rather than competitors, this kind of helpfulness—organized and ongoing—can work. On the other hand, groups may not be your thing; you just don't feel comfortable functioning as a team. You prefer to operate solo. Or with only one or two close friends. I can relate to that. As I've said before, any suggestion offered is strictly a suggestion. You may not elect to follow it, or you may adapt it to better suit your needs. Please remember that.

STEP 1:   Invite ten or twelve women (or two or three, if you prefer) over for coffee to explore the possibility of networking. Select women who are ambitious and sharing, and tell friends to invite the women they know who fit the description. If the response is big, split into small sessions so that each person gets a fair hearing, and every identity has a chance to be known. Introduce yourselves, tell about your work and your goals. This is a preliminary "interview" to feel each other out. You may start with a lot of people, but the number will whittle down quickly, as people lose interest in making a serious commitment. And that part of it is *crucial*: Stress clearly the need to make and keep a pledge to the group. The network is only as strong as its weakest link. At the end of the get-together, come up with a time and place for the first formal meeting.

STEP 2:   At that first meeting (perhaps at breakfast), set the dues ($20 yearly seems reasonable) and plan the next meeting's agenda. Even then you'll be evaluating members for their level of contribution. How can this woman add to the network? Does she have friends who are helpers and available to be called upon in crunch times? Is she connected with people in positions of influence who could lend their expertise to the group from time to time? Is she trustable, dedicated to this idea of one person helping the other?

See to it that phone numbers (home and office) are exchanged so that everyone can be contacted one way or another. As the group settles in and gets to know itself, members will feel more and more committed to one another. That's the secret of a small core group (five to seven members); the intimacy cultivates a bond of sisterhood. You will probably decide to meet once every few weeks at first, to keep the momentum. But timetable decisions are up to you and your group, of course.

STEP 3:   At the first *working* meeting, you'll probably focus on career issues. But as the group builds mutual trust, other concerns will take the floor: child care, child support, adult courses. Soon you may want to spin off subgroups that target one interest: travel, investments (see Resources), theater, children's activities. They will probably want to meet separately according to their own schedules, but the main group must always be foremost in everyone's priorities.

STEP 4:   The network exists to serve its members in as many ways as they choose. One of its prime functions is to be a web of services and solutions, so as you expand your membership (watch and see how word spreads about a good thing), be careful to build in a variety of occupations, ethnic groups, and interests. (Members contact their friends and they do the same, and so on—which is the way job interviews materialize and slightly used automobiles find buyers.) You're building a bulletin-board operation through the cooperation of like-minded women willing to make an effort on behalf of the person who needs it at that moment.

STEP 5:   But don't stop there. The meetings can also help smooth over the rough spots of being single. Use them to rehearse first-date conversation, career events, phone calls that loom large. Setting up an effective network is not a piece of cake; you and a handful of other women will probably find yourselves doing most of the work at the beginning. But after a few months, your efforts will pay off. A helping network will be in place and functioning.

STEP 6:   Before you forget, make a card for your Old Girls' Network (OGN) and write on it every member's address and phone numbers. Add it to your single file.

In time, even though you're constantly screening, some

members will probably drop out, no longer motivated. Crisis? No—opportunity to bring in fresh blood and keep the group healthy. New people bring new ideas and other ways to improve the network. Listen to those suggestions. Your group's longevity will depend on its ability to adjust and adapt.

Expanding your life doesn't always come through people, though. Reshaping strategies requires time alone, too. Solitude allows you to digest changes and integrate them into your psyche. After hearing me out, visiting with yourself periodically could become a lifelong habit, no matter whom you love or how many friends you have. Daily meditation will fill some of this need. So will periods of retreat, when you spend the day in a park or hiking alone. As the growth process becomes a way of life, these times of aloneness will appreciate in value.

EXERCISE 5:
ADVANCE YOUR CAREER

If I were asked my favorite bit of advice, it would be to develop a career; I firmly believe that not much else you can do on your own can bring such satisfaction. In later chapters we'll go into this more deeply, but this section alone should start you thinking more seriously about the work that consumes most of your waking hours.

STEP 1: For openers, focus on your job. Literally. Close your eyes, lean back your head, and concentrate. How did you get it? How long have you had it? Is it interesting/appropriate for you at this point in your life? Is it the right field, the right position? Don't rush the answers; let them simmer. And while you're feeling contemplative, give a thought to the fact that a "just-a-job" work life leaves you famished for the excitement of a man, while a meaningful, absorbing career can bring with it compensations that release you from that form of slavery.

STEP 2:   List three other career possibilities that interest you. If you're currently negotiating for a salary increase, or are unsure about your work for other reasons, now's a good time to spend real amounts of time and energy to look into those career paths. But don't give it up prematurely. (A steady job gives the security to explore alternatives without pressure.) If the local adult school offers courses in these fields, see if you can audit the first few classes and then, if you're hooked, enroll for credit. If you decide to enter one of these fields, the additional education may give you a leg-up at a job interview. This is the kind of situation where your OGN excels; ask their advice. And find out about salary potential, advancement possibilities, qualifications. Talk to people already in the field you are considering. And read the excellent books available for people who, like you, are at a crossroads. (See Resources.)

STEP 3:   But if you're content where you are, this is a time to think about advancement. That means setting goals, of course, and—yes—writing them down. Suggestions:

- Work overtime this week—it earns extra money and the added respect of your co-workers and employer.

- Enroll in a class this semester to work toward a master's degree—it will boost your earnings, position, and morale.

- Subscribe to a leading professional journal and/or newsletter.

- Join a professional organization in the field. (If there's no chapter in your area, contact national headquarters and ask about starting one.)

Your work—"career" is the word I prefer—should be a solid, exciting, strong element in the center of your life. It can be a sanctuary when the rest of your world seems to be falling apart, a source of emotional enrichment, and a support system. But it must never prevent you from reaching your potential as a rounded person by becoming a defense barrier or hiding place. There will be periods when you work hard and long, but that must not be all the time. Any dimension of your life that becomes so large it chronically overshadows the others destroys the balance you are striving to achieve. In all things, you will find moderation to be the ultimate sophistication.

AVOID SELF-SABOTAGE

Fear of success—not fear of failure—can stand in the way of anyone's career. You, as a single woman, may be giving this fear a special twist: undermining yourself unconsciously out of fear that success will keep men away. Well, the facts are otherwise. Successful people gravitate toward successful people. (Men are no different—unless insecurity is a problem. Healthy male achievers are drawn to women who are similarly productive.) So do all you can to avoid shutting yourself out of a very sweet part of life—and some very sweet men.

1. Start a scrapbook of your achievements—at work and elsewhere. Tangible reminders such as congratulatory letters, special honors, commendations from your employer, diplomas, and awards will keep your ego boosted and ready for the next climb up the mountain.

2. Reevaluate your career expectations. It helps to create a graph of positions in your company so that you can plan your spot two years from now, five years from now, and so on. Be careful not to be grandiose—use the insights

triggered by the exercises to stay realistic—but be just as careful not to sell yourself short. You could wind up in a position no woman has ever held. Why not?

3. Visualize yourself as a confident person and keep that image foremost as you fall asleep each night. As you wait for sleep, see yourself in your mind's eye as a key person in your office, managing work flow and employees with respect and firmness. See yourself in a dialogue with your parents, pitching your political views. Imagine winning a debate with your boyfriend. Picture how gracious you would be with them all and how scrupulously you would keep their egos intact.

And while you're visualizing, picture your life as a child's seesaw, with work in the middle, as the fulcrum. In a very real way, work's satisfaction gives balance to relationships by keeping expectations reasonable. Friends and family are asked only for what they can give, a man is expected only to be half of a love partnership. Work's gratification frees the people in your life from having to be your sun, source of all your pleasure and energy.

And work gives you your own corner, a domain you alone rule. Even if the kingdom is a single desk, it is yours. Work frees you from role-playing and encourages you to express your individuality. In its unique way, it gives you security and a sense of purpose because you're contributing to something larger than yourself. We women lose ourselves so naturally in nurturing the people we love; what a joy to have a part of life that actually strengthens personhood. You needn't be a high-powered executive to gain sustenance from your workday; with the right attitude, any decent job can make you more of a person. As the Chinese say, one can use stone to carve jade.

Living *as if* you will always be single is another way of saying take charge of your life now. If you bring away only one nugget from these strategies, let it be the resolve to live your life *as if you will always be single.*

You're in pursuit of something great, staging your private revolution. You're changing the basic patterns of your life, and because the challenge is ongoing, along the way you're learning to handle the setbacks that must come with such a venture. You'll make mistakes; plans will take wrong turns. So what's new? It's only logical that the more you attempt, the more mistakes you'll make. But as long as you learn from them, they'll work for you. The real test is whether you will quit. Only quitting turns your attempts into failures. Staying with them shortens the gap between where you are and where you want to be. Refuse to be vanquished, no matter what. Don't settle for mere coping. You want better than that; you want to prevail.

When you think about it, living As-If is such a radically new way of looking at the world that it's tantamount to citizenship in another land. You say you'd rather live in the Country of the Married? Or keep renewing a Singleworld visa to avoid full-fledged citizenship?

Believe me, I resisted my singleness the same way. That's why insight into the biggest What-If question of all made me do a flip-flop in attitude. Suddenly I saw the wisdom of embracing the very thing I had been fleeing for years. I realized that living as a "temporary" in the single community was keeping me rootless and anxious, back in the waiting room. You and I both remember the void there, with virtually no power and just the faintest hint of identity.

Well, the next chapter makes all of that history and might convince you once and for all to settle into your present moment much more contentedly. When you think of it, isn't that the best thing you can do with your life right now?

THREE

SYNTHESIS:
SHAPING THE SELF

You are on the verge of the most rewarding find of a lifetime, the one discovery guaranteed to make you happier. You're about to find that beneath insecurities and fears, beyond well-intentioned excuses and half-hearted resolutions, lies a solid and thoroughly likable person. It takes a lifetime to truly know yourself, so you're not going to make this total discovery overnight, no matter how much insight you bring to these exercises. But you are going to understand yourself better.

Oh, I know, you're thinking that "finding yourself" went out with "flower power" and other 1960s slogans, or that you already did all this—in high school. But the kind of self-exploration I'm talking about doesn't go out of style. It's always with us and it's endlessly fascinating. If you've given up on the search for self, it's time to try again. This time, with persistence and patience and faith.

Discovering parts of yourself is a synthesis, as new truths

emerge and then blend with the "you" you already know. The process of opening petals is lifelong—and be glad it is. Appreciate having many chances to know who you are.

Why start the journey now? Because as a person on her own, you have an advantage. I won't say it's impossible to develop yourself when you're partnered, but it's more difficult. Now, while you're without the inherent distractions of a man—sharing his interests, considering his needs—you have more time and energy to find out what makes you tick. Remember the Chinese word for *crisis* as composed of characters for danger and opportunity? The chance to know yourself is part of the opportunity you gave yourself when you picked up this book. You see, each stage of life has its own reason for being, and a single space in life is a time to pin down the selfhood so elusive during the search yet so trustable once defined.

The identity that emerges from that search will:

- become a fixed frame of reference in the coupled phases of your life, when it's even more crucial to keep your self-balance

- help you choose a partner (how can you know another person if you don't first know yourself?)

- serve as a bulwark against the negativism of limited people who see no further than "single" when looking at an unmarried woman.

Like a career, family, and friends, this grounded sense of self will be the bedrock on which you build the rest of your life. Pondering the human psyche has kept thinkers busy for centuries, so I will not dare to supply ultimate answers in one chapter. What I can do—and what you will in time do for yourself—is to help gather around you those things that encourage your selfhood to shine. Putting them together takes a bit of doing, but I promise that your single-mindedness (in both senses) will pay off with strong feelings of confidence.

WHY WOMEN WAFFLE

The letters I receive, together with two decades of research and extensive life experience, convince me there's a very real reason why many single women shy away from knowing themselves: You'd rather "stay loose"—without too much definition. Whether or not you realize it, you've built into your personality a "margin for error" open for revisions and alterations by The Man Who Isn't There. I don't usually pass along horror stories, but we all know about the woman who made herself over in the image of each man she loved—and in the process forgot who she was. Even if *you* haven't gone that far, you've probably experienced the queasy feeling in the pit of your stomach when you were in love, the signal that comes with giving away too much of the self you're afraid to own. It's the dark side of the passivity and procrastination we've talked about. In Chapters One and Two it threatened to keep you in the waiting room; here, it could steal your identity.

COMPROMISING POSITIONS

Haven't we all—at least once—come perilously close to losing our identity to a man? You can't build a self if you're busy giving it away. So if you can relate to several of the following situations (I certainly do), take stock of current romantic involvements (no matter how one-sided or new) and promise yourself you'll *be yourself* from now on. Toward that end, a checklist of danger signals:

- you're deliberately holding back part of yourself (your laugh, your politics) because he may not like it;

- you're angry because deep down you know you shouldn't hold back—but you're fearful and can't seem to stop yourself;

- your tastes suddenly change; you're into acid rock when you really prefer classical music;

- you get a perm, change your hair color, alter your way of dressing, talking, or behaving—because he likes you better that way and you're afraid you'll lose him if you don't change;

- you have few opinions—until you talk to him;

- you're drifting away from your friends because he doesn't like them;

- people say you've changed since you started seeing him (and they don't mean for the better).

And while we're on the subject of self-knowledge, let's look at it through a cosmic metaphor. Too often, a woman gets caught up in a man's orbit and plays moon to his sun. Her movements are not her own; she depends on him for groundedness. Many actually believe that without a man in their life (even The Man Who Isn't There), they will be spun out to the far edge of the universe with accompanying loss of status, respect, and a comfortable niche in the social environment.

It's easy to see how this kind of thinking embedded itself in the female mentality. A woman used to be a man's property and, therefore, had no identity without him. Literally. (In some societies that is still the case.) Gradually, American women are working their way out of this morass. But the evolution won't be complete until we've internalized the belief that each of us belongs first of all to herself. (That is the essence that remains individual, autonomous, unique, and the reason I believe all people are basically single.)

You must create your own orbit and make *yourself* its sun. I promise you that your solar system will not rotate on a lonely orbit. It's a people world, single or married, so the challenge is to balance alone time with the good people you put into your life. Your solar system will be animated by the energy of a support network, community involvement, components that give you connectedness. But *you* will supply the groundedness. Like moving out of the waiting room, building your own life by defining your selfhood in no way precludes you from sharing love. And this way, when it comes into your life, you won't give up anything; you'll *combine* orbits. (That is synergy, one plus one equaling three.) Any man worth wanting will be relieved that he doesn't have to drag you along as a shadow as he goes about his life or have to be the center of gravity for your life as well as his.

As I've said before (and will probably say again) many women believe that an interesting, fulfilling single life—the kind you can build when you know and understand yourself —practically guarantees spinsterhood. (Remember that word?) The truth is just the opposite: Knowing and growing *increases* romantic possibilities; passivity and procrastination shut them out.

SOLITUDE

The path to the self begins with a long look at your past as well as your present—to see who you have been as well as who you are becoming. The exercises and suggestions in this chapter will help. But before we get to them, there is a prerequisite: You must learn to become comfortable, really comfortable, being alone. It is indeed a "people world," but the journey to the self is traveled single file.

In this society, being alone gets bad press. We're afraid to walk into a cocktail party by ourselves, embarrassed when we are solo and run into friends at the movies (which you promised—with a deep breath—to see alone occasionally). You must learn to ignore the feeling that to be alone means to be rejected, that it's the condition of last resort. (Chapter

Five deals with the difference between aloneness and loneliness.) You must acquire the self-discipline to turn down boring people and resist "buffer" activities (dates made solely to avoid being alone with yourself). Society makes it too easy to feel rejected, a loner, second-class for being alone, but you can't live your life according to public perception. Acknowledge prejudices as part of living—and, with practice, move beyond them to live as you see fit.

A BIT OF IRONY

With all this talk about alone time, you're justified in feeling baffled. Who is this Susan Deitz, a loner who's trying to make me her clone? Not at all. Actually, my mission is to gently swirl you out into the world. But to get there you need a sense of who you are. And that requires time spent with yourself. So we come full circle, back to solitude. Understand that it's not solitude for its own sake, but as the springboard out of preoccupation with self—aloneness as liberating process, you could say.

MAKE YOURSELF COMFORTABLE BEING ALONE

Think of this section as a limbering-up strategy, designed to help you feel better in your own skin. The following situations are "teeth-gritters" for most single women, and I've suggested ways to feel more relaxed in them. The theory is simple: Turn distress into success. But the doing is not so pat. Feel free to add to the list.

SITUATION 1:
GOING TO BED ALONE

This can provoke all sorts of fears, from immediate physical ones (what if somebody comes through the window?) to rejection (what if I have to sleep alone the rest of my life?). Above all, keep in mind that you can always have *somebody* to sleep with. There's nobody who can't find a body. You're deliberately choosing to sleep alone; you're not a victim. Whether you've been accustomed to another warm body or have been sleeping solo for years, there are ways to climb between the sheets alone and be glad of it. (Once you're asleep you're on your own anyway, it's the "drifting off" that's not fun.)

- See bedtime as a chance to be utterly selfish: Watch the telly till three in the morning, light a fragrance candle, luxuriate in your lacy sheets, sleep in the nude—things you might not do if somebody else was around to see. It's eat-crackers-in-bed time.

- Play music—buy a clock radio that plays for a designated period and then shuts off, or play a tape or record that makes you smile. Robert Browning said, "He who hears music feels his solitude peopled at once." You can sing along, too. Who cares what the neighbors think?

- Afraid of the dark? (Don't be ashamed, most of us are to some degree.) Give in and leave a night-light on in the bathroom or hall and keep your door slightly open.

- Install a phone by your bed if you don't already have one. Then you can "reach out and touch someone" without getting up. Develop your support group to include people you can reach in the crunch moments. (In my widowed years I dated a man who owned a bar. It was great being able to have a friendly humanoid to talk to at 4 A.M.)

- Keep a notepad and pen by the bed. Your mind is often clearer in that twilight time before sleep comes, and ideas are freer to bubble up.

- Read in bed—all night if you want. The best part is that you don't have to use one of those pea-sized book lights. Think how much your eyes will appreciate this!

- Try "dial-a-joke" or "dial-a-prayer" (depending on your mood) to combat what I call the "tigers that come in the night" and a friend calls the "Oh my God's."

- There's nothing wrong (and everything right) with getting up, making yourself a cup of tea or warm milk, and reading *The Power of Positive Thinking* or the Bible. Turn your energy outward—say a prayer for somebody else, send your positive thoughts to a friend who needs them. It can only help.

- There's a time for everything, and this is your time to go to bed alone. One thing is certain: Things change. While you have the chance, get the goodness out of this end-of-the-day communion with yourself.

SITUATION 2:
GOING TO A PARTY ALONE

This is the biggest challenge of all, because it involves other people and their perception of a woman socializing alone. And so much of the outcome depends on what's inside your head. Feeling rejected, out of place, or like a loser means almost certain rejection, awkwardness, exile—to one degree or another. If there was ever a situation for a belief to become reality, this is it. Because on the other hand, feeling good about yourself, secure in your own niceness and adequacy, generates an aura around you that magnetizes. A ready smile, bright eyes, friendly expression, calmness—all are intriguing. You may not be an instant hit the first time you party without a man, but poise and confidence will grow with practice. (So accept all invitations to go out alone.) Only nonfriends will care that you are not partnered, and they don't count in your scheme of things. Tips:

- Tell yourself as you walk into the room that you have a delicious rendezvous after the party. (Maybe you will.) This ploy helps put the shoulders back and chest out where they convey confidence and a healthy ego.

- Think uplifting thoughts while you are making an entrance; they will show on your face and in your movements. (List the thoughts and memorize them a few hours before the party.)

- When you arrive, immediately locate the host and say a hearty hello. Any host worth his or her canapés will take you around and make a few appropriate introductions, especially if you don't know many of the guests.

- Offer to help with the serving of the food. Nothing puts you into the action like becoming a participant.

- Bring a gift—a bottle of wine or a bouquet of flowers, a casserole to warm up. Making the presentation fills the first few moments that could be awkward, endears you to the host as an appreciative guest, and gives you an excuse to talk and smile.

- Mingle, mingle, mingle. Use your mobility to the max; exploit the advantage of being dateless.

SITUATION 3:
BEING ALONE FOR A WEEKEND

Most of us are fine on our own for a little while, but we are lost when the days stretch out ahead of us, a virtual desert of nonstop hours daring us to bring it alive. Possibilities for structuring the time:

- Make a mental note to meditate twice each day—morning and evening.

- Tackle a chore you've been postponing: closet-cleaning, bank-statement sorting, magazine clipping, photograph cataloguing, vacation planning, budget reviewing. (In fact, now might be the time to make a list of such odd things to be done in leisure periods like this.)

- Rent a fitness video or audio tape and actually do the workout! There's no law against doing it twice a day, either—and on consecutive days.

- Pack a lunch and bring it to the park. Listen, really listen, to the sounds of nature; touch the leaves, feed the squirrels.

- Call your local museum and ask about special movies and weekend programs.

- Plan a dinner party. Yes—make lists: guests, groceries, menu, wines, and anything else that can be listed!

- Rent a bicycle and ride through the park. Stop at a playground and watch the children at play.

- Spend an hour browsing at your local bookstore or public library. The real trick in our society is to utilize the devices that compensate for our isolation (telephone, radio, Walkman, television) with dis-

cretion, in a way that doesn't separate us from ourselves. As diversion, entertainment, a touch of
fantasy, they work well. But a difference in degree
is a difference in kind; overdosing on technology is
a form of addiction. A word to the wise.

SITUATION 4:
BEING ALONE WHEN YOU'RE ILL

Involuntary alone time becomes the ultimate test of your support system. That old negativism creeps under the covers
when you're sick and encourages you to think the strangest
thoughts. Lying in bed, bones aching and feeling miserable,
you tend to see marriage (to any man) as the solution to
everything. This tests your ability to uproot negative thoughts
and replant them with positive replacements. It's easy to wallow in self-pity when alone and sick, but you can do better:

• Remind yourself you would feel just as awful if you
  had a husband. He'd be at the office and you'd be
  just as you are—alone.

• Pick up the phone and call the network of friends
  you've talked to about just such days as this. (Their
  office and home phone numbers should be on a
  bedside list. If that list is not yet there, I have a
  hunch it will be the next time you are laid low.)

• Call the local deli to make a delivery. (Chicken soup
  should be in it.) And while you're calling, ask them
  to throw in a candy bar or bananas. It's indulgence
  time; the calories will have to look the other way.

• With the pad and pencil you keep by your bed
  (ahem!) make a note to call your parents when the
  rates go down—or when you think they'll both be
  home. A family conference call feels so good. Your
  mom will undoubtedly suggest medicine and foods,

and write them down too. You never know; you just might try them!

TIP: **After you've dialed a number, lie down with the receiver to your ear. Speaking while nestled under the covers feels cozy and restful. Prop a pillow under the back of your knees while you're on your back, and don't let the one under your head come down below your neck.**

• Feeling sick is a low time when you're not expecting a mate to come home soon and supply companionship. So, if you're not cranky or contagious, ask a bosom buddy (one of your best on that list, remember?) to share a barbecued chicken or pizza pie. You two can have a hen party, and her visit will end the dragging hours of feeling every ache magnified. Keep making calls until you've corralled someone. (If it's feasible, your folks would be thrilled to be asked over. Don't worry about appearing babyish; a little healthy dependence is good practice for relating skills.)

With a change in thinking and a formulation of strategies, you can go far to smooth over those rough moments alone. But there is a type of isolation that resists eviction, the alienation that comes from being out of touch with the inner self. No condition is as painful, confusing, and corrosive to relationships. Until you can tune in to your inner voice, that blend of intuition, insight, and instinct, there is nowhere you can hide from this awful separateness. When the mind and the emotions are not connected, self-knowledge and human closeness are just not possible.

The next time you are by yourself, listen for that small voice. It may not always broadcast what you want to hear, but its very existence—and your ability to tune into it— provide baseline wisdom. *My* inner voice tells me that once you start listening to *yours*, you will never again feel the extremes of loneliness. (Chapter Five holds more thoughts on this.) The more you listen to that voice, the more confidence it will inspire. It will never fail you.

This next exercise gives you a break from the world of words. Make sure you are in a quiet place before you begin, and give yourself plenty of elbow room.

EXERCISE 1:
PICTURE YOURSELF

STEP 1:   Take out a clean sheet of unlined paper and a pencil, pen, felt marker, or crayon, and draw a picture of yourself. It can be any shape, size, or style you wish. Don't worry about professionalism; this isn't a test of artistic skills! Draw yourself the way you see yourself; a self-portrait is what we're after. I do ask that you finish this in ten minutes or less. That's all I'm going to say for now. (And don't read ahead; that's cheating!)

STEP 2:   On another sheet of paper (or the same one if you have room), draw another picture of yourself. This one is to be you ten years from now. (Again, limit yourself to ten minutes.)

STEP 3:   This time, draw a third picture of yourself as a woman about seventy. (Same time limit as above.)

STEP 4:   Now, look at the sketches. Did you draw a face or a full figure? A stick figure or a fleshed-out one? Is your body proportioned? (Taking into account your artistic strengths and weaknesses, that is.) Did you draw yourself as a fat person when you are really medium-size? Or vice versa? Does your likeness take up most of each page? Or is it a forlorn little figure almost lost in the whiteness of the paper? Are you alone in the sketch? Or do you have "props"? If so, what are they? A briefcase? A baby? A friend? A man? Are you standing beside a house, a tree, a desk? Which facial feature is most prominent? Are you smiling or frowning? Are your eyes open or closed? Is the sketch realistic or impressionistic?

STEP 5:   Ask yourself the same questions with the ten-years-later and older-woman sketches. How did you change yourself to show the passage of time? Do you have wrinkles? Are you shorter or taller? Bette Davis once said she'd end up as a lonely old woman on top of a hill. Where do you end up?

Don't look to the bottom of the page for answers. There are none. This is not a quiz with a score. Nevertheless, it is a *picture*, and if not worth the proverbial thousand words, still exceedingly valuable. This cuts to the essence of your self-image. And you can analyze the clues. Look closely between the lines for the truths.

EXERCISE 2:
TREE'S A CROWD

Your pedigree is yours alone, and tracing your roots is a great way to gain perspective on yourself. (Besides, it's fun to dig up gossip about your ancestors.)

STEP 1:   There are many other people who are digging for family facts, so many that there's a national organization whose purpose is to help people track down their own genealogy. The National Genealogical Society offers charts, books, a correspondence course, and other research material to help you do it yourself. (See Resources.)

STEP 2:   Tap every living relative (especially the older ones, of course) for information about your family. Seek out the family archivist, the aunt, uncle, or cousin who knows the most about your family (including why great-aunt Sally ran away when she was fifteen).

If you're part of a clan that came over on the Mayflower or had a great-great-great grandfather fighting in the Revolutionary War, someone in your family may have already done a lot of research to become a member of a special society like the DAR (Daughters of the American Revolution). So don't reinvent the wheel; build on what other relatives have done. If you're the first one in your clan to dig for information, it's even more fun—almost like a detective story.

STEP 3:   Gather information about your family. Here are some suggestions:

- Check local courthouses for birth, death, and marriage records.

- Visit an old graveyard and make a rubbing of a relative's tombstone or copy down any relevant birth and death dates you find.

- Look through family photographs and ask questions of the "family archivist" about the background of each one. If past is prologue, then these photographs will show you where you're going. The more you know about your relatives, especially ones you resemble, the more you can learn about yourself. You can build on their decisions, avoid their mistakes. These glimpses of the past can introduce you to almost-forgotten relatives, too, and help you see the relationships among them.

- As you discovered above, the pictures you draw tell you about yourself. Family photographs do the same. If you don't have anyone to ask about some snapshots, try to figure them out yourself. In contemporary photographs, notice things about yourself—

telling patterns. Are you standing to the side? Even your own childhood is prologue, you know. It's another way of learning about the elements that made you who you are.

• It might be expensive, but you could travel all the way back to "the old country" to seek out long-lost cousins or family homesteads. (You could combine this journey with your "momentous trip" in Chapter One.) Contact the Genealogical Association and see if they have local representatives. Through them you might meet someone in your area who's doing the same thing. As you begin exploring your family tree, one thing will lead to another until you may be taking a real as well as a metaphorical journey. (This could give you the impetus to start saving money seriously.)

STEP 4:   Interview each of your parents (separately) on tape about their history and backgrounds. (Write your questions beforehand so you save time and tape, leaving some room for spontaneity, of course.) Getting to know them as individuals will help you understand them better. I promise you, you'll discover things about them you never knew, explanations and personal asides that will allow you to see them out of their roles and labels. And as you do, you'll feel yourself relating to them more as friends than caretakers. Your growing process is helping them to grow, too, to relax and be themselves.

STEP 5:   Go on to tape interviews with your siblings, a favorite uncle, your grandparents, a female cousin you've always idolized, an aunt who is a role model. As these family members reveal themselves, their insights will shed light on parts of you that may have been hidden or misunderstood up to now. If you have limited tapes and time, talk with your parents and grandparents first. Even an hour-long conversation will give you lots of information—and a memento you will always treasure. It will be even more precious to your children, giving them a sense of continuity and pride.

STEP 6: Create a family network from what you learn. You can start by drawing a family "tree." (You don't have to make a real tree, but simply list the names and dates and indicate the relationships of each family member. See Re-

---

AN ALMOST—FAMILY TREE

This is something you can do if you have the time. (I hope you do.) Since you are making a concerted effort to get to know yourself, it would help to go beyond your family for information. Arrange to interview a favorite teacher (or a few teachers with whom you've felt that special chemistry) or a first employer who will tell you about yourself as you were then. Tape the interview, if possible, and again, go with a list of prepared questions.

These people will have perceptions that could never occur to your parents. A teacher can tell you things about you at thirteen that no one else can: whether the boys walked you home, how you spoke up in class, whether you were a happy teenager, if you were as you are now—all sorts of interesting things. Talk to old friends, former classmates, the family you used to baby-sit for. Collect their names and create an "almost-family" tree on a separate sheet of paper to record significant relationships of your past. Put the tapes you create into a separate box, labeled and dated. They are irreplaceable because people never speak the same way twice. And you want their voices, as well as their words, for your children.

sources for a home-study course.) Start as far back as you can, at least with your great-grandparents. Go a step further with living relatives. Put their addresses and phone numbers on the "tree" too. You're building two family networks here. One is for the past, the other for the present.

STEP 7:   The best use of this new knowledge is when you *contact* your discovered relatives for a family reunion. If you can, make it a big shindig. (Ask the local paper to send a photographer.) But the gathering doesn't have to be an extravaganza; a simple invitation to your relatives for a visit will be as celebratory. Some may live near; some may live far away, so work out the housing arrangements with them and ask your friends to board some guests if necessary.

You may learn more about your background when you talk to a cousin you haven't seen for twenty years. He'll call you a nickname or refer to a distant summer that all of a sudden makes some large pieces fall in place. The *process* of this exercise is as important as the findings, because it will lead you to sides of yourself which may have always been puzzling.

———

You are making a family of friends; now, make friends of your family. And I mean true friendship—the kind that encourages frank talk. (Most of the steps in the next exercise are addressed specifically to those of you who have children.)

EXERCISE 3:
FAMILY COUNCILS

Your children will give you a bright-light picture of yourself—that's for sure. It's from their perspective, of course, but it's an unsullied slant, unadulterated by the influences that cloud the minds of most adults. You could do a lot worse than walk around this world with the self-image given to you by your children.

STEP 1: Ask your children if there's anything they'd like to know about you. Suggest that they make a list of their questions.

STEP 2: In privacy, read the list and make brief notes of your replies. Prepare your thoughts, giving yourself plenty of room for spontaneity, but develop a point of view about each question—even if it stirs up some dust. Controversy can resolve into even deeper closeness.

STEP 3: Then call a family meeting. Ask your kids if you can tape the session, and do it only when everyone feels comfortable with the idea. Arrange it on a night when there's no school the next day, and tell the kids to keep the evening free—the whole evening (Friday night or a holiday eve is perfect). Later you might want to treat your questioners to an ice-cream soda. Give them as much time as they need for this discussion. Don't rush them, and don't you rush, either, no matter how antsy you get. This is a rare opportunity to show your kids the person behind the mother role. It would help if you know yourself well so you won't feel shame or guilt when you answer. But if you do feel twinges, admit it. They'll love you even more for not trying to be superhuman. And above all, make your answers honest; no one sniffs out duplicity like the young.

STEP 4: Throw out for discussion the idea of making this a regular ritual for everyone to air gripes, ideas, questions. If bimonthly sessions seem too often, plan at least one additional council to this one, say about three weeks from now. Suggest that everyone start keeping an agenda of issues they want to discuss then.

STEP 5: Go out for ice cream—as a family. And a family that likes itself better. Chances are you'll know yourself better after even the first family council.

STEP 6: Celebrate this new-found insight by calling your folks and suggesting that the next clan gathering be held at your house. Hosting a family get-together is another way to elevate you to full adult status in your tribe. After all, developing yourself the way you are is hard work; you're making a lot of changes. Equal footing in the family ought to be part of your reward.

EXERCISE 4:
GREAT TRANSFORMATIONS

Think back to the second exercise now, back to that person you were beginning to uncover when you talked with a cousin you hadn't seen since childhood, and recall that almost-forgotten part of you he brought to mind. This next exercise asks you to think of the moltings in your life, the times when you've shed the old and started growing a new skin. Through those changes you can plumb the layers of your current persona.

STEP 1: Write down all the names you've ever used. (Include even the most childish nickname.) Have you ever changed your first name? Legally or informally? Did it stick? Who called you that? What about your last name? (Marriage doesn't count.) Circle the name you like best, and think about why you like it. Is it the name you're called currently?

STEP 2: Next, think of personality changes, times when you've made a conscious effort to change some important facet of your character. I don't mean every New Year's resolution you've ever made, but an effort to transform yourself. Include the changes that didn't stick—that time in college when you started dressing entirely in black and smoking cigarettes (in a cigarette holder, no less), or right before your divorce, when you vowed to be nothing but the perfect wife. And include the changes that *did* become a part of you. To make the unraveling simpler, divide your life into decades and see if you can find at least one change every ten years.

STEP 3: Study this list of "great transformations." Look for trends. Have you been running away from a character trait that haunts you, trying to alter the unalterable? At what points in your life have you changed the most—when there was a crisis (read "opportunity")? Do you change voluntarily or only when some near-catastrophe pushes you toward it?

In a sense, we all reinvent ourselves every day, but to make sense of these new selves, you need to understand whether you're using them as a cover-up or as a route to self-development.

How often we race around keeping appointments with co-workers, teachers, baby-sitters, friends—you name it—but forget to honor the most important appointment of all, the one with ourselves, the one that needs quiet time.

EXERCISE 5:
MEDITATE

Establish a pause in your routine. Arrange it at the end of your workday, after dinner or just before bedtime. Since your celebration of self comes in the early morning, it's best to place this ritual at the other end of the day. It is very important to integrate your period of meditation into every day, without fail, since the results are cumulative. (That they are astonishing is for another book.)

Yes, this is time with and for yourself, no one else invited. (Though at some point you may decide to ask another meditator to share the moment. What intimacy energy-sharing can develop!) Meditation is the answer to life too often lived fast-forward and too seldom given time for review. Its disciplined quietness clears the mind and allows important issues to bubble up through the jumble of fleeting impressions and stray thoughts that accumulate.

Meditation is not a dark ceremony of secretive cults. Actually, any directed mental activity qualifies as meditation. It doesn't even require a special mantra or Sanskrit word to be effective. The point of meditating is to return sovereignty to the mind and acknowledge its limitless potential. Meditation is no more than an instrument to change what you think and how much you think.

1. Find a quiet place (phone off, windows closed).

2. Sit in a comfortable position with your feet squarely on the ground, legs uncrossed.

3. Close your eyes and put your hands on your knees. Let your body relax.

4. Become aware of your breathing; count "one" as you exhale. Count "two" when you exhale the next time (up to ten), then start again at "one."

5. Concentrate on your breathing. If thoughts arise, that's good, but stay focused on the breathing. If you forget your count, that's okay too, but—again—go back to the breathing. You might notice that your breathing slows down. This is a natural and restorative result of relaxation.

6. Do this five or ten minutes a day at the same time of day, and several times a week, if possible.

7. It's important that you not be distracted. If you need to stretch or move, do it quickly and return to your breathing routine.

Once you develop this skill, you can use it whenever you need it: walking, or standing in a line at the supermarket (imagine how meditation could help you in a car stuck in a traffic jam!). You're extending your ability to concentrate for longer periods and you're quieting the mind for new ideas to emerge. Now, relax and begin.

———

Knowing yourself is only half the victory; utilizing your insights to create a nutritive environment for that selfhood completes the task. In time, knowing what you know (and all you will know by the end of this book), you will gain the confidence to reach for better housing, more enriching relationships, more gratifying work, and, yes, a better love partner. And this reaching is in no way a product of vanity or narcissism. No, this is the real stuff, the confidence that comes from a strong sense of self.

You don't want to be a hothouse rose. You should be in the living room of life, where you are husbanding your resources, protecting yourself—doing for yourself what a good man would do for you. And since only a well-nourished self can thrive on its own, it's time to talk about feeding ourselves.

F O U R

SELF-FEEDING: GETTING WHAT YOU WANT

Women are the feeders of the race. We nurture men with our faith and support. We encourage friends with counsel and good cheer. We give children love and guidance along with their fruits and vegetables. We nourish souls, big and little, by creating a calm and optimistic environment around them. But when it comes to giving *ourselves* a complete and happy life, well, let's just say we need practice.

It's a new concept, feeding ourselves. It takes training. But because we are already care-givers, new skills aren't needed; it's just a matter of using the old ones in a new way. For starters, this means thinking of ourselves as *worthy* of care, as deserving.

We women seem to suffer from an unfortunate misunderstanding. So used are we to feeding others that we believe someone (a man, our children, our friends) will in turn feed us. Maybe they will, but we can't assume they will know

what we need—or when we need it. Think of their love as
the finishing touch, the gravy. We're responsible for the meat
and potatoes (or tofu and vegetables, if that's more your style).
So you have to know what you want—which means getting
to know your tastes—and then you must go for it. I have no
doubt that you will; all you need is practice.

But I'll have to add the usual refrain: There are no quick
fixes. Like everything else, learning to feed yourself takes
focus and time. But once you begin, you'll see your life choices
as a menu, setting in front of you an interesting array of
possibilities. These strategies will help you take advantage of
them. One thought to keep in mind: In the preceding chapter,
I mentioned that the worst form of aloneness is alienation
from your own feelings. Well, the worst kind of *hunger* comes
from not feeding yourself. Both of these "worsts" come from
within. So that's where we'll make the changes.

ATTITUDE ADJUSTMENT

Are you a victim of the "too's"?

Women tend to be too tolerant, too flexible, too
compliant, too cooperative, too understanding, too patient. Gloria Steinem says that women suffer from ter-
minal gratitude, and I say it is an overdose that mires
too many of us in the status quo. We're so very thankful
to be where we are that we forget about moving ahead
toward our goals. Know the limits of your goodness.

Is your motto "Every woman last"?

You may at some point get around to feeding yourself, but only crumbs, the leftovers. And only after everyone else is taken care of. You're too busy worrying about
others' emotional requirements to realize that you're mal-
nourished. You'll never thrive until you give to yourself
right along with others—one for you, one for them.

Are you worried that putting your own needs first will make you selfish?

When flight attendants explain airplane emergency procedures, they tell passengers traveling with small children to put on their own masks first in the event of an emergency so they can help their children. The same principle applies to ordinary living. Unless you take good care of yourself first, you really can't take care of anyone else. (We'll talk more about this at the end of the chapter.)

Do you own your own impulses?

Or do you ignore your womanly intuition and listen only to the mind's rationality? Well, rationalism can be wrong, whereas your inner voices never fail. Part of being female is a connection to the life force, the energy that springs from the very source of life and gives you life-bearing capacity. That connection can be a powerful ally; lean on it. Life's cafeteria can be very confusing, and as its number of selections increases, the tougher the choices become. Your inner voices can make the winning difference in the decision-making process. Respect your hunches, instinct, intuition; feast on them happily. Never ever be embarrassed or apologize for their power in your life. The nonrational dimension can help you give yourself what is best for you.

There are two tasks ahead. But they are not the deadly dull garden-variety type; you'll be stimulated by both of them. You may even be inspired to rethink (or renew) some close relationships because of them. That will depend on what you discover. Anyway, back to the tasks.

You must first realize that you need to feed yourself (a process already under way) and then determine the diet right for you. Like real food, emotional sustenance has certain minimum daily requirements: respect, love, and trust. And like those real foods, emotional needs are given color and zest by life's seasonings, humor, and adventure. All of these are necessary to full emotional health; you need the whole package for total nourishment. But the amounts of each vary, and finding your personal balance is what elevates self-feeding to an art.

MENU

Independent Study

First Move

Life-Support System

Single Nutrients

Self-Maintenance

EXERCISE 1:
INDEPENDENT STUDY

What better way to begin than by feeding the mind? Either through a home study course or through a plan of learning you set up yourself (with help from your Old Girls' Network). Don't be scared off by the words "independent" or "study." (If it's been years since you stretched your mind, ease into this gently; don't sign up for quantum physics first thing.) Likewise, the "independent" part is meant to make it easier on you. Signing up for a home study course (or designing your own) implies that *you* choose the field, you set the schedule, and you decide the work pace. (I taught myself speed-writing years ago while I was pregnant, and I'm still using what I learned.) This particular exercise is not in "steps," but a series of strategies. Begin with the one that most appeals to you.

TAKE A CORRESPONDENCE COURSE   Correspondence courses run the gamut—from diamond-evaluating to zoo-keeping. Tuition is usually cheaper than for university study. (Most correspondence courses cost below $1,000.) They usually take from one to two years to complete. And some employers may even reimburse tuition if the course advances your job skills.

Important note: Don't enroll in any course without first checking its accreditation with the National Home Study Council. Write NHSC, 1601 18th Street, N.W., Washington, D.C. 20009. Request their directory of home-study schools. It's free, and could be the first step toward making "free" time count. (When you think of it, time is never free—it's much too costly to squander.)

CREATE YOUR OWN COURSE   If you don't have time for a correspondence course, design your own curriculum. It can be as low-key as you want. If you've always wanted to learn about butterflies, go to your local library and look up "butterflies" in the card catalogue. Then check out books on the subject and get a sense of what's available. If you want to invest in your own books, a reference called *Subject Guide to Books in Print* will come in handy, because it lists all the books currently on the market according to subject. If even that sounds too formal, make a list of books you've always wanted to read. They can be the "great books" or not-so-great books. The important part is that you set a definite goal for yourself—like reading one book a month—and meet it.

BUDDY UP   Just because your study is independent doesn't mean it can't be shared. Here's a good place to put a "buddy system" in practice. Mention your studies at a meeting of your network; maybe someone there wants to study butterflies along with you. And if there's enough interest, you could even form a splinter group focused on them.

JOIN THE CLUB   If you have a VCR, consider joining a club where you find out about educational cassettes as well as entertainment films. If books are your thing, make inquiries about several clubs before you enroll. If you're looking into record clubs, ask for referrals at your local record store. And bring up the subject with your network. (Now that you've built these connections, use them!) Some clubs sound good in the advertisements but turn out to be leeches. Others make great offers, asking nothing of you beyond the initial purchases (usually to buy three or four books or records). There are clubs for special interests, a history book club or jazz record club, for instance. In the same way that a subscription prods you into going to concerts, membership in a club keeps your reading and learning patterns regular (if you know you have a new book arriving next week, chances are you will try hard to finish the current one).

MUSTER SELF-DISCIPLINE   Sitting down alone to study requires self-discipline, which means that home study is not for everyone. But before you write yourself off as a student, try this: imagine doing something you love—skiing down a challenging slope, fly-fishing, or reading quietly, turning the pages of an engrossing novel. Try to remember the feeling of concentration that accompanied these activities. Relive the total absorption that came along with it. If you felt that once, you can feel it again. Now, while it's vivid in your memory, consider this plan of action:

1. First, choose the subject you truly want to learn more about.
2. Establish a quiet workplace, a corner of your bedroom or a desk in your living room that you associate with mental effort.
3. Set definite goals—a chapter completed by the end of the day or a unit by the end of next week.
4. If your attention is flagging, again summon up that feeling of concentration. The more often you recall it, the easier it will be to relive.

5. Push yourself gently, and don't forget that taking breaks actually helps maintain a high level of concentration.

6. Keep your ultimate goal in mind, and remember that the completion of each step is in itself a goal that brings its own sense of achievement. And that feeds the ego some pretty nice feelings.

EXERCISE 2:
FIRST MOVE

Before you can feed yourself you must reach out and take the spoon into your own hand. In other words, you must seize the initiative and take responsibility for *beginnings*. Until you do, you'll never be able to help yourself to the bounty around you.

I know it isn't easy. We women are used to being the "asked" instead of the "asker," and we've lost touch with the exhilaration of starting things. Men, on the other hand, have always known that kicky feeling because they've held near-exclusive rights to making first moves. Well, get ready to share their fun.

STEP 1: Phone a member of a group you belong to and suggest that its next meeting be at your home. While you're talking, arrange to meet for lunch with her or him to discuss an idea you've been working on. In other words, make the call and do the inviting.

STEP 2: Set up a business breakfast or a lunch with a co-worker, possibly someone you've wanted to know better but haven't because both of you are waiting for the other to make the reach. Have your calendar near the phone so you can set a date and time on the spot. (Or do this in the office, if that's more convenient. Either way, it gives you the same valuable practice.)

STEP 3:   This is simple—repeat the first two steps over a period of one or two months, making several calls each week and setting up at least three appointments. (Maintain a chart of dates and results.) Keep the situations relatively simple and unpressured: a parent-teacher committee meeting or a planning group for a charity function, for instance. Save big-league invitations—your supervisor, the man who interests you— for later, when you've had enough practice to initiate smoothly.

STEP 4:   After a few months of entry-level initiating, you are ready to phone a man. *Not for a date,* but for a relatively benign event. You might want to start by taking a male relative out for his birthday, or a male co-worker (or friend) out to lunch. Make this event during the day to keep the lid on man-woman dynamics. This is only a dress rehearsal, but you could rehearse even *this* call with a friend—perhaps someone from your network. Go through your opening lines, the small talk you'll use to break the ice (if you don't know him very well) and ways to arrange the details. The idea is to become so comfortable making the first move that you can reach out smoothly, in your own style.

STEP 5:   Now, call a man for a date. Try not to break mental stride from the previous step, because you'll want to use the same casual tone of voice. This is nothing to get heart-stoppingly nervous about. You're not asking for some monumental favor; you're giving this fellow a chance to share your company. In essence, you're creating a space for the two of you to learn more about each other. Keep that attitude, and you're on your way to conquering fears.

STEP 6:   If it would make you feel better, write out a few phrases to help you through the first few minutes of the call. It makes things easier if you can refer to some experience you've both shared. (If you're on the same committee of your neighborhood block association, open up the call with talk about the last meeting.)

STEP 7:   Have a clear idea of what you want to do on the date so that you can give him the details. Arrange for transportation, parking, and reservations (make them in your name). Let him know how to dress (casual or not) and about how long he'll be away. Because *you* are the initiator, *you* do the planning. But on the other hand, don't take over. Keep the mutuality in this call by asking him his preferred time and date; part of getting closer is working out details together. Ask him to a specific event, but graciously leave him room to turn you down—and then suggest a better time to get together. Yes, you do the pursuing. In your own way, naturally, but don't give up without a second try.

STEP 8:   Because you're doing the *asking*, you'll also do the *paying*. (You've already had practice taking your parents out to dinner and/or picking up the tab for a friend's lunch occasionally. If not, try those less emotionally charged situations first.)

- Tell him up front that you'd like it to be your treat. That way he knows what to expect and you can both relax. There's nothing magical about picking up a check. The key is preparation.

- You shouldn't find it necessary to tell a waiter beforehand that you want the check brought to you, but if you'd feel more comfortable this way, do it quickly and unobtrusively. If the waiter places the check near your date, firmly ask, "May I have the check?"

- If your "date" (maybe you'd rather call him "friend") reaches for the check, gently remind him that it's your treat, but allow him to pay for some part of the outing if he insists. Be flexible. You don't want to be rigid and overwhelm him with a preconceived agenda!

• Take care of your part of the payment quickly. Carry cash and credit cards in an accessible part of your wallet. Don't further the stereotype of the scatter-brain frantically scrounging around in her bottom-less satchel.

• Have dollar bills on hand for tips and parking. Try to behave as if you've done this before—even if you haven't. And if at any moment you're stumped, handle it lightly. What a great chance to share a laugh. We're all learning new roles; he'll respect you for keeping a sense of humor about an awk-ward moment.

• If you're a traditionalist, you may want to hand him the tickets. It certainly isn't necessary, unless that makes both of you more comfortable. It's another chance to confer.

• He'll probably take you to your door, but when he thanks you for the evening, tell *him* how glad you are he could come and how much you've enjoyed being with him. Try to act natural, as if you're say-ing good night to a good friend.

• For a follow-up, send him flowers or a plant, a friendly card or note. Or phone him again to thank him. By now *you* should feel easier about reaching out to him, but *he* may still feel baffled and a bit ill at ease. (Many men I know are flattered when a woman makes a move and expresses interest, and often they go out with her when under usual circumstances they probably would not have called her.) It doesn't matter who makes the first call. What happens after that is all that counts. Now, sell that to your ego.

• Treating isn't limited to occasions when you do the asking, by the way. If you're seeing someone frequently, occasionally reciprocate.

Reaching for the check is a significant symbol of the distance women have traveled. Just a few years ago, we would have bought a new blouse in anticipation of an evening with a man. Today we use the money to finance the evening! One small step for us, a leap forward for womanhood. That single gesture goes further to inspire admiration—from ourselves and the man involved—than any piece of clothing ever could. And that's an understatement.

Making the first move gracefully is an art. The more adept you become, the more changes you will notice in the people around you. Some friends and even more family members may feel awkward dealing with the assertive you. They're accustomed to old dynamics.

Since you definitely will not regress to passivity, pretty soon you may have to do some fancy artwork in your address book—deleting some names, adding others. (This is why I suggested it be refillable.)

It's always sad to lose a friend, but when it happens like that, the reason is positive. You've outgrown a dialogue with that person, but don't think of yourself as cold-blooded because you write them off. As you grow you'll discover that you do not fit with everyone. And although a little attrition is inevitable, your best friends will stay your best friends. The nucleus of family and close friends will not alter their feelings for you, nor you for them. Because they know and love the *real* you, they are with you for the long haul, adapting to your growth and rejoicing with you. That nucleus may even grow along with you, responding to your impetus. You'll see; you may well become an example and a catalyst for change.

LEARN TO SAY NO

From time to time, you may need to end things, as well as begin them. Phone calls, for instance. How many times have you been involuntarily glued to the phone, pressed by a zillion other things you should be doing—all because you couldn't conclude a conversation? How many times have you let a friendship (or a romance) linger far too long because you couldn't muster nerve to call it quits? Consider this:

- It's easier to effect the ending if you've brought about the beginning, because the power already lies with you. That goes for socializing, as well as phone calls.

- Be frank but be kind. Don't apologize or lie or give unnecessary excuses; if you have to go, you have to go. Be steadfast.

- Don't worry about making the other person feel rejected. If the conclusion is handled sincerely, you won't hurt the other person's feelings, and you might even gain her or his respect.

- Regard saying goodbye as another form of initiation. Once again, you're deciding your destiny rather than letting someone *else* call the shots.

EXERCISE 3:
LIFE-SUPPORT SYSTEMS

A singleness equated with isolation is as doomed as a marriage expected to bring unremitting bliss, since either way of life is no more (or less) than the sum of your choices. Right now I am going to interest you in forming a support group of specialists. The services they can put into your life will be one of the prime ways you can give yourself the self-reliance we're aiming for. After all, you and I are not building a sham independence of bravado that cowers in the lonely night and trembles at the thought of going it alone the next day. No, this is a joint venture to establish a bred-in-the-bones independence that comes from an examined and prepared life. The phrase "real thing" may make you think of enduring romantic love, but here in this context it applies to authentic independence. You could experience love several times in one life span, but you need to build this practical groundedness only once.

To create your personal support group, you're going to locate an all-night drugstore, a dry cleaner with convenient hours, a physician who (preferably) works as part of a team and will make emergency housecalls, a deli/restaurant that delivers, an attorney, accountant, a tax specialist (if appropriate), a spiritual leader, and a house of worship. If the idea of having such a group available makes sense, putting it in place should be done now—before the need arises.

STEP 1: List the services already in your life: a favorite drugstore, a local butcher who explains the difference between a shank and a loin and doesn't put his thumb on the scale. In other words, begin with the people you know and trust. Then, start filling in the empty spaces. An ophthalmologist, gynecologist, dentist, travel agent?

STEP 2:   While you're doing this, rethink those services. Are you satisfied with them? Think back to the reasons you chose them in the first place (*if* you chose them). If they no longer fill your needs, look for replacements. (Make a note to ask your OGN, family, and close friends for referrals.)

STEP 3:   In some instances you can expand your system through contacts already in place. For example, the bank official you already visited might supply you with the name of a competent and understanding attorney. The general physician you currently see may give you the name of a specialist she or he knows and works with; the family attorney might recommend an accountant. From these referrals, make a list of two or three names in each category. Yes, write all this down. You can never be too rich, too happy—or too organized.

STEP 4:   Phone each of the referrals and explain why you are calling. They will be flattered that their professional advice attracts you—but if they're too busy to talk, make an appointment. (Make it clear you don't need their expertise right now—and don't want to be billed for the time—and chances are you'll get what you need then and there, over the phone.) Run down their hours and their fees. In return, tell them what you need and expect. (Write this out before making the call.)

STEP 5:   After a few minutes of conversation, you'll have a sense of the compatibility level between you two. (Personality and temperament are sometimes just as important as education and experience. If those factors are high up in your priorities, give them extra weight when you're making a final selection.) Mark each name A, B, or C according to compatibility, availability, fees, and so on. These people will be working for you, so in effect the conversations are interviews. Important ones. So keep your manner professional but not belligerent. You are consuming their work-time, remember? Be appreciative (not cowed or obsequious) and pleasant.

Reminder: As you make final choices in the categories, write each name and all details on a card for your single file. You might want to cross-reference resources, filing cards un-

---

EXAMINATION TIME

Once you've interviewed and put into place those experts, think about the ones who help maintain your physical well-being. Make a list of the examinations basic to your health: PAP test, gynecological exam, dentist checkup, ophthalmologist, mammogram, annual physical workup. Next to each one, write the doctor's name, address, telephone number, date of last examination, and date of next examination. Make two copies. Tape one list in your medicine cabinet where you will see it every day and put the other in your address book. (Giving a third copy to your folks is an option that could either give you added security, or be an invitation to nagging.)

- If you don't want to bother making a list, simply write appointment dates on your calendar, and put it where you can check it at the start of every week.

- Each time you keep a medical appointment, ask the receptionist to hand you (or mail) a reminder of your next appointment. Some offices do this routinely, others leave it up to the patient. Be smart; always request an appointment card.

- You do all you can to keep up with your children's examinations; do the same for yourself. Scheduling and keeping every health-related appointment is nurturing the self you are working so hard to define.

der the category and also the specific name of the person. Be sure to make cards also for friends you can depend on to make sick calls when you need them. Their names and numbers should be on the list you keep by your bed. (See Step 7.)

STEP 6: If this sounds like too much work, remind yourself that problems have a way of surfacing at the worst possible times, and now while life is relatively calm is a good time to put these "solution resources" in place. If you wait until you're in a crunch, you'll have to take what you can get. Planned in advance, your system of resources can be top-grade. So persevere until you have the people you select alerted to your needs and committed to meeting them when the moment comes.

STEP 7: Type the final list, with names, addresses, business phone numbers. (Get home phone numbers, of course, for those sickbed pals.) Make two duplicates of the original.

STEP 8: Put one copy next to your bed, in the drawer of your night table, give one to your parents, and put the third copy next to your kitchen phone.

STEP 9: Recheck and update the list every few months so that it's accurate and fast-working when you need it. In other words, call each person on the list to verify phone numbers and addresses.

EXERCISE 4:
SINGLE NUTRIENTS

Now that you've assembled a group of medical experts, I'm going to suggest that you find the need to use them as seldom as possible. Which is a provocative way to suggest that you feed yourself well—literally.

1. Give mealtime character by thinking about its goodness. Appreciate the taste of the food, the love you have put into its preparation, the experience of actually taking this nourishment into your body. Reflect on the blessing of having food while so many do not, of having good and healthy foods that you enjoy. Eating alone can be a communion, a time to ingest the meaning of nourishment, along with the food you're eating. (Reading during the meal is okay sometimes, but it can distract you.) Concentrate on the event itself and you'll elevate the act of eating to its highest purpose.

2. Be your own guest. You deserve the good dishes and cloth napkins as much as your guests. Have wine with dinner if you feel in the mood, or a cocktail in the kitchen while you're preparing the vegetables.

3. Invite people over for dinner often. Having someone to please makes cooking more fun.

4. Eat more potatoes, not less. Bake them in a toaster oven with an aluminum nail to cut down on cooking time. (Microwave potatoes are not memorable.) Your basic potato is a source of potassium, and they're the perfect meal for one—self-contained, neat. If you substitute low-fat cottage cheese or yogurt for butter and sour cream, the calorie count plummets.

5. Broccoli is a near-perfect food. Peas are very high in fiber. Kidney beans are a good protein substitute. Learn about foods through the Center for Science in the Public Interest, a fount of straight talk about nutrition. The Center's posters, for instance, deliver the facts colorfully and specifically. (See Resources.)

6. Frozen and convenience foods are expensive and high in sodium. Instead, cook fresh foods and freeze small portions in sandwich-size Baggies.

7. Take a daily calcium supplement if you don't drink three

glasses of low-fat milk a day (or its equivalent). Make it a point to take a multivitamin-with-minerals daily.

8. Substitute toasted whole-wheat English muffins or slices of whole-grain bread for empty-calorie snacks.

9. Add fresh fruit to plain, low-fat yogurt. That way, you lower the sugar, fat content, and price.

10. If you like to bake but hesitate to do it because you're the only one around to eat the results, motivate yourself by donating your breads and cakes to a local Meals on Wheels or food kitchen.

11. Consider getting your friends together and starting your own food cooperative to buy fresh foods in large amounts and save. (See Resources.)

12. Walking after dinner is a healthy habit to develop (good for digestion), and a good way to sort out the day's events. Sometimes, bring along your earphones and listen to tapes of music or books while you're out moving the bod. They make ideal companions because they don't expect answers!

13. Most important, start eating as if food is fuel for your body—no less, not much more. If mealtime has become too big an issue in your life, it's time to reexamine your pleasures and see what's lacking. If you feel you may have an eating disorder, seek help from your doctor, nutritionist, or seek out a weight-loss support group.

EXERCISE 5:
SELF-MAINTENANCE

After you've fed mind and body, scrutinize the part of you that people see. Your image may be only skin deep, but it's all the world has to go by to form a first impression. Might as well make it an invitation. When hair, clothes, accessories, and makeup reflect the woman within, she is truly liberated in the sense that she is freed from those superficial concerns and can go on to the more important and interesting things in her life.

STEP 1: Make an appointment at a beauty salon to discuss the right hair style for you, the best color, and cut. Don't go to one at random; ask well-groomed friends for their favorites. (If you see someone whose hair style you admire, muster up courage to ask her where she gets it cut.) Look for a style that frames your face and fits your routine. (If you swim or work out regularly, you'll probably want it short.) Notice what the stylist does—how he or she blow-dries your hair, for example. By being eagle-eyed, asking questions, and making notes, you can do a pretty good approximation of their styling. Make regular appointments for a trim; maintenance of this sort becomes part of a beauty regimen that will in time become automatic and require minimum thought and energy. The initial decisions are the big ones.

STEP 2: Have a free cosmetic makeover at a local department store or at a Merle Norman store. (Usually the only "string" attached is a small makeup purchase—and it's probably time for a new lipstick or blush, anyway.) Watch carefully (take notes, if you want, so you won't forget the tricks). And be sure to ask for a chart of the colors most harmonious to your hair and skin tones.

Take from these experts what you like and practice with your image until you develop a look that you like, probably a little less contrived than their interpretation. You'll know when you have achieved your personal best because it will tell the world exactly what you want to say about yourself and it will feel appropriate for you.

STEP 3: Visit the best store in town and ask to see a suit that's right for you. Go from there into a "right" dress. Chat with the salesperson. (The aim here is to get an opinion on the way you are perceived, not to pay big bucks for top fashion.) Observe well-dressed women wherever you go. Analyze how they put themselves together. It usually takes years to find your look, and even then you may find it modifying as your tastes grow up. Basically, you're after a look that is fashionable but not faddish. You want to look attractive, well-put-together. There is nothing more appealing than a woman whose style is individual and *personal*. The insight needed to make that kind of fashion statement is a result of dedicated searching and trial and error—the same principles that govern discovery in your tastes, needs, and priorities. The outward sign of a clear sense of self is a distinct, appropriate image.

EXERCISE 6:
LEARNING TO COMPLAIN

Opening your mouth is not only for feeding yourself; it's also for complaining. (This exercise is the last one in this chapter because of its delicate nature.) Let's face it: Most women do not have experience expressing negative opinions; our function as the calmer of troubled waters is so deeply ingrained that it is almost a genetic trait! We have been conditioned to skirt around confrontation and head-on collisions in any form. So it is only logical that at those rare times when we have no choice but to gripe, we under- or overreact, either suffering in pained silence or raging in inappropriate aggression. Well, it's time to make your opinions heard in a style that represents you as you would like. You're going to practice this art form until you get it right.

STEP 1:   Speak to the people who serve: waiters, counter-men, mail carriers, delivery people. Make a comment about a missing item or late delivery. Fight the old impulse to clam up. Notice your gestures, your tone of voice, your inner tension. Don't create an incident if one is not called for (the object here is to learn how to complain only when necessary) but do look for opportunities to speak up. Stay low-keyed, but make sure to get the results you want.

STEP 2:   Next time you eat out, ask for your sandwich to be toasted, or for extra mayonnaise. Requesting small details is in the same category as making a complaint. Asking for what you want may sound elementary, but some women feel so itchy speaking their minds (in public, particularly) that they do without their preferences. Believe me, the more often you ask, the easier it gets. Again, for emphasis: Ask for what you want, when you want it. Like most simplicities (eating when you're hungry, sleeping when you're tired), it's anything but simple. I know.

STEP 3:   Now, you're ready for a full-blown complaint. Make sure you have a valid complaint—don't invent one. (In this less-than-perfect world, it won't take long before you find the real thing.) When the dry cleaner returns your favorite suit with two ivory buttons missing, fight the urge to either say nothing—or raise your voice. You'll get more satisfaction using the "steel fist in the velvet glove" approach: outwardly gentle, inwardly immovable. Do not walk away from the dialogue until you have written assurance of comparable replacement or payment for a full set of buttons of similar value.

STEP 4:   Don't waste energy. Make sure you complain to the right person. If you don't get satisfaction from the counter clerk, ask to speak to the manager. State your case clearly and concisely. There is no need to overstate; facts will speak eloquently. And don't let yourself be distracted into complaining about the slow service, surly help, or inconvenient hours. Repeat your primary complaint until you receive full satisfaction.

Once you see the results, you will rather enjoy exercising assertiveness muscles. They may be a bit stiff from disuse, but they'll limber up quickly. Practice, practice, practice. Feminine assertion is an acquired skill. The power of complaining, like any power, must never be abused, however. The more effective you become, the more responsibility you have to be considerate to the people around you. And not surprisingly, effectiveness actually makes life easier. The more you assert, the more people will be aware of you as effective, treat you more carefully, and give you less and less cause for complaint!

———

BE GOOD TO YOURSELF

This is not an exercise, but a commandment. You *must* be good to yourself. Only a very few people, those closest to you, can even begin to know what that means in your personal terms. (And even they cannot be mind readers.) Only *you* can give yourself all the things you need in order to grow and thrive—all the time.

I'm going to throw out a few suggestions for enriching your life. Choose only ones that please, like wildflowers you would pick when you are out walking.

- Invest in (at least) one piece of silver or gold jewelry. A young friend of mine says she realized one day that her only real pieces had been given to her by men—her father and her boyfriend. Without knowing it, she had been waiting to be presented with the next piece by a man. So it was a breakthrough when she herself shopped and paid for a heavy silver cuff bracelet.

- Buy yourself fresh flowers for no reason at all—especially in the dead of winter when their color and life boost the spirit.

- Give yourself the gift of regular exercise—every other day, at a minimum. Fitness and stamina are not just modern jargon; they actually make you a candidate for long life. Any objections?

- Find a fragrance that strikes a chord with you, and wear it often—not just for special occasions. One particular scent gets to be associated with you and becomes your trademark, another dimension of your identity.

- Break the Puritan ethic and indulge in a massage. A combination of Shiatsu (acupressure) and the more rigorous Swedish system feels best for me, but find your special favorite and stick to it. Being massaged weekly is less of a luxury than you might imagine; it actually promotes circulation, tones muscles, and firms the skin. After one or two trial sessions, you'll probably decide to spend hard-earned money this way rather than accumulate yet another piece of clothing that will hang in your closet. Being massaged is a good way to become familiar with your body, since most masseuses will let you know facts about your particular set of muscles. Get the name of a licensed professional from a credible source and give it a try. You may become such a believer that you'll add her to your life-support system. Massage plus meditation, as regular parts of your routine, complement one another, exercising body and mind into harmony.

- Copy the following and post where you see it often. *"Happiness comes from your decisions; it is neither gift nor blessing. Your life is the sum of your choices."*

- Test different approaches to reaching your goals. Don't be reluctant to change serving lines in life's cafeteria.

- Make resolutions twice a year, adding your birthday to New Year's Eve. Ring in your own personal new year by nudging yourself to keep the promises made December 31.

- Always, always, save time for yourself. Refresh yourself by reserving a few moments every day (preferably at the same time every day) for personal prayer or meditation, private thoughts. Gradually, this period of sanctuary from daily life will become a necessity. It is also a privilege.

That said, a giant-size disclaimer: Being good to yourself will *not* make you selfish. Good, healthy self-interest makes you

> less of a martyr (single parents, please note)
> less of a frump (if you've given up on your appearance)
> less dependent

In a delicious twist, treating yourself right actually makes you *less* selfish, because the better fed you are, the more you have to give to the people who look to you for nourishment. As you ingest more satisfactions delivered from your own hand, you'll develop more faith: in what life can offer, perhaps in God, primarily in yourself. Confidence in your own effectiveness brings with it greater optimism about the future.

As you think of yourself as more precious, you will be more discriminating in the things you give to yourself. You will sustain yourself with balanced helpings from life's bounty. For if you are not wise in your own behalf, who will be?

YOUR PERSONAL SUPPORT SYSTEM

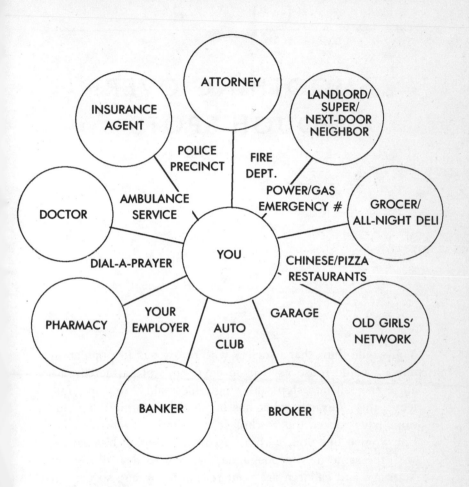

YOUR FAMILY:

BEST FRIEND:

CO-WORKER:

PRIEST/RABBI/MINISTER/GURU:

THREE FRIENDS YOU CAN COUNT ON:

FIVE

SMOOTHING OVER:
ROUGH SPOTS

You would think that a society with nearly half its population unwed would rouse itself from daydreams of partnered paradise and fall into step with single-file reality. And in some ways, this is exactly what has happened: Enormous revolutions have rocked the workplace, the family, even romance. But women like you, without a partner, are still bombarded with the same tired propaganda that blasted dear old Mom: Marriage and children are your reason for living, so get out there and grab a man. On and on it drones, from hundreds of sources, in countless forms.

As a single woman today, you don't buy the party line, though, because you've seen the generation of women who surrendered identity too soon. You've promised yourself more. But pioneers pay a high price. You're constantly being judged by an old, outdated stereotype which weakens your resolve and makes the rest of life's rough spots that much rougher.

As I enter another decade in the world of singleness, I'm more certain than ever that pressure to join the married mainstream is responsible for much of the discontent there. *Recognizing* this is a giant step in your growth because it lets you leave despair behind and start changing the attitudes that have blocked your peace of mind. I'm talking about changing your *own* attitudes, because changing those around you is too much to ask; popular perception is not known for quick shifts.

But public opinion isn't the only roadblock to contentment. Loneliness is a real mischief-maker in single lives. And an unbending "old maid" mindset creeps into your awareness now and then. Shyness and defensiveness wreak their havoc, too. Not to mention jealousy and bitterness. We're going to exorcise these hobgoblins—admitting they exist so that we can end their tyranny—so you can get on with your life.

That's not to say you'll be able to smooth over all the rough spots in one sanding. Many have been around a long time, and they won't disappear overnight. But you *will* be able to get a handle on them once you tune in to them; skills you learn here will take away the power to make you their victim. And I won't use up precious time identifying the roots of these problems, either, because the whole point here is to *do something* about them.

The problems that come with being a single woman can wake you in the small morning hours and make your heart race. But if it helps any (and I think it does), please know you're not the only one facing them. There is a sisterhood of women out there who share your concerns. Believe me, you're not the only one nodding your head right now. (What I would have given for these strategies during my young widowhood.) I hope the suggestions here will become a connecting bond, and that all of us can work out the rough spots together.

THE DIRTY DOZEN—
12 ROUGH SPOTS YOU CAN
SMOOTH OUT

LONELINESS
(L-ONLYNESS)

ALONENESS
ADDICTION
(HERMITUDE)

RIGIDITY
(OLD-MAIDISM)

COMPETITIVENESS
AND JEALOUSY
("THE GREENS")

THE END OF LOVE
(PREMARITAL
DIVORCE)

BITTERNESS

COMMITMENT
PHOBIA

SHYNESS (SH-I-NESS)

REJECTION

DEFENSIVENESS:
FORTRESS
THINKING

PUBLIC OPINION
(RAISED
EYEBROWS)

SELF-PITY
(GENERIC BLUES)

You can jump directly to your worst demon and its solutions. But I urge you to read the entire chapter—even if a specific rough spot isn't bothering you. You know I don't believe in wasting time, so I don't make this suggestion idly. It simply makes good sense to add *all* of these ideas to your storehouse of answers to the questions of your life.

I hope that merely seeing these rough spots in print takes away some of their power, and that the irreverent names attached to some of them will reduce their negativism even further. The names are not meant to make fun of you for feeling shy, lonely, rejected, whatever—but to inject levity in an otherwise long-faced list. Maybe they'll help you take a half-step backwards and look at these rough spots a little less emotionally, as snags needing solutions and nothing more. That said, let's get to disarming them.

LONELINESS (L-ONLYNESS)

Touted as the biggest demon of all, loneliness is often attributed to solitary living. It's the "only" in the "lonely" that makes it so unbearable, or so the reasoning goes. That's the easy explanation, the one commonly accepted, but I don't buy it. From all I know about single living, it is not living alone but feeling "different" and "left out" that explains much of the pain of loneliness. I don't rule out vestigial feelings of dependency, either, those yearnings to be taken care of that lodge themselves in the pit of the stomach and refuse to budge. They contribute to single loneliness, too.

Many women confuse those longings with loneliness. And it turns out to be a self-fulfilling confusion, because we devalue every form of companionship while waiting for The Man Who Isn't There. We consider ourselves alone if we are with someone other than a "live one"—and have been known to break appointments at the drop of a hat when an eligible man calls. Of course, conditioning has something to do with this kind of thinking; women over forty-five are more likely to be its puppets. (But all of us have had our strings pulled this way.)

If you recognize yourself in that scenario, take another look at the first two chapters and remind yourself of the possibilities friendship offers. You may be inspired to take a few chances! Look, every woman reading these words wants a love partnership; it's as normal as blueberry pie (or is it apple?). But when that need shuts you out of enriching companionship and distorts your thinking, it's time to rethink what is going on.

One of the great ironies of loneliness is that much of it has to do more with how you feel about yourself than with external factors. Think about that. And while you're in the mood for soul-searching:

STEP 1:   In a quiet place, sit or lie down comfortably and close your eyes. In your mind's eye, visualize yourself as popular and beloved, surrounded by trusted and loving friends. You don't need to know who they are, because the faces need not be limited to real-life people. The point is to place yourself in the center of a group of people who genuinely care for you, to revel in happiness and contentment. This scene doesn't need to be photographic; concentrate on the picture and the feeling. Do this for at least three minutes, every other day.

STEP 2:   With that vision in mind, write down reasons why people should be drawn to you. Mentally drink them in.

STEP 3:   The next time you're about to enter a room full of people or attend a meeting, remember this visualization and your reasons for being loved. Walk in with a friendly and receptive mindset—even though the stomach may be churning. I know, it's not easy. But one successful adventure ("successful" as in meeting good people—not necessarily the man of your dreams) will give you the courage for the next. Each one becomes a practice opportunity. And if you learn this visualization habit, it stands a good chance of materializing; by cultivating the feeling of being loved, you can become more lovable. You are mobilizing the forces of self-love (the main point of the exercise), which, when nurtured, make you more generous and loving with the people around you—who themselves want to be loved. Don't we all?

Other loneliness strategies:

- Go back to your interest inventory in Chapter One and see what you like to do that you haven't been doing. Make a concerted effort to follow up on at least one of the activities. The goal? Greater involvement with people. Sometimes loneliness can be banished with a single phone call or visit.

- Concentrate on the positive side of loneliness: freedom. Unfettered by another's needs, you're free to use time *your* way. Think about that, too.

- Make plans for times when you're most vulnerable. Do you feel more alone at certain times of the day? Sunday evening is a low time for many single women—there's something about facing a blank week. Well, arrange to alternate phone calls on Sunday with a friend. And use Sunday evening to schedule into the coming week a dinner out, a hen party, an adult class. You must *agree* to be lonely; do your best to refuse its negativism. But a certain amount of loneliness is inevitable in anyone's life —it seems to be part of the human condition.

- Use alone time to become compatible with yourself. Read through Chapter Three about avoiding the worst kind of loneliness, alienation from your feelings. When you know the person you are, you'll be able to live with her more comfortably.

- If you think you'll feel less lonely in a different apartment, house, or town, consider a move. Of course, you can't expect your problems to go away with a change of scenery. We take ourselves wherever we go. On the other hand, don't stay put if you definitely feel your living situation is a contributing factor to your loneliness. One of these hypothetical situations might apply to you:

  1. *You're living in the house where you and your husband lived. He died over a year ago and the children are on their own. The house is big and dusty and lonely.*

     You might want a smaller living space. If so, research your move carefully, considering all the areas where you could live: near your children, a walk away from your work. Living someplace where it is easy to get out and meet people could be a major step toward curing your loneliness—as long as you remember that it is up to you to make those critical first moves.

2. *You've been out of college for ten years, successfully building a career in a city far away from your hometown. Several of your best friends have just moved away, you know you're ready for a major job shift, and you're thinking about relocating.*

Study the possibilities carefully. Would you consider moving back to your hometown (or closer to it)? It's important to maintain your independence, but you may be eager to put down roots. The issue is whether you want to do that where you are or in a new community. And the answer will be clearer after you have actually visited a few of the places you are considering.

3. *You don't need a total change of scenery; maybe just a roommate. But this can be a big decision.*

Check your telephone book for roommate services or post an ad in a club newsletter, on a college bulletin board in your favorite bookstore, or the health-food store where you shop. Inquire at your town hall; some cities have shared-housing resource centers. You might even consider buying a house with a group of people.

There are even faster ways to outwit loneliness when it is the more occasional kind. We'll talk about them at the end of this chapter.

THE FRIENDLY
NEIGHBORHOOD PUB

It used to be that unmarried people could find instant companionship at a "singles bar." You may not have been in the habit of spending the night with a stranger, but somewhere in the back of your mind you knew the option was there for you. You knew that if nothing else, you could always go there to rub psyches with other humanoids and feel less alone.

But one-night stands are now as extinct as saddle shoes. Only a madwoman would consider anonymous sex these days. And the same wariness has filtered down to even the most casual encounter in or out of a bar setting.

But there *is* a way to keep the benefits of that setting without endangering your health. When you need company, frequent a neighborhood pub. Becoming a local "regular" will make you feel better about walking through the swinging doors alone—and you will be more likely to know (or know someone who knows) people you meet there. If you like to meet people in bars, adopt one favorite spot. There's a different feel to an encounter near your home, a homier and more relaxed tone. Even your mindset is different.

But the perils of casual sex remain the same. "Never" is the motto—without exception.

ALONENESS ADDICTION
(HERMITUDE)

It's healthy to be able to live on your own without feeling lonely, as long as you don't take it to an extreme. But if you become so adept at being alone that you never want to be anything else, solitude becomes *hermitude*—a degree of self-sufficiency that shuts out the world.

Symptoms: You don't want to see people as much as you used to. Dinner is always yogurt in bed or a sandwich in front of the television set. You haven't gone out with friends in months. You work, come home, wash out your nylons, feed your cat, and go to bed—sometimes without washing off your makeup. No one complains and no one criticizes ... because no one is there. But no one gives a damn, either, when you don't show up at aerobics class three weeks running. You've become so proud of doing everything yourself that you don't feel the need to include anyone else. Independence has become a mission, and give-and-take is no longer part of your vocabulary.

The catch is that while you're reveling in your hermitude, you're losing your natural resiliency. As rabid as I am on independence, I am convinced that healthy doses of *inter*dependency are actually regenerative. The trick is to strike a balance between the two by sharing some of your life on a regular basis.

- Invite a friend for the weekend. Try to smile bravely at the messy bathroom and dirty dishes, reminding yourself that disorder is a sign of life.

- Take a trip with someone. Share a room (or a cabin if you're on a cruise). Split the responsibilities for planning the adventure; the point is to learn to rely on someone other than yourself.

- Rent a cottage or a ski lodge with friends. That will

mean group shopping, group outings, group dating, group talking, group living.

- Consider a roommate or the possibility of shared housing, mentioned above.

- Don't be reluctant to ask for help with your storm windows or your dog's bath. People like to do favors for each other. Don't you feel good when you're asked to pitch in?

I bet you never thought I'd say it, but you can be too independent. Being Single Superwoman and doing everything yourself actually limits your life. If you won't open up your world and let other people inside, you're closing yourself off. Wholeness that keeps people out needs to be reexamined because it has become a distortion of itself. Imagine your life as a full circle, and always, always, make room to include good people. You can retain your identity while being inclusive.

RIGIDITY (OLD-MAIDISM)

Women are no longer called spinsters when they don't marry by twenty-one, but that doesn't mean old maids are a vanishing breed. There are plenty of them. (And, so you won't think I'm being sexist, they have plenty of male equivalents, the "old bachelors" out there.)

Being an old maid has nothing to do with how many times you've been a bridesmaid or missed catching the bridal bouquet; it's a matter of attitude. You probably know some married old maids, women who get so used to doing things their way that they can't share any part of their lives even when they have the chance. The hallmark of old-maidism is the need to run the whole show.

If you can't share what you have and get along with

someone under the same roof, you could wind up rigid and all by yourself. You'll never be really close with someone unless you can yield a portion of your sovereignty. And if you just shuddered, take heart. There are ways to avoid ending up an old woman alone on a hill.

- Beware the unbreakable routine. If you grocery-shop every Saturday morning religiously even though you could occasionally shop after work, hear me and bend your own rules. Above all, never hide behind your schedule when an opportunity for human contact comes along. You know by now I'm not suggesting you drop important work for a "clutter" date. I am suggesting that you be loose enough to put off the laundry when a friend calls for lunch. There are really very few "musts" in your routine. Most chores can be rearranged and shifted in your schedule. Sometimes deliberately forget to do one, and note that the sky doesn't fall. Stay flexible.

- Don't get too used to doing things one way. Stay up later than usual one night—watch the late-late movie. Volunteer for a crisis hotline and put yourself on call one weekend a month. Your biorhythms may be thrown for a loop, but you'll prove to yourself that they are at *your* command and not vice versa.

- Look through your home for signs of superneatness. A compulsively arranged refrigerator (milk on the right, water on the left) means that you're bored and rigidity is setting in. Get into a sport or hobby fast. And show yourself that lightning won't strike if you leave your bed unmade and dishes in the sink for two days running. They'll be there in the morning, but you'll be a more companionable person.

- Search your soul. See if an excessive number of your satisfactions revolve around creature comforts. I'm talking about becoming a couch potato by sitting in front of the television set and having dinner there (then dessert, nine-o'clock snack, and midnight snack). Not that there's anything wrong in relaxing after a hard day of work, but there's a lot more to life than being stuffed and comfortable. It's time for intellectual stimulation or physical exercise.

- Consider taking a pet into your home. Too much bother? Then try a bird or a fish—or an ant! Truman Capote wrote that love is a chain; if you can love a bird, you can love a dog, a tree—yes, another person. Deliberately put love objects into your life so that you don't get rusty. The art of loving needs constant practice.

- Become an "aunt" or "godmother" to a friend's child. And that's not admitting that you'll never have any kids of your own. What it denotes is a woman clever enought to seize an opportunity to express her lovingness.

- Become a "big sister" or foster parent, as a way to try parenthood and see if you would like it on a full-time basis. You'll also help yourself break out of a rut and see the world through young eyes. (More on this in Chapter Seven.) And at the same time you're fighting your own rigidity, you're influencing a growing person. That should make you shape up!

- Reread the suggestions, especially the ones that hit home. It wouldn't hurt to spend some time right now dreaming up ways to put them into action.

COMPETITIVENESS AND JEALOUSY ("THE GREENS")

Single women would have achieved much more solidarity by now if not for the competition they were taught to enter in early childhood. In a million ways, from subtle to overt, we are brainwashed to believe that looking better and being more clever than the next woman will charm a man into choosing us. I'm not telling you anything new or startling, but since sisterhood is an important part of this book (and your future), let's dump the garbage that has kept us from a feeling of community with one another. By seeing other women as competitors, you're perpetuating old ways of relating that do nothing but keep you competitive and frazzled and less than excited about woman-to-woman relating. We're turning every day into a race for men when all any of us needs is one good one.

The way to resist the rat race and the jealous "greens" is by remembering that you are one of a kind, unique in all the world. To compare yourself with another woman is an exercise in futility—and that's one exercise I don't recommend. Like each of the women you know, you have your own life plan to play out. Boosting your personal strengths and building on them will bring more gratification than molding yourself into someone else's pattern. And since self-development is a process without a finish line, a life lived true to it will have no time to worry about a possible rival. There are none; it's you and your goals. Period. But if you thrive on competition and you must compete, then compete with yourself. Hold an inner Olympics to surpass your last achievement. And while you're doing that, remember to be gentle with the runner-up.

But despite the best intentions, the green-eyed monster will surface from time to time. And when it does, there is a way to make it a positive learning experience: Cool down and use your head to pinpoint exactly what it is you envy— *then strive to emulate it.* If you see your "competition" as younger, prettier women, notice the components of their attractiveness and then maximize your own best points. Learn the makeup techniques right for you, exercise, get enough sleep, and, for Pete's sake, keep on piling up life experiences. Interesting people are rarities. To chew your fingernails over snowbunnies with their carefree smiles and seemingly poreless skin is only an excuse to regress to the waiting room and sit out the best dances. (Reread Chapter Four.) When you're living in the present and feeding yourself generously, there is no time (or reason) to salivate over someone else's portion.

But there are still times when you find yourself wanting what you can't have. For example, maybe you envy the incredible figure of your aerobics teacher. But think about your life and hers. She leads aerobics classes five hours a day, five days a week. You take them twice a week, one hour at a time. You're forty-five and have two children. She's twenty-five and never married. Of course you're not going to look like her. Nevertheless, you can twist your jealousy into a determination to step up your own exercise campaign. You'll see that it's (almost) impossible to be jealous when you've done all you can do with what you have.

Besides, you might not want the package that comes with those women who give you the greens. They have their own private demons, and you might not want to trade. In the final analysis, all you can do—the best you can do—is to work on yourself. If you need a reminder of your special assets, go back to your lists from Chapter Three; you may be able to add some you've discovered since then.

The next time you take a walk, make it a point to pass a playground and watch the children at play. They are a perfect example of true single fulfillment because they live in the present moment and are totally absorbed. Think of that as you work for whatever it is you want from your life; keep your mind focused on what you are doing and possible ways to do it better. As you improve yourself, admire your efforts. We're all in this journey together—and it's not a race.

THE END OF LOVE
(PREMARITAL DIVORCE)

Of all the rough spots that single women confront, a breakup hurts the most. No matter how gently it comes, the end is painful. You are a victim of divorce. It doesn't matter one iota if it isn't legal divorce, if no attorney is needed, and if no children are involved. The pain is there.

You've probably been a part of more than one premarital divorce and vowed never again to leave yourself open and vulnerable. But whenever a special man appears, you fall back into the same pattern. Because you so desperately want it to work, you throw your all into the relationship. You drop your single buddies in favor of coupled friends; you drop out of groups and activities that once interested you. Your world is now his world. So when the relationship is over, the world turns to ashes. You feel scattered to the winds: hurt, angry, resentful. Somewhere deep inside you know that you are still okay as a person and aren't being rejected because of some intrinsic worthlessness, but the fact remains that your entire world must be reconstructed. The challenge is to summon up the energy for the job, especially when you know the whole process could happen again . . . and again, a future of ecstasies and agonies.

There *is* a way out, and it is certainly not to stop risking your heart. By maintaining your own spheres of interest, friends, and activities, your world won't end if and when love ends. Keeping that balance requires a conscious decision not to wrap your life around your man's, to fight against the tendency to lose your very soul in the heat of togetherness —a tendency you and I know is a major flaw in the female psyche.

Keeping a separateness within the togetherness is actually generosity. Your self-interest reduces the pressure on a man to be all things to you. It definitely makes you more interesting, and it distributes partners' rights and responsibilities more evenly. And the biggest plus of all is that it equips you to handle the terrible moment when someone you love makes a choice you don't like.

But all of that is for the future. To deal with your ache right now:

- Think back over the days immediately following the split to find a moment of calm, peace, relief. However fleeting, that moment nurtured can become the linchpin of a gradual but steady recovery.

- In your affirmation each morning, repeat the words (mentally or aloud), "It's over, and I'm glad." Repeat them, until your body resonates with them. Keep the flow of breath steady and deep. Resist the tendency to take shallow, irregular breaths.

- Remind yourself that love is not the only adrenaline. Too many women make love the only part of their lives in which they accept a challenge. Once you dare to find new interests and friends, love will lose its preeminence among the emotional stimulants.

- When you feel you must cry, let the tears fall. Cry hard. You'll find that you can't cry hard very long; the body stops itself. By giving vent to them, crying jags become shorter and less intense. The feeling of emptiness slips away faster if you allow yourself to play it out.

After some time elapses, you might want to reexamine your "divorce" by asking yourself:

1. What can I feed myself (not food!) to fill the emptiness? (This is a good time to reread Chapter Four.)

2. What is my next goal, now that I am again in charge of all my time? Is there something I put on hold for the sake of this relationship? Is this a good time to do it?

3. What was my part in the ending? How much was I a contributing factor?

4. Will I choose a different kind of man next time? Will I be a different kind of partner? Will I invest myself more wisely in the relationship?

5. Looking back over the experience, what would I change? Am I making efforts to better my chances for happiness the next time?

6. How can I stay optimistic and avoid feeling bitter as I start over?

Depending upon how long ago you suffered through a premarital divorce, you will respond to what I am about to say differently. If it's recent and the hurt is fresh, you may not hear the essence of my words clearly. (If that is the case, I suggest you put a paper clip on this page and make a mental note to reread it another day, when the passage of time and the influx of new satisfactions have given you a different perspective.) But if you feel ready to dissect a painful episode now, read on. And hear me out. This is not pap and this is not feel-good time.

Looking back at the love stories that have crossed my desk as advisor to the single world (and remembering romantic highs and lows in my own life), I can honestly say that each wrenching of the heart adds something to the loser. Oddly enough, I have observed that loving and losing is more of a growth experience than winning; the pain does the magic. In the process of being torn from the beloved (the reason doesn't matter in this discussion), the loser gains insights and wisdom. It's commonly thought that the one who loses love also loses part of the self. And, in a way, that is true: Shared dreams, shared experiences, leave with the lover. But that's small stuff compared to the main event—a growth period that widens your understanding of life and self and (dare I say it?) love. You are more for the experience.

I'm not advocating a life pattern of loving and losing. Certainly not! After the third such experience, it's time for healthy introspection, perhaps some time with a professional therapist to find out what's going on. But take my word that the loss of love can be an augmenting experience. Sad, heart-wrenching, of course. Painful beyond belief. But not an excuse to give in to bitterness and feel hatred for all men. That's too easy and cheap a reaction, given the beauty possible between a man and woman. The goodness in what once was surely deserves another chance.

BITTERNESS

Of all the aftershocks of divorce (whether premarital or post-marital), bitterness is the most destructive, because it's sneaky. As it clouds perception, it silently fulfills its own prophecy: People stay away. Potential friends and lovers keep their distance from the embittered, affirming her negative view of the world. And the circle of cynicism completes itself.

But when you are content, you view life's happenings evenly and fairly, putting blame where blame is due and assuming your rightful share of responsibility for the mistakes inevitable in a full life. Bitter or optimistic, the choice is yours. And believe me, it is a choice, because there are ways to remain hopeful even when life tosses a curve:

- Ask yourself if you blame men, fate, society, or your parents for your lacks. If so, write the ways they are hurting your chances for happiness and the ways you can overcome them. Since you are the only person you can change, heal the woman in the mirror.

- Read the control exercise in Chapter One to remind yourself how much power you have over your life. Then make concrete plans to put this power into action.

- Think in the present moment. Resist the tendency to taint today with yesterday's hurts. Become too busy pursuing possibilities to relive disappointments. When you think of it, there is no other way, really, since yesterday is gone and tomorrow is out of sight. The only viable choice is to dig into today and see what it can yield.

- Admit your part in mistakes, and work on changing your patterns. If the error was a poor choice of a friend or lover, it's time to analyze the reason for the choice and resolve to do better next time.

- If you detect a pattern of wrong choices, make that the topic of discussion in your next network meeting. If you're up for it, a bit of group therapy can do wonders.

- Pinpoint the occasions when you're most likely to blame an event or outcome on somebody else. Those are the times when you feel like somebody else is in control. Bitterness cannot coexist with positive action.

- Beware the "might-have-beens." Like bitterness, they are signs of powerlessness. No one who takes charge of her life has thought patterns that dwell on yesterday. The past is for educational purposes only, to improve today and tomorrow. Life is not a gyp; it does not cheat us. We cheat ourselves when we chain ourselves to bitterness and regrets. You deserve better.

COMMITMENT PHOBIA

Without a mate, and often without children or nearby family to keep them accountable, many single women become quite adept at "slip-sliding away." (This isn't a built-in character flaw; it is acquired, the dark side of flexibility.) This is an enhanced ability to sidle out of commitments and a decreased ability to follow through (as in, "I'll call you soon and we'll do lunch"). Every year of living solo compounds the fear of commitment. I remember panicking at the thought of showing up on four consecutive nights for a meditation course. (That gut reaction alerted me to a fear that could ruin the good things I was so earnestly building.)

Toning the commitment muscles takes time, patience, and gentleness with yourself. (At least, they worked for me.) So when you begin your commitment campaign, center the first few battles around nonemotional issues:

- Arrange with a friend to exercise together on a schedule (every other day, if possible) and to pay a "fine" (say, ten dollars or dinner out with wine) every time you show up late or not at all. That should keep you diligent.

- Listen to your words when you make your next promise. Whatever it deals with—a phone call or a meeting—write down the specifics and make no other plans for that time. It's reserved. No backing out if a man calls for a date, either. This is a much bigger project than one date; it goes to the essence, the very heart of your character.

- Subscribe to a series of concerts, movies, or lectures. (The nature of the series is secondary to the fact that it is ongoing and money is paid in advance.) And unless major illness strikes, be there.

Every time. *Alternative:* If a one-ticket outlay is more affordable and a one-time commitment easier to swallow, that's better than no commitment at all. So buy the one ticket. And show up. You will build up financial and emotional reserves in small steps like these. (Progress is slow, but it will come.)

Now that you've gotten the message, supply the projects. Strengthen your follow-through in ways only you know are necessary, and *don't quit* for a spur-of-the-moment impulse. You'll respect yourself for doing what you said you'd do, and that's one of the best feelings you can feed yourself.

WHEN HE WON'T COMMIT

If commitment is an issue for you, how can you expect *him* to follow through without a qualm? And how can you be certain that you are not *choosing* men with commitment phobia, so that *you* can wriggle off the hook when crunch time comes? If you're having trouble pinning yourself down, it's going to be even more difficult wrestling a lover to the proverbial mat. The only way out is to teach *yourself* to follow through first, then look for a man who recognizes and admires that quality.

Let's assume you have begun flexing your commitment muscles and are curious if the man in your life is able to do the same. You could start your research with some minor tests:

Ask him to help move your sofa to the other side of the room, or to baby-sit a younger brother (or nephew) while you go to the supermarket (assuming you know the man to be mature, reliable, and childproof). Each time you see him —the man, not the nephew—involve him in one or two small chores, and watch his reaction. Does his jaw fall when you ask him to come with you to visit a sick friend? Does his smile freeze at an invitation to co-host a party with you? Do his knees knock when your folks are in town and want to meet him? Note it all, but don't say a word. It's not time for talk—yet. These tests are preliminary fact-finding forays into his commitability. (If it's questionable at this level, you would do well to reconsider the future of the relationship.) But on the other hand, *he* may be capable of growing into a larger sense of responsibility.

If you sense that is happening, the relationship is at the next stage, and it's time to ask more of him: dinner with your folks, a weekend at your brother's home, joint membership in a coed bowling team. If he passes these tests, you might consider him for a partnership in a summer rental to see if he's ready to deal with issues of money and emotions, the big tests.

If you're beginning to feel it's time to discuss the main event—love and the rest of it—don't expect him to bring up the subject first, especially if he's still a little commitment shy. *You* will have to break the ice. And what better way than by candlelight, in a private, at-home dinner for two at your house? Lead up to the issue slowly, and present your point of view as gently and firmly as you can. Relationships can be talked to death, so don't make this a filibuster, simply a low-keyed dialogue about shared feelings. (If you can, rehearse this conversation with a friend or member of your network to iron out excessive verbiage and tears. Preparing in advance will get the main points clear in your head. When they are, the rest will fall into place as talk progresses.) But, again, first things first: Work on your own issues about commitment before you work on your man.

SHYNESS (SH-I-NESS)

Philip Zimbardo, acknowledged expert on the subject, says that shyness strikes men and women just about equally. The significant difference between them lies in the rewards given by society for displaying one's nervousness: Men are branded wimps and often lose out in the race for desirable women.

And shy women? Ah. That's the rub: Shy women are given society's seal of approval, because shy behavior is lady-like behavior. Women have always been permitted—yes, even encouraged—to be reticent in social situations and passive in mixed company. Men bought this double standard, vowing to "date" (sleep with) bold hussies but, when the time came, to settle down with a woman whose reticence would make her a "suitable" wife and mother. Both sexes were caught in the shyness bind.

Now the kicker. As women freed themselves from underdog status and moved up into the male role of initiator, they needed a hefty dose of assertiveness, an underdeveloped trait in females. We told ourselves that we're unshackling from other restraints, why not this one too? So we set about making ourselves heard. In the work world, our assertiveness is rewarded. But outside of the office it's another story—and probably a familiar one.

At the slightest hint of our forthrightness, we interrogate ourselves: Am I coming on too strong? Too fast? Am I the kind of woman he'd like to marry? What will he think of me if I call him? (Or ask him to dance? Or act aggressively in bed?) Am I acting unladylike? Is he going to reject me? He says he likes it, but am I too assertive for my own good? Self-interrogated by questions that only he can answer, you hold back, paralyzed, afraid to make even the smallest of first moves—and find yourself reverting to the old shy ways as an oasis of comfort and safety. You feel sure he will approve of a shy little buttercup for a companion.

As Zimbardo says, shyness comes from being I-oriented (as you may have noticed from the many *I*s in those questions), and female insecurity adds yet another reason for us to concentrate on ourselves in social situations. The harder you try to stop thinking about yourself and your new assertiveness, the more self-conscious you become. But there are pattern-breaking devices:

1. Shift the focus from you to the other person:
   - Face to face with a stranger, think in terms of sharing what you have. Begin by sharing a smile, an affectionate pat, a compliment, a news item.
   - In social situations, look for people who seem awkward and ill at ease and do something to make them more comfortable. This distracts you from your own feelings and at the same time brings out warmth and gratitude in the people you help.

2. Imagine yourself on the stage of life, an actress whose role is to act poised and confident. Play your part to the hilt; you may ham it up at first, but with practice the poise will become a part of you and integrate into your personality. This is an example of change happening from the outside in.

3. Make yourself a more interesting conversationalist. Read the newspaper daily, read current magazines, tune in to the television/radio news while you're dressing for work and again before you go to sleep. (If the news is too disturbing before sleep, listen only in the morning. But do stay informed.) And work at not being timid about giving opinions; a point of view defines you.

4. When you are stymied for a response, simply repeat a version of the last comment made to you ("So, you're *really* going back to school?") while you think of something else to say. You can't use this ploy often, but it's useful for an awkward pause once in a while.

5. Take small steps when making first moves:
   - Don't approach a man and ask him to dance right away; instead, ask if you could sit with him and talk awhile.

- Rather than asking for a date when you phone a man, ask him for advice or an opinion or simply say hello.
- The purpose of a first move (in person or over the phone) is not only to get to know him better, but for him to get to know the *real* you. So whatever makes you more relaxed, use it. This has nothing to do with being deceptive or phony; on the contrary, what you are after is showing the real you!

Above all, don't reproach yourself for being shy. You can't expect to unravel eons of conditioning in an afternoon. These strategies work when you are ready for them. Outwitting shyness is a gradual process; there is no one timetable for reaching the objective. So be gentle and patient with yourself, but *persist*. (My zodiac sign is the Ram, which could explain my passion for persistence.) You need practice in the art of making the first move, and to get it you must continue to deliberately put yourself out on a limb in all kinds of situations. Your network discussions will give you some of that practice.

IT'S IRONIC

Since time began, it's been the shy male of the species who got left behind. Now it could be our turn. Think about that and stop worrying what he will think. Just be your own sweet, feminine, assertive self.

REJECTION

In the preceding chapter you learned how to invite a man to go out with you. Although much of the time he accepts (how could he resist?), there comes a time (it may already have come) when he'll refuse. That "no" can feel like a major crisis. It shouldn't, but it usually does. It hurts to have an invitation turned down, of course, but it's not the end of the world. Men go through that trauma all the time! And it's nothing new to you, either; it's just coming from a different source. I'm sure you've asked a female friend or a relative over for dinner and had them decline. And I'm equally sure you've had work proposals fall flat. But you didn't go into a deep depression over *those* slammed doors. Ideally, the same will hold true when you ask a man for a date. In time, you can develop a thicker skin and not be devastated by a male turn-down. Believe me, when you can handle a man's "no" and not go to pieces, you'll be able to survive other kinds of rejection much more easily.

Here are some things to keep in mind:

- Depersonalize rejection when it comes. Think it through: Most of the time the man in question doesn't even know you very well. He's not *rejecting* you as a person, he's refusing one particular invitation. Haven't you done the same?

- Find out what he's really saying, listen to the tone of his voice. There's a "no" that means "don't call me again" (you probably won't hear that one very often) and there's a "no" that means "not this time, maybe next week." If he sounds inviting, promise yourself you'll make a second call sometime soon. (It wouldn't hurt to write his number on your calendar for a follow-up call in two weeks or so.) And notice whether a headache develops around the time you're due to make it. (See how it disappears the moment he accepts.) And when you know him better, share a laugh about your fear. He'll understand. Men have been battling that devil for ages, remember!

• Your first invitation is spadework: Even if the first call doesn't pan out, chances are good that the man in question will remember you the next time he has a movie pass or a dinner party invitation.

• Decide to ignore rejection. You've heard stories about a manuscript being rejected by scores of publishing houses before finding a publisher. Naturally, the novelist was tempted to quit, but chose to "keep on keeping on," as the song goes. People who persist usually get what they're after. And if they don't, at least they harbor no regrets for not having tried hard enough.

• To keep rejection to a minimum, review the steps for asking a man for a date (see Chapter Four). Have notes at hand with opening lines and the small talk that follows, and practice them with a friend or in front of your group. Be prepared. Use any and all of your strategies. (Think this is overkill? Men have been onto these tricks for years!)

• Finally, keep your options open, and don't give any particular invitation too much importance. If one doesn't work out, another will. None of this "last-chance-for-happiness" thinking. The best things happen at random, so all you can do is involve yourself in your life and let nature take its course.

If all you wanted was a husband, any husband, you'd certainly have been married by now. (You're *not* single because no man wants you; anyone who knows you knows that!) You are single because you refuse to settle, a strategy that takes guts.

DEFENSIVENESS: FORTRESS THINKING

By now you've gotten the message: Most rough spots are not harmful in themselves, only when they get out of hand. The same thing applies to feeling protective about your identity and accomplishments. You've worked hard to get where you are, and the instinct to hold on to your turf is natural, normal, adaptive. But when you become hypersensitive about who you are and what you've done, when you become *defensive*, you undermine the very goals you've achieved. It's a perfect illustration of how a difference in degree becomes a difference in kind.

For women, especially single women, this can be a sore spot as well as a rough spot. Because liberation is still new enough to make us unsure it's here to stay, we come on strong, shouting: "I am strong; I can do it myself." It's understandable, but not a very good idea when excessive. We are not islands, we cannot set ourselves apart from the human crowd. Nor would we want to. Genuinely confident women do not need to be defensive. Once you feel really good about your job, your friends, your home, the balance of love and work in your life, you won't bristle at unintentional slights. You'll be able to laugh them off and thus take your place among the greats. But this kind of self-assurance can take a while to achieve. Until you reach that balance, consider ways to smooth over sharp edges:

- Think of the last time you felt sure of yourself and truly confident. That picture is the real you, and the more often you dwell on it, the closer you will come to being that woman—all the time.

- Do what exhilarates you—and do it often. Dancing does it for me, every time. On the dance floor I am as close as I can be to the peak picture I have of myself. Do whatever it is that does that for you.

- Learn to trust your instincts. Consult them when you need an answer and listen to them over the din of outside opinions. Confer with yourself before making any decision of major proportions.

- Analyze what's making you feel defensive. Is it not having a man in your life? Is it being unmarried and "different" from family or friends? You're not looking for excuses; you're looking for understanding. Level with yourself and work to break down any walls you have put around yourself.

- Observe yourself the next time you're out with a man. Are you on the edge of your seat, afraid he will jump on your bones? Relax. My survey found that single men—most of them anyway—do not expect sex on the first several dates. Could it be that you secretly do? That desire might be a key to understanding your defensiveness. I've noticed that those women who are most outspoken about their liberated state have secret yearnings to return to a "little girl" state and be taken care of by "daddy." That sort of "opposites thinking" could be true for you, too, regarding independence or some other part of your life. It's worth examining.

- When you find yourself tightening up (physically as well as mentally) in response to a remark or action, stop and think instead of blowing up. Are you sure of your position, confident of your opinion, secure in your decision? If so, there is no need to be defensive. You are doing what you think right. Period. No one else's judgment or opinion should make any difference. (It's easier said than done, of course, but after a few stop-and-think reactions like this, at least you'll be slower to retreat to your fortress.)

By all means, build a strong foundation, but don't build walls so thick no one can come through them. The lasting cure for excessive defensiveness is to feel comfortable and integrated with the life you've made for yourself. It may take a long time to achieve, but activating the strategies here should help. And as you snuggle into life as a secure, confident woman, you'll find fewer instances where defensiveness is needed— at least to the degree where they become rough spots. Remember that only the weak feel called upon to defend their position. You don't qualify.

HOW TO IGNORE PUBLIC OPINION (RAISED EYEBROWS)

An eyebrow raised in disapproval at the wrong time can be devastating to an unmarried woman, no matter how steeped she is in security and self-esteem. As I said earlier, negative perception of a woman on her own can make the rough spots rougher. Such a woman can evoke a lascivious leer, unadulterated pity, gossipy curiosity, overwhelming motherliness (I should say smotherliness), uneasiness, jealousy, and hostility. The range of reactions is as wide as the horizons open to her. But you know I won't close this chapter without helping you chip away at society's negativism.

- Consider yourself an emissary from the single world; carry your self-reliance and contentment to the world at large. By living well you will send the message that being single is indeed an enjoyable alternative to being married. Make the richness of your life a beacon of hope to women still unsure of their single selves.

• Make full use of your network and personal support system when you need a friend. Society is coming around to a more sane appraisal of unpartnered women, but it's taking time, and you can still find bias and condescension if you don't choose your friends selectively.

• Use the strategies in this chapter over and over again. You'll find that sanding the rough spots *within* your control will help you handle the ones you can't do as much about. Be creative with the solutions proposed here: overlap them, mix them, adapt them to fit the shifting situations in your life. Only you know the answers that fit best in your own life. Only you can arrange them to work for you.

• Review your personal belief system in the Introduction and the expectations in Chapter One. I'm certain you can see more possibilities in life now, proof that upbeat thinking makes answers easier to find.

• Practice positive behavior. Act *as if* (remember?) your life has no limitations. In fact, do something that at first thought (and a few weeks ago) would have seemed "silly" and out of the question: Try out for a dramatic role with your local theater group, paint a landscape, plot a short story. The worst that can happen is an imperfect attempt; you can always improve with practice. But if you don't try, you've lost the chance. And who knows? Your "silliness" may explode a limitation. What a victory that would be.

SELF-PITY:
QUICK FIXES FOR THE
GENERIC BLUES

Some low feelings are perennial; they crop up no matter how many times you think you've weeded them out of your secret garden. They are the generic blues: a vague, unspecified unease. Low-grade though they are, they make an ideal breeding ground for bona fide troubles and escalate a simple problem into a full-blown case of self-pity. So it's important to deal with them at the first sign. (The following list isn't meant to work out long-term problems; those require second and third opinions and sometimes professional intervention.) But for the moody blues, minisolutions:

- Get on the phone and talk to your parents, gather your children and read them a story, or visit a neighbor. Talk and interaction are instant mood-breakers.

- Go for a brisk walk, no matter the season. Tuck a key and some cash in your pockets so your arms can swing freely. Fresh air and motion work wonders, and natural light is known to lift seasonal depression.

- Invest in a pair of walking shoes; they put a spring in your step (which can put a smile on your face). You think I'm kidding? Try it.

- Use a technique professional counselors use: "runaway thinking." Exaggerate your problems to the nth degree. Blow them up in your imagination until they're so farfetched and absurd that even you can laugh at them.

- Meditate. Pray. Whatever you may call it, use the power of your mind to heal yourself.

- Turn on the kind of music that stirs your soul.

- Go to the local hospital and look at the newborns. Then just *try* to be pessimistic.

- Make a call to a dedicated fan. In my life it's my mother, who never fails to lift my spirits by reminding me how much she admires what I've done with my life. (Not bragging; it's true.)

- Rent a video tape and watch a good movie.

- Buy travel books and start planning next year's momentous trip.

- Buy a trashy romance novel and spend the evening snuggled in bed drinking hot chocolate and losing yourself in an improbable romance.

- Treat yourself to something special, some little luxury: a ten-dollar lipstick you usually don't allow yourself. Rationalize the extravagance by comparing it to the national budget deficit.

- Reread old love letters—or, better still, write one to the man of your dreams, whether or not he exists. (If he doesn't, this might help to define him— just don't make him *too* wonderful to be human.) If the letter is to a real person, wait a day or two to mail it. What seemed fun at night might not look that way in broad daylight.

Shortcuts like these give a quick charge, but their effects fizzle fast. The real stuff, habitual positive thinking, takes repetition and discipline. So use each ritual in your daily routine to talk yourself into good spirits. As you apply your makeup each morning, think about the day to come with optimism and cheerfulness. Coffee breaks and trips to the ladies' room can also give you a chance to psyche yourself up while you're doing something mundane. If you have a difficult task ahead (a phone call to a disgruntled customer), do it early in the day and get it over with; don't fret about it till 5 P.M. The deeper this discipline is in your thought patterns, the more available the solutions will be.

SWEET PAYBACK

Sunday is traditionally a day of rest. I suggest you add to it one more tradition, one with repercussions far beyond the obvious. Every Sunday night on the brink of a new week, make it a ritual to count your blessings. Do this in full consciousness, wide awake so that you can relish every one. And don't leave any out, even the ones that came with your heritage. Give thanks for this free country, with its economic and social mobility. Be grateful for good health and the options it gives you. Include your most valuable assets: the ability to reason and take risks, the impulses to laugh and cry. Name every person you care for, whatever their status. Each one of them is another reason to make the most of your life. Last, but not least, enumerate the advantages of being single, the freedom and autonomy inherent in being at the helm of your life.

It's easy to fall into a semislumber that merely gets you through the days, numb to the potentially zesty moments. Going through the motions is pushing away the days without making much of them. I wish for you more than that. Yes, I know there are problems in your life. There are in mine, too. No one gets through without their share. And even when the biggies have retreated and no crisis is pending, there are still minor-league worries and irritations that sap energy and good will. But I believe that each of us has a mission—an obligation, really—to pay back the positive energy that entered us at our birth and continues to animate us. The repayment needn't be a continual or ever-conscious effort, but we should remind ourselves of the debt often enough to keep the payments going.

There is no alternative to being grateful. There is so much misery in the world. Listen to the news, read the papers, eavesdrop on conversations around you; catastrophe and chaos are everywhere. So think about all you have, and come up with ways to share some of it. What goes around comes around. Your contribution will come back to you at the most unexpected time, in ways you could never plan.

If, as we said, most of the rough spots of singleness are the result of society's disapproval of the uncoupled, then revenge is called for: Your life can disprove those skewed perceptions. And if living well is the best revenge, then *knowing* you are living well certainly must be the ultimate and the very sweetest payback. Strive to be happy; count your blessings.

SOLVENCY: TAKING MONEY SERIOUSLY

As you're edging out of the waiting room (and you are), take another minute to look over your shoulder and see if you've forgotten something. You may notice a green package, a seemingly innocuous bundle as potentially dangerous as a time bomb. That package symbolizes money matters left unresolved for one reason or another. Ignore them too long or treat them too carelessly, and all the precious dreams you are nurturing will go up in a puff of smoke.

What's that you say? You pay your bills and save a little when you can? Well, that's not good enough for the kind of life you've begun building. Your future peace of mind depends on the kind of financial decisions you make right now, as you are molding life predicated on the As-If approach. The choices you make in this chapter can evolve into a rock-solid financial foundation that will mean security for the rest of your life—whether you're married or single, wealthy, or like the rest of us. We're talking long- and short-term planning, from monthly budgeting to retirement planning, from today's credit management to the kind of saving tomorrow that can allow you to start your own business . . . or whatever. (You supply the word.) As you may have guessed, this is not interim, while-I'm-single stuff. This is for the long haul and whatever it may bring your way.

And so, this chapter is a series of steps similar to the ones financial planners use with their clients:

1. Collect your financial records.
2. Set financial goals.
3. Identify financial weak spots.
4. Produce a written plan.
5. Follow through.
6. Periodic review.

If that seems like a lot to accomplish in one chapter, it is. We're doing big things here. The financial plan that will emerge is a substantial starting point, but it is *the process of exploration to create that plan* that will leave you a changed person. I doubt that you will ever look at your money in the same way . . . and I'm optimistic that because of this one chapter you'll take a more lively interest in all things financial that affect your life.

WHAT YOU'LL GAIN FROM A FINANCIAL FOUNDATION

- More money—money works harder when you know how to use it
- Greater self-assurance
- More goals achieved

- Clearer priorities
- Respect from others—and, more important, from yourself
- Access to a wider range of men (let's face it, that never hurts!)
- Financial autonomy
- Greater equality in a love partnership

Because of its value, this last advantage should be amplified: When you do meet a man you love, your sound financial condition will empower you to ask of him greater emotional involvement. You're probably saying that you shouldn't have to buy emotional responsibility. But whether or not women admit it, before we claimed parity in the workplace we felt compelled to contribute up to 75 percent of a relationship's emotional currency because of the big disparity in the earnings level. That imbalance is leveling out as women earn more, but it won't achieve a fifty-fifty ratio until we assume total responsibility for our finances. Fiscal maturity will also earn us a place in decision making, both in relationships and in the workplace. Remember the fiscal Golden Rule: The person with the gold rules. In other words, financial soundness is going to buy you something beyond price: partnership.

Curious? Primed and ready to start? Not quite yet. There's gold in these pages, and I want to be 100 percent sure you don't have one foot in the waiting room, still ambivalent about going for the gold. A last look back at your outdated money mood:

WHY YOU IGNORE
MONEY MATTERS

1. Finances are dry and boring.
2. Finances are unfeminine—they are a man's job.
3. I'm not worth the effort they require.

4. Financial prowess scares off men.

5. Numbers give me the willies.

6. The subject rattles me so much I don't know where to start.

7. Finances are too private to discuss—even with someone in the field.

8. I'm not sure of myself in this area.

9. I'm terrified of what I'll discover.

10. I'm not sure I deserve to have real amounts of money under my control.

Now for the fun—putting each of these illogical gems to rest. This is the psychological part of your financial foundation-building. It's important; if you don't have the will, you won't care about the ways.

1. *Finances are dry and boring.*
   Money is so much more than mere currency. Solvency equals independence, autonomy, dignity, mobility, equality, self-worth. Believe me, it's not dull.

2. *Finances are unfeminine—let a man take care of them.*
   If you believe dealing with money is a man's role, you're still in the waiting room, helpless until the right man comes along. Remember, you're not dooming yourself to eternal spinsterhood by making the present secure. If you still think you are, reread Chapter Two.

3. *You're not worth the effort they require.*
   No wonder you fritter away cash. Somewhere deep down you're unsure whether you deserve a financial future. Review Chapter Four to remind yourself that a solid financial future is another way of feeding yourself. Eat!

4. *Financial prowess scares away men.*
   Wrong. There's nothing as appealing to a secure man as a capable, organized woman who takes care of herself.

5. *Numbers give you the willies.*

If sheer fear is your problem, there are books to help you overcome it. Or go back to school or take a correspondence course in algebra. The new, expanded you will feel less intimidated by mere numbers.

6. *You don't know where to start.*

Start at the beginning—with Step 1 in this chapter. You'll soon see that finances are not hopelessly confusing.

7. *Finances are too private to discuss.*

These days, money is much more a private matter than sex, but that doesn't mean you can't talk things out with a qualified professional. When you keep the questions to yourself, you lose a chance to get a second opinion on money matters—and even professional money managers know to ask for one.

8. *You lack confidence in your judgment.*

You're as capable of figuring out finances as anyone else (man or woman, single or married). But you *do* have to make an effort—and you will, after this chapter. For starters, begin reading the business pages of your news-paper and subscribe to *Changing Times, The Wall Street Journal,* or *Money* magazine. And consider a course in investing or basic accounting.

9. *You're terrified of what you'll discover.*

Most people are pleasantly surprised when they add up their assets minus their debts. Besides, if you do have some financial weak spots (and who doesn't?), the best place to discover them is on paper, privately.

10. *You're not sure you deserve to have real money.*

With an attitude like this, no wonder you've let your finances drift away from you. It's time to realize you're as entitled as anyone else to a strong financial future.

For most of us, insecurity about finances comes from a complicated combination of reasons. But the result is uniformly the same: The time bomb continues ticking, and many women let their peak earning years pass with only partial fulfillment of their own potential. They have a job and a bank account, not a career and a financial plan. The truth is, society doesn't consider you a whole person without some money in your own name. How much? That depends on many factors. What's important is that you base that number on your own needs. For instance: Think about the feasibility of saving enough money to keep you going for a year if you suddenly lost your job or decided to change careers. If that is out of the question right now, write it down as one of your long-term financial goals.

More eager than before to start? Good. But where you start in the chapter depends on your financial experience. A wide range of women will be reading this book, and because time is money, there's no point in going over yesterday's news. These broad categories will help you place yourself and get to the "meat" without wasting time.

> **TIP:** No matter where you fit in the following groups, take a minute to look over the steps you passed. Finding one gem of new information will justify rereading what you already know.

And unless you already have a functioning financial plan, we'll all meet again at Step 4 to produce one.

- *If you're new to the job force and aren't making much money yet:* You want to manage cleverly what you have while learning ways to make more. Best to begin with Step 1, gathering receipts and records, and move on after creating a budget out of the information they yield.

- *If you're making good money now but feel that your financial life is out of control:* Jump in at Step 2, where you'll really be prodded to deal with nitty-gritty questions about financial goals, both short- and long-term.

• *If you earn a decent amount of money, have a budget and other basics under your control, but would like to fine-tune your financial skills:* Step 3 is your launching pad, where you'll scrutinize each building block of your financial foundation. This is the place to locate the weak spots and learn how to strengthen them. (Again, take time to scan the preceding steps.)

STEP 1:
BUDGET AND NET WORTH STATEMENT

Whether Chief Executive Officer of a large company, a computer programmer, or a counter clerk, the way to manage your finances is by monitoring (1) *what comes in* (salary, dividends, and other income), and (2) *what goes out* (rent, food, savings, other expenses). It's that basic! And as I explained before, you'll do this in a series of steps:

PART A: You'll begin by drawing up a net worth statement. You'll need several sheets of paper (one for the totals and the rest for scrap paper), a few pencils and an eraser, all your financial records (that means bankbooks, IRA statements, real estate mortgage, stock certificates, bill of sale for automobile, receipts for clothing, credit card bills, charge account statements and other unpaid debts—and an open mind. But before you make the first entry, invest in an accordion-pleated, legal-size file folder. Label the compartments separately in alphabetical order with the various categories that make up your budget and net worth information, for example, "bank account statements," "IRA and other retirement account information," "insurance," "investments," "stocks," "taxes," "will." This organizer will be invaluable in this chapter—and long afterward.

1. The first step is to tabulate your net worth—a professional way of stating what you have minus what you owe. Sit down at an uncluttered table with all these documents. (Use the form below as a guide.)

2. Check recent statements and passbooks for savings and checking account balances. (Call your bank for the most current figures if you're unsure about a deposit or a recent interest payment.)

CHART YOUR NET WORTH

ASSETS

1. Checking account, $ _____
   money market/   _____
   savings account,   _____
   certificates of
   deposit,   _____
   other savings   _____

2. Stocks, bonds,
   mutual funds   _____

3. Pensions, IRAs   _____

4. Home/real estate   _____

5. Car   _____
   Furniture   _____
   Household
   furnishings   _____
   Clothing   _____
   Other household
   items   _____

6. Any other assets   _____

                SUBTOTAL: $ _____

LIABILITIES

1. Mortgage or real-estate loan $ _____
2. Car loan   _____
3. Credit-card or charge-account debt   _____
4. Amount owed on furniture or appliances   _____
5. Amount owed on goods and services   _____
6. Taxes due (income, property, school)   _____
7. Other outstanding debts   _____

SUBTOTAL: _____

FINAL TOTAL
(*subtract liabilities from assets*): $ _____

3. Write down the current value of any stocks, mutual funds, bonds, certificates of deposit, etc. (To find the value of U.S. Treasury bonds and certificates of deposit, call your bank.) For the value of corporate stocks and bonds, consult today's newspaper, call a broker, or give a ball-park estimate.

4. Write down the values of your pension and IRA accounts. You can find the exact pension value by asking your employer or by looking at the last annual statement from your company. For IRA values, consult either statements sent periodically by your bank and/or call your broker if you have IRAs in stocks or mutual funds. Again, you can estimate this figure since stocks fluctuate.

5. Do you own your own home or some other property? (Real property is probably your largest asset.) For an idea of the property's worth, contact a real estate agent or the property assessor in your town, or refer to your last property tax bill. That bill or the assessor will give a low-end estimate, while a realtor will come up with the more realistic figure of what price your home would sell for now, under current market conditions.

6. Estimate the value of your car, furniture, other household items, and clothing. (If you have already done this for a homeowner's insurance policy, you're a step ahead.) The idea is not to put a value on every single thing, but to approximate the resale value of high-ticket items such as automobile, antiques, coins, and jewelry.

7. Do you have other assets? Estimate their value and add to the total. Be as precise as possible, but don't spend inordinate amounts of time assessing values to the last penny. Add these in one column; the final total represents your total assets. (If we were to go a step further, you'd differentiate between assets that are liquid, which means they are readily convertible to cash, and assets that are fixed, tied up in long-term investments, such as real estate and long-term certificates of deposit.)

8. The next part is easier to compile: Add up your liabilities (debts), using bills, installment credit contracts, promissory notes, and other written agreements to find the total.

   • Do you have a mortgage or other real estate loan? What do you owe?

   • Do you have a car loan? Write down the balance due.

   • What do you owe on credit cards, charge accounts?

   • Write down what you owe on furniture or appliances.

- Do you owe anything on goods and services (for example, physicians' or attorney's bills)? Write down the balance due.

- Write down taxes due over the next year on income, property, and school.

- Write down any other outstanding debts.

9. Tally these in another column. The total represents your liabilities. Subtract liabilities from assets. If there is an overage, you have a positive net worth, and would be able to pay off your debts if you decided to convert assets to cash.

If you owe more than you are worth, help is on the way. Keep reading. Save this basic information—your net worth sheet is a financial profile-at-a-glance. It helps prove to a bank or other lender that you're worthy of credit, and it's useful when you're setting financial goals. Because it governs your spending habits, you should update your net worth statement at least once a year.

PART B: Next, you'll create a monthly budget. Chances are, a budget is more familiar to you than a net worth statement. In fact, you may already have one. If you do, you might want to use it to help you prepare this version. (It will be interesting to compare the two.) Or, if you've done all this and are satisfied you've been thorough, move on to Step 2.

- List your total monthly income, including regular take-home pay, interest, dividends, and miscellaneous (loans repaid, consulting fees, etc.) $ _____

- Tabulate your monthly expenses:
  Savings   _____

Rent, mortgage,
maintenance   _____

Utilities and phone   _____

Food   _____

Life insurance   _____

Household furnishings   _____

Insurance—homeowner's,
renter's, car   _____

Loan payments   _____

Clothing   _____

Transportation (gasoline,
airplane tickets, etc.)   _____

Medical/dental (fees not
covered by insurance)   _____

Spending money
(entertainment, extras)   _____

Miscellaneous (including
home and auto repairs)   _____

TOTAL $_____

Give this breakdown serious attention. It is proof in your own handwriting of what you lay out every month. (You'll probably have to track your expenses for several months before you get a real sense of where money goes and at what rate.)

It's important to realize that a budget is more than just a monthly record; it is also a conscious choice about the amount of money you are willing and able to spend in a given area. After you've monitored where the money is going for several months in a row, you can make a budget that gives you *control.*

YOUR FINANCIAL FOUNDATION

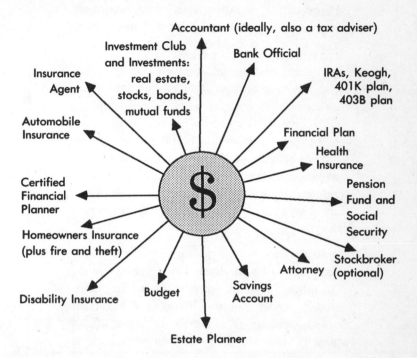

So, after you've kept a budget for two or three months, come back to this step and use a new sheet (but the same format above) to write down what you *ought* to be spending in each category. Trim the fat from your budget. (If you notice you're spending too much on gasoline, for instance, figure out what you'd save in a carpool, and start or join one.) Set up a budget that's realistic, but not rigid or austere! You will only follow it if it is livable. The goal: to live beneath your yearnings.

BUDGET TIPS

• Be sure to file every paper in your accordion folder. Being methodical now will mean easy access when you need it.

• Make sure this budget (and all financial records) are neat and clear. That includes your checkbook, the crux of daily record-keeping. Reconcile your balance with the bank statement every month without fail. If you often forget to record checks, order a checkbook that makes a carbon copy of each check you write. Also, remember to record every cash withdrawal you make from an automatic teller machine (ATM).

• If you need help with the budget or net worth statement, call your local Cooperative Extension office, listed in your telephone directory (usually under county listings) or reached through your state's landgrant university. (Call a nearby state university or college and ask to be directed to the "landgrant" university.) In some states, Cooperative Extension offers individual budget counseling, budget workshops, and fact sheets of financial information written for the lay person. It's reassuring to know of a place besides an accountant or CPA's office where you can find help with money matters.

STEP 2:
SETTING FINANCIAL GOALS

Now that you've assembled basic financial records, it's time to ask yourself what do you want to *do* with your money. Financial goals are like ladder rungs, each one leading you closer to fiscal independence. On the bottom rung is an adequate amount of money to meet current needs, on the next a separate fund for unexpected expenses, and after that—well, that's up to you.

1. First, list the major, predictable expenditures coming up in the next *one to three years*: a new washing machine because your old one is creaking and grinding; a new car because the odometer in yours shows 125,000 miles; a credit-card payoff because you've been making minimum payments too long.

2. Next, think of how you'd like to spend your money *three to five years* from now. (You see what I mean about finances being anything but boring?) The truth is, financial goal-setting is a time to think about hopes and dreams and priorities. Some expenditures you could face in the next five years:

   • college tuition for your kids

   • a new house—you never meant to live in this one as long as you have

   • a fur coat (or a shearling if that's better for budget)—because you've decided to be your own Santa Claus

   • medical care/nursing home for your parents

   • a cooperative apartment—a home to *own*

   These are only suggestions. List your own goals, then rank them in order of urgency. But don't imagine you can only have one. Options come from thinking ahead. So if you'd rather not have to chooose between college for your child and good care for your parents, *begin planning now so you won't be faced with that excruciating choice.*

3. Finally, list longer-term goals, ten years from now. Too far ahead to make specific plans? A decade is only a hop, skip, and jump away when you're planning to buy a business or take the voyage of a lifetime. And it *is* possible to map at least the general direction you want the future to take. At the worst, you'll have to alter plans and downscale dreams. But the thinking you put into them will definitely not be lost, because it will guide you to the self-assessment that is fundamental to financial solidity.

STEP 3:
IDENTIFYING FINANCIAL
WEAK SPOTS

Here you'll explore most of the components of that strength. You'll also expose any weak spots in your financial projections by asking hard questions. They may not always have pretty answers, but the payoff is big. After you've gotten through this step, you'll be much better able to reach your goals.

You'll need budget and net worth statements from Step 1 and the goals you listed in Step 2, as well as savings information, insurance records, investment certificates, tax records, retirement information (such as IRA certificates), and a will or estate plan, if you have one. If you don't have any of these papers, don't worry—you'll find out the way to get them.

At this point, you may want to venture outside your

four walls and keep appointments you set up. Call an accountant, tax specialist, broker, investment counselor, or financial planner. If you're already using specialists (you may have made the contacts before this book or when you set up a support system), you should by all means continue working with them. But I urge you: Before calling experts, become knowledgeable. No one on the outside, no matter how well trained, can understand what you expect from your money as well as you. You'll learn enough to ask the right questions of a professional through the preparation you are now making. As you tackle each component of your financial foundation (savings is the first), keep a separate list of Things to Do. This will give you a head start at your meetings with these experts, and show them that you have done your homework.

Once again, if you come to a section you feel confident you have mastered, by all means move on to the next. I don't want you to be bored for a moment!

FINANCIAL BUILDING BLOCKS

Savings Account	Up-to-Date Tax Information
Insurance Coverage	Retirement Plan
Credit Control	Up-to-Date Will
Investments	

SAVINGS ACCOUNT

Of all the building blocks, this is most crucial, since a sum of accumulated money provides a buffer between you and the jungle out there. Without savings you're back in the waiting room again—and you know how I feel about that. (Women who don't save regularly usually don't have investments or retirement plans, either, a sorry lot who wind up eking out their golden years.) Tomorrow, I want you to open a savings account in your name. If you already have one, then take $25 to the bank and deposit it in the account. Tomorrow. Add to it regularly every time you are paid. (If I could provide you with gas money for the trip to and from the bank, I would— I feel that strongly about the benefits of savings fever.)

Each endorsement of each salary check should include the phrase "pay myself first" as a reminder to deduct a set amount each time you are paid and tuck it into your savings account—before it's used any other way. Even if you must reduce eating out or clothes shopping, save you must. First things first.

When it comes to savings instruments, it's not necessary (or particularly savvy) to keep all your money in a savings account. Bank money-market accounts and money-market mutual funds invest in short-term securities and usually pay a better rate of interest, but that rate will fluctuate more. Bank certificates of deposit (CDs) are receipts for money you lend to a bank or savings association and offer predictable rates for six-month or longer-term deposits.

Shop around for the highest interest rates. Ask whether they are compounded daily or represent simple interest. (Avoid the latter if at all possible.) Remember, you are interviewing for the most secure and best-paying bank, so sit down with an official at each office, your list of queries in hand, and fire away. Timid mice don't earn respect—or high interest. (By the way, if possible do all your banking at one bank. You'll become known there by using its services and dealing with many different people. Go to the banker you already know and talk things over. He or she is already slightly familiar with your life, so answers may be easier to come by. But if this bank is paying lower rates, forget friendship and go for the gold.)

Discuss savings options in your Old Girls' Network and

SAVINGS SENSE

- Save all windfalls that come your way. Unexpected money should never see the light of day.

- Save the equivalent amount of maintaining a habit (a pack of cigarettes a day adds up quite nicely).

- Save the amount of any installment payments after you have paid off the debt. You won't miss the ready cash, and you'll be one step further from consumerism.

- Set up a totally separate savings account for the inevitable replacement of big-ticket necessities, such as an automobile or washing machine. Figure out what monthly payments on each of them would cost for a year, and then arrange with yourself to put that amount in this special account.

  Important: The minimum amount in the *other, primary* savings account should equal two or three months of your net salary. No less—and possibly more. You'll sleep better knowing it's there. (So will I.)

with your parents. Get several opinions—and facts. Not until you have a solid base stashed away in a basic savings account should you even entertain thoughts of risking your money in higher-interest but less secure investments. Seeing the numbers grow in your bankbook gets to be a minor compulsion, which leads to some very lovely peace of mind.

INSURANCE COVERAGE

Like savings accounts, insurance protection is another area women often ignore until they're in a bind. They don't know much about the types of insurance available to them, and they feel awkward calling an agent to come and talk to a lone person. (Your OGN solves this problem because any insurance rep would jump at the chance to address a group of working women!)

With *health insurance*, you have several choices: fee-for-service plans such as Blue Cross-Blue Shield or fixed-fee plans like HMOs (health maintenance organizations). Your choice depends to a large extent on what your company offers. If you don't have a family physician and you have the opportunity to join an HMO, consider it—there is usually no deductible and it covers basic checkups and other routine health care. Now that you're thinking of these things, make a note to ask at work and also make a phone call to Blue Cross.

For *disability coverage*, read the fine print in your company's policy. This coverage is especially important if you're a single mother and sole breadwinner. But it's also crucial if you're your sole support. Find out how much income you'll receive if you can't work—and how long you'll receive it. Does the coverage become partial? When and how long does partial coverage last? As a single person, earning power is your single greatest asset, and you need to be adequately compensated if it is interrupted. If your company's policy doesn't provide any (or enough) coverage, it may be worthwhile to put this security blanket in your hope chest. Talk to an insurance rep about costs, possibly a group fee for the network group.

You need *life insurance* to cover lump-sum expenses (such as funeral and debts) upon your death and also for any ongoing support you're providing for a child or other relative. Life insurance is not an investment tool. You should be familiar with the two basic types of life insurance—term life, which is cheaper but accumulates no equity, and whole life, which does build up a cash reserve you can draw upon but has more expensive premiums. For more information on how to determine the type and quantity of life insurance you should buy, read up on the subject (see Resources). And talk, talk, talk until you feel comfortable talking about insurance.

When you're ready to buy, it's a wise move to call the local office of a reputable national agent—Nationwide, Allstate (Sears), Kemper, or Travelers—and make a date to visit them. (For a list of financially stable insurance carriers, check the directory published by A.M. Best & Co., found in the reference area of most libraries.) When you talk with an insurance agent, take a list of questions with you, and don't be too proud to take notes during the discussion. The first meeting will give a picture of your insurance needs, but resist the temptation to purchase on the spot. Instead, call an accountant to discuss what you've been told, since there are all sorts of tax advantages and other financial nuances to insurance as it is sold today. Talk the matter over with family and business colleagues. Listen, read, ask questions, take notes.

CREDIT CONTROL

Credit can be a liberator—or chain you to sleepless nights. It should be a safety device to be used in crunch times and a tool to get you what you want. It should be an aid. But our society makes it much too easy to get deeply in debt, lulled into a false sense of buying power. (When you figure that you pay as much as 18 percent interest on some charges, you can see who has the real power.) Too often it only represents a burden.

In the real world, the basic credit equipment is at least one major department-store charge account, and any one of the Big Three: American Express, Visa, or MasterCard (the last two are available through banks). If you're new at this, apply first to the department stores, prove your creditworthiness by paying your bills on or before the due date for at least six months, then apply for one of the Big Three, bearing in mind that American Express expects payment within thirty days (they do offer installment payments via their Optima card), while most issuers of Visa and MasterCard hit you with the 18 percent figure. All three charge an annual membership fee.

Plastic is part of the TNT in that green package beside you in the waiting room; credit is noted for its fickleness. Like Lady Luck, it goes with the person best prepared to handle it.

Still, having credit cards and charge accounts in your name can be a lifetime asset. (Smart cookies keep them *in their maiden name*, even after they marry.) Respect these plastic passports, because they can help you acquire that income-producing real estate or form that company. They can help you get where you want to go. So do what it takes to become credit-worthy at worthy institutions, and by all means build a family of credit cards. But *do* leave home without them.

INVESTMENTS

Your economic life is a progression, and investing your money in stocks or mutual funds is an important step. Like credit, investing can give you a high degree of financial sophistication—or leave you financially adrift. So here, more than anywhere else in your financial life, it is vital to plan. If you begin investing too soon (before you've saved enough), you could undermine your financial security. If you begin too late (and keep too much in your savings account), you lose the advantage of a higher return on your money. And if you jump into investing without adequate forethought and research, you may acquire the wrong kinds of investments. But don't get me wrong—investing is a healthy habit. It gives your money the chance to make money for you.

So how do you know when, where, and how to invest?

First of all, by understanding yourself (an entity you're getting to know better, I trust). If you sleep better knowing your financial risks are nonexistent, stay where the rate of return may be less but your money is secure. If you're more daring (and can sleep no matter what), you're ready to think about investing.

Once you've thought about your capacity for risk, check to see that you have the following reserves:

- six months' net pay (twelve is better)

- health insurance

- life insurance

- disability insurance

- retirement plan, such as pension, IRA, 401K, or Keogh plan

- ownership of your own home (house, condominium, or cooperative apartment)

You should not consider investing so much as a penny until you possess *all* the above. (Even with that shock insulation, a prudent woman will think a hundred times and talk with twenty people about any venture that carries even the most minimal risk.) Insured accounts at your bank are the safest way to earn money on your money and still sleep soundly. The stock market has become so sophisticated and volatile that it barely accommodates small investors anymore. Talk this over with a friend who is a business person, and get a second opinion if mine sounds too conservative. And then get a third . . . and a fourth.

Bounce the idea around in your Old Girls' Network, because I'm going to suggest forming an investment club out of its membership. As part of a group venture, investing can be an exciting (and safer) experience. But any risk-taking should come about only after all of you are savvy about no-load funds, dollar-cost averaging, junk bonds, and the rest of the jargon. If your group does its homework, an investment club can turn out to be profitable. But if you're a novice and want to function independently, stick to bank certificates of deposit, a savings account, or interest-paying checking accounts. At least for the moment.

Another avenue to explore is investment opportunity at work:

- stock purchase plan
- profit-sharing plan
- matched savings plan
- payroll deduction savings plan

For more facts, make an appointment with your company's benefits representative. Revealing yourself as serious about finances can't hurt in the image department. As usual, go with a list of issues. And a sharp pencil.

UP-TO-DATE TAX INFORMATION

The more money earned, the more gobbled up by taxes. Change the earnings/tax ratio by bringing in an expert; by now you're in on the secret that an independent life is only as smooth-running and manageable as the specialists behind it. Certainly in money matters, specialized knowledge is crucial—even if your income is smallish right now. The object is to train yourself to find answers, so that as your earnings grow, you are accustomed to conferring with people who can manage them. A skilled accountant can also be a knowledgeable tax advisor, which is why it's so important to make this choice with deliberation.

Begin by raising the issue at a meeting of your Old Girls' Network. Ask the group for the name(s) of certified public accountants specializing in your field of work. Inside knowledge of your field on his part can make a big difference in your taxes. Having your own accountant may seem like a luxury, but it usually saves you more than the fee. Sit down with two or three CPAs well in advance of April 15; talk to each of them, see their offices, get an idea of how each handles your questions (yes, go with a prepared list). Go in with your head high, no matter what your net worth statement might show, because in time you are sure to become a bigger client. Besides, you deserve to be treated well no matter what your tax bracket.

Note: To learn the language of the money professionals, consider attending a seminar sponsored by your bank or some other financial institution. Learning how to use your money is a fascinating education—and, incidentally, not a shabby way to meet men. The payoffs of your curiosity could be splendid and unexpected! Many times these seminars are given during lunch hours (brown-bag it and take notes between bites) or right after work. Whenever they're offered, forgo a boring date or a hairdresser appointment—and be there. The thrill of having money smarts is high up there on the list of excitements.

RETIREMENT PLANS

If you're under forty, that does not mean you can skip this section. It may be a long way to retirement, but women are living longer than ever before, and that means more years to support ourselves *after* retirement. And the truth is, neither a company pension nor Social Security will provide enough for you to live on. (Many company pension benefits are reduced once you start receiving S.S.) Your youth is no reason to avoid thinking about your retirement. In fact, it's the reason you may even enjoy those golden years—if you start planning them now. So by all means, stay with me till the end of the chapter even if you are in your twenties.

First of all, determine how much money you need in order to retire. Ask yourself:

• How many more years until I retire?

• How much income do I want when I retire? You may want to refer to your budget, deleting expenses you'll no longer have and adding ones you will. (Medical expenses are usually greater—which is where adequate medical insurance comes in.)

• How much money will my assets be producing (including your home, especially if you plan to sell and move into something smaller)?

• How much income can I count on regularly from a company pension plan and/or Social Security, and from my IRAs, 401K, or Keogh plan when invested?

• How much surplus will I need to enjoy my retirement? (This is the time to travel and catch up on the pleasures you've been too busy for. A Senior Scrimper is not what you want to be.)

Until a couple of years ago, the best way to supplement pension and S.S. income was with an individual retirement account (IRA). But rules have changed and contributions are no longer tax deductible if yearly earnings exceed $35,000. For that reason, the 401K and 403B plans, where money is taken out of your paycheck at work and remains tax deductible, have become popular. All these plans leave your money untaxed during the high-income years on the theory that your income (and tax bracket) will be lower in later years.

Self-employed persons have access to Keogh savings plans, which allow investing from 10 to 15 percent of net income in various savings instruments. IRAs and Keogh accounts can be held in a bank, mutual fund, or other financial instrument. Ask your accountant for advice on all these options and on anything else that is not crystal clear. You should finish this chapter with a list of all those issues that are not yet completely clear to you.

If you need more motivation to get going (and even if you're already raring to go), ask yourself the following questions compiled by the Older Women's League (OWL):

- How many Social Security credits have you earned on your own?

- Can you keep up house payments on your own? Can you pay apartment rent the rest of your life?

- Do you know how poor you have to be to qualify for Medicaid?

- Do you think you can keep or get a good job when you're in your fifties, sixties, or older?

- How long do you have to work on your job before you are entitled to a pension?

- If your job provides a pension, do you know how much you will lose if you take time off to have children?

- If your parents were seriously disabled, could you afford to take care of them at home? Could they afford nursing home care, or would that expense be yours?

- Can you imagine yourself in a nursing home? If not, what alternatives are you planning?

These aren't exactly subjects you want to think about before a night on the town. But they need to be faced head-on.

UP-TO-DATE WILL

An up-to-date will drawn up by a competent attorney is your ultimate As-If strategy, indisputable proof that you are thinking about your singleness as an integral part of yourself.

Put fear from your mind, the panic that says a will could hasten death or make your singleness lifelong—you're too

TRACKING YOUR
SOCIAL SECURITY

Before you need to is the time to confirm your Social Security number and examine the earnings record that will determine the amount of the check coming to you in older years. (You need to have worked forty quarters to qualify for a monthly payment.) So write down this address and send a brief letter asking for an up-to-date earnings statement. It's free. And write a note to yourself next January in your calendar to write again. Make it a New Year's resolution of the highest order: the kind you keep.

> Social Security Administration
> Office of Central Records Operations
> 300 Greene Street
> Baltimore, MD 21201

Give your Social Security number, your name, and birthdate.

A brand-new service from the Social Security Administration now lets you know—at any age—information which used to be available only when you were nearing retirement. You can find out:

- your monthly retirement benefits at ages 62, 65, and 70

- your survivors' monthly benefits if you were to die this year

- your disability benefits if you were to become disabled this year

Call 800-937-2000 and ask for Form SSA-7004.

Finally, for a free pamphlet outlining the general benefits of Social Security, write:

> Social Security
> Pueblo, CO 81009

sensible for that. As a responsible person, you have a duty to put your life in order through every means available, and a will is a significant one. If you're the parent of minor children, you must settle the crucial question of guardianship before any other. (I remember how large that question loomed in my mind—even after I had it settled. The thought of my child being reared by anyone other than his mother was almost too painful to entertain. Needless to say, I did not take trips to distant lands during my years of solo parenthood.)

To help get relevant thoughts in order, purchase an estate-planning notebook. And read up on the subject of will-making, then talk to an attorney. Once the will is drawn, store it in a safe-deposit box. (If you haven't already done so, reserve that indispensable item at your local bank. Depending on the size, it costs around $25 to $30 annually and is a secure resting place for all your papers.)

With the shadow of death removed, the project of drawing up a will becomes an opportunity to look at the big picture of your life, another reason to set goals and work toward them. Looked at that way, the document predicated on death becomes as dynamic as the rest of your financial foundation and a vital part of the ongoing process of financial planning.

As you finish Step 3, look at it as a whole to locate weak spots that could undermine the goals you set in Step 2. Ask yourself: *What improvements do I need to make in each crucial area?* Be as specific as you can. Your findings will come in handy for the next step.

In the meantime, you've been doing a lot of thinking, so pause a minute and take stock of your accomplishments so far:

- You've drawn up a net worth statement and a budget and monthly cash-flow statement.

- You've identified short-term, intermediate, and long-term financial goals.

- You've analyzed financial problems and started

thinking about investing, savings, insurance, wills, Social Security, and money professionals.

• You've made a list of weak areas that you'll work to improve. I bet you feel far removed from that timid woman who sat beside a time bomb, vaguely aware of its potential but confused and unsure how to defuse it. I know it's been slow going. At times, you probably felt itchy and anxious to get this over with. Well, we're on the home stretch now. So you've earned a celebration: a fifteen-minute walk or a double-scoop ice-cream cone (even if it's February), maybe even an outrageous nightgown. Give yourself the fruits of your labor.

STEP 4:
PUTTING THE PLAN
IN WRITING

Let me make this perfectly clear: Your final financial plan at this point is not one paper, but a series of plans, each one focused on a different building block. Read on.

1. Go back and formulate a conclusion about each building block. For instance: Do you need to set aside more in your savings account or start a college tuition plan for your toddler (it's never too early)? Do you need more health insurance? Have you vowed to reduce the amount of plastic in your purse? Now, write your ideas and plans for each building block on paper (one sheet for each). Staple them together and leave them on your desk, where you'll always be reminded of their resolutions and promises.

2. But that's not all of your written financial plan. In a legal-size file folder (preferably one with sides) collect the following:

Bankbooks

Will

List of financial goals

Insurance policies

Keogh statement from bank

IRA statement from bank

Charge account cards (retail stores, etc.)

Estate planning book

Stock certificates (clipped together with information about your stockbroker)

Pension plan from your employer

Copy of health insurance policy—and ID card clipped to it

Social Security card (stapled onto larger sheet)

Budget form

Net worth statement

Credit-card account numbers (master sheet)
(for American Express, Visa, MasterCard, Discover)

Other relevant documents: real estate deed, mortgage, leases, jewelry appraisals, government bonds, bank loans)

Every one of those papers, where possible, should be at least in triplicate with copies in your safe-deposit box at the bank, in a fireproof metal strongbox at home, in your parents' residence (or safe-deposit box), and of course in this comprehensive Plan of Plans. Each one should be recorded and kept current in your estate-planning book (naturally there will only be one original of most documents, but make photocopies). Make as many duplicates as you need for your peace of mind, but always keep the original in *your* possession.

3. Inside this folder should be a master sheet listing its contents. (By the way, label the folder "Financial Folder" or the equivalent.)

4. There should also be another master sheet in the folder listing your Keogh and IRA accounts. Record each account number, dollar amount, and rollover date.

5. Credit and charge account cards should be listed on their own master sheet, giving name of creditor and account number. (It wouldn't hurt to enter the expiration date also.) Leaving most cards in the folder will keep you out of impulse buying and excessive debt. The only ones justified to be with you all the time are your gasoline credit card and one of the Big Three—for emergency purposes only.

6. By the way, this is a good time to memorize your Social Security number. And write it on its own sheet for this file. This should make a total of four separate master sheets.

7. In your estate-planning book, enter the names of insurance beneficiaries and those who you want to assume power of attorney should you become disabled. Keep the book in this folder.

8. Review—and type—all the information above whenever possible. Legibility will encourage you to pore through this material more often. Each time you consult your budget (at least monthly) to make sure you are on track, also take a look at your list of goals and the rising balance in your savings account.

After this plan becomes part of your life, you'll probably set up your own systems suited to your particular needs. But for now, and until/unless you've located a certified financial planner with adequate motivation, interest, and training, this series of simple plans will do very well.

STEP 5:
TAKING ACTION

Realistically, very few of the objectives you've set can be realized quickly, but speed is not the issue here. Persistence is the key to financial solidity, and that can only be measured in months and years.

You can build your budget into your finances immediately, of course, and once you see yourself staying with it and depositing money into your future every time you get paid, you'll move into a frame of mind that would rather bank the bucks than buy the blouse. And if that sounds farfetched, try it and see. Your only regret will be that you didn't start thinking that way sooner. (But *Single File* hadn't been published, so your excuse is legitimate. Besides, regrets are useless.)

Eventually, though, you may decide to add a certified financial planner to your network. (One recent survey indicated that 35 percent of Americans who seek professional advice use one.) A good financial planner has a working knowledge of all areas of financial planning, from taxes to cash flow, investments to retirement planning—an advantage which lets you see your total financial picture. Some planners who are also stockbrokers or accountants will share their expertise as they work with you, a big plus they have over other, more generalized planners. But a word of caution: Although the field is growing quickly in recognition and prestige, it has as yet no state or Federal regulations. Check to see if the planner you're considering has the designation of CFP (Certified Financial Planner) or ChFC (Chartered Financial Consultant) after the name. (Ask reliable friends for an informed recommendation.) Organizations to contact for a planner are in the Resources at the end of the book.

You should be aware that financial planners set their

fees in one of three ways: fee-only, commission-only, and fee-plus-commission.

Fee-only planners charge a flat fee, usually based on an hourly rate, and receive no commissions. The fee ranges from $500 to $1,500 but is usually not more than $75 an hour.

Commission-only planners produce a plan without fixed charge but collect a sales commission on many of the services they recommend. With this method you may never feel quite certain that their recommendations are in your best interest. Before signing any agreement, be sure to settle on the amount of money to be paid.

Fee-plus-commission planners charge a set amount for the plan and also take a commission on the services you use.

Be prepared to pay hidden costs, such as attorney's or CPA's fees.

Above all, review the planner's experience and his or her recommendations. Question the planner about the length of time he or she has been in the community. Ask to see a sample plan and a client list, and be sure to talk to some of the people on it. Ask about the planner's areas of expertise, previous occupation, and the estimated length of the planning process. Make certain that you are to receive a written plan at the end of your work together.

(By the way, if you find yourself stimulated at the prospect of a new and growing profession, you may want to become part of it through a correspondence course that will ultimately accredit you as a Certified Financial Planner. It's a burgeoning field, ripe for women. After completing the requirements, you could use your weekends and evenings for consultations. And when your reputation is better established, you will have the option of making financial planning your full-time work.)

If using a financial planner sounds expensive, there is another way to utilize money professionals to get a workup of your finances (in computer printout form). The service is not personal, but it is an inexpensive way of monitoring your finances and a first step toward having your own personal financial planner. (It could be the right financial service for you at this stage.) If you want to know more, contact:

Financial Planner
700 Brisbane Building
403 Main Street
Buffalo, NY 14203
(716) 842-6860

STEP 6:
REVIEWING

The final step is to look over your plan, at the very minimum once a year. Any significant change in your life (a birth, marriage, career move) or in the world around you (inflation, major tax changes, etc.) should send you back to the plan for review.

Rethinking your fiscal well-being on a regular basis is as imperative as having annual physical checkups, because your financial picture tells you whether you're moving ahead toward your goals. That's the whole point, to use money to get what you want. Once you take charge of your finances, you'll never think the same way about your money. And once you start thinking in terms of investment rather than consumption—thinking rich, I call it—you'll be a different breed of spender.

THE NEXT STEP:
MAKING MORE

Let's assume you're efficiently organized and dripping with money smarts, but the money under your control is still not exactly "significant." Angry, discouraged? Great! You're ripe for upward movement.

There are a zillion possible ways to bring in more money. These are only a few imagination-stirrers:

1. *Finish your schooling.* A college degree will get you two-thirds higher pay than a high-school degree; that's fact. And when you get that far, you may want to continue on into higher education with a focus that really motivates you. Do it. This is where your bank connections will come in handy, for an educational loan.

2. *Look into a higher-paying job.* You may have convinced yourself that you love your job and will stay put no matter what the salary, but an in-depth look at your finances, like the one you've just experienced, may change your mind—or at least open it to the realization that you work in a "female ghetto" position, as a teacher or secretary, and that insight may push you to expand your goals.

   If you're thinking seriously about changing jobs or fields, look in the library for *The American Almanac of Jobs and Salaries* or ask the librarian for other reference books. (*What Color Is Your Parachute?* is an excellent guide when you decide to job-hunt. And everyone knows of it.)

3. *Negotiate a raise.* Notice I didn't say "ask." Negotiating means you prepare your reasons and achievements in advance. It assumes that you state your requirements clearly and concisely and begin the discussion with a positive attitude.

To negotiate effectively you must know comparable salaries in your job market. (Again, *The American
Almanac of Jobs and Salaries* is a good resource.) Check
the posted salaries in large companies in the same field
or in government jobs, and don't forget classified ads,
employment agencies, executive search firms, and college placement offices. The first person you should turn
to is a friend in a position similar to yours. And let the
word go out via your network.

Your employer wouldn't be discussing a raise unless your work is satisfactory, and that alone should give
you some confidence. If you are asked why you think
you're "worth" that kind of money, say, "That's the market value in this area." Your research will back you up.

4. *Become a salesperson.* I'm not talking hosiery or cosmetics;
   I mean computer sales, high-tech sales, commercial real
   estate. Automobiles are being sold by women right now.
   Why not you? Yes, there is still discrimination against
   women selling big-ticket items, but it has diminished,
   and will lessen even more as more women prove selling
   power. Persuading and convincing have always been
   necessary for females, since for too long our effectiveness needed to be routed through a man. We needed
   skills influencing him, so it's a logical evolution for women
   to sell in the marketplace.

5. *Join or start an investment club.* Your Old Girls' Network
   will probably yield five or six live wires interested in
   pooling money and making more. But don't stop there.
   Reach out to co-workers and relatives who are business
   people and interested in making money; invite them to
   join. Naturally, don't make any investments right away.
   Use the first few meetings only to establish guidelines,
   goals, and maximum dollar amounts of contributions to
   the general fund. (For brain-picking, ask one or two
   stockbrokers to share their smarts with the group at the

early meetings.) When you do make an investment, consider using a discount brokerage house, which eliminates personal brokers and research departments—but also nearly half the fee. This will challenge the club to do its own research and learn about the companies that make America run. On the other hand, you may be able to negotiate a favorable fee structure with a full-service broker.

A few interested people coupled with a first-rate stock letter and information from the National Association of Investors (see Resources) can form a functioning nucleus. (An old and respected investors' newsletter is ValueLine, Inc., 711 Third Avenue, New York, NY 10017. It is not inexpensive, however. Consider asking for a back issue of the newsletter to discuss at one of the first meetings.) I can guarantee that this venture will be a practical and exciting education in economics—and a lot of fun, too.

6. *Move into ownership.* This first taste of entrepreneurship may inspire you to think about buying a business. Small steps can chip away at the fear of ownership so prevalent within our sex. (Make them bite-size at first, but keep on biting.) Ask your Old Girls' Network members and friends for their experiences with ownership. You might sniff out other curious women interested in going into a joint venture with you. Don't get discouraged easily, but on the other hand don't make financial commitments too quickly. Go heavy on research and preliminary talks with bankers and accountants. And go slow on action.

> TIP: Now is a good time to make your Single File cards for the professionals you contacted in the process of completing your financial plan. You may upgrade or change them later, but have at least one name for each category in your file to begin with. Your accountant is the critical choice, but even if he or she does not work out, it's not the

end of the world. Mosey around your support system for a replacement.

UP, UP, AND AWAY!

This could be you: making more money than ever and moving away from the pack, only to discover that in pulling yourself up you're pushing men away. In the small hours of the morning, you catch yourself wondering whether the old days of money blindness were better than the isolation that solvency is bringing.

In your heart of hearts you know there's no going back—even if you wanted to, which you most definitely do not. But there *are* changes that can make men more comfortable in the present.

- Stop flaunting credit cards, especially if you have one of those "gold" cards. Credit is a privilege, as is earning enough money to deserve it. Be proud, but don't push it. Never use your credit rating to diminish a man.

- Learn to become comfortable with your new earning power; let it become part of you, like a subtle shade of lipstick. Don't hide it but don't show it off, either. Like your singleness, let it be simply another fact of your life in the overall picture.

- When you meet a man who interests you, and you make the first move, handle the financial end of the evening as discreetly as you can. Especially if your salary is higher than his. It may be as simple a thing as handing him the tickets when you're treating, or letting him cook dinner at home for the two of you instead of dinner out. He'll admire and appreciate your tact and consideration.

Of course, there are some men—the insecure and the weak—who will indeed be intimidated as you rise. Others, earning less than you but fulfilled in their work and happy with themselves, will remain open to the possibility of a relationship with you. And there is a smaller group (that dwindles as your earning power rises) who will be undaunted because they earn still more. Yes, dear Reader, there is a smaller chance for the financially secure woman *who insists on marrying up*. But if, as you soar, you keep your eye fixed on the goodness and compatibility of a man rather than on his tax return, you will have access to many *more* of the good men who do indeed exist, because you have liberated yourself from the income needs that have been restricting your choice. Solvency is a many-sided freedom, and this is one of its best aspects.

Learning to tend your money is in some ways linked to learning to tend your other needs. The way we plan our finances is a significant measure of our ability to nurture and feed ourselves—and our selfhood. We've got a way to go, because in general we still earn less than men, but we're definitely on the path headed in the right direction. Upwards.

Money is a form of energy, and so demands respectful treatment. Like time, it is a commodity to be neither squandered nor hoarded, but prudently accumulated to create wealth, stability, and opportunity. Handled with intelligence, money can make the difference between reality and dreams, influencing your life as surely as attitudes and beliefs. Over time, solvency evolves into a bedrock degree of security and financial autonomy that puts you in charge of your life. And that's where I want you to be.

SEVEN

CONNECTEDNESS: PUTTING DOWN ROOTS

You can be sure that when Gloria Steinem takes off her glasses and curls the ends of her lightened hair, feminism is changing before our eyes. The vitality that made sisters of us all, women tethered to each other by indignation and conviction, is becoming more personal. The battle for total partnership is being fought in corporate offices, day-care centers, private homes —no longer by bra-burning mobs in public squares—and it will ultimately be won by women (single and married) working together, helping each other, drawing strength from the simple contacts of daily life.

Now, while you're single, you have time to forge the kind of connections your own mother would never have dared dream possible. This, after all, is what the women's movement had in mind all along, for women to form a chain connecting their careers, children, communities, and churches, and to link their independence with causes that span the globe and bind together the primal family of womankind. Single women connecting with the world—well, why not?

(The components of your personal connectedness are up to you. The ones described here are only a beginning. It would be a tribute to my beliefs if you decide to concoct your own styles of connecting, ones that fit *you*. If you feel like sharing your personal connections, write me about them; I'd be proud to feature them in my column. As long as they are founded on a common purpose or need, the links you've discovered will help us all.)

Look at it this way: You have a choice. You can use your newfound confidence to move away from others, or you can build bridges that link you to the world outside your door. Connectedness is often lacking in the single life, but it doesn't have to be. The seedlings, the possibilities, are everywhere, it's just that they're usually undernourished. Once you discover how much connectedness gives back to you—in stability, continuity, groundedness—you'll understand how it can make you whole, happy, and self-possessed. And that's the bottom line, single or married, woman or man.

Your mission, dear Reader, as you probably know by now, is to make yourself whole before marriage, without a man. It's quite a challenge. But believe me, independence is much easier when you're in the flow of things, and the amazing thing about putting yourself there is that it does not demand superhuman effort. You begin with your career, your children, your community, and your church—the basics already in place—and start looking at them as heartlines, each one a way to break down a rather large and impersonal world into smaller, manageable worlds that rotate on friendliness and like-minded companionship.

CAREER AS CONNECTION

Goal-oriented, ongoing, meaningful work is the ultimate connection, the taproot into the world around you. By its very nature it places you in the middle of a varied support group, from the bank clerk who cashes your check and the salesperson who sells you clothes for the office, to the people who work alongside you. The routine of work itself is a bridge to the outside world, pulling you out of self-absorption and prodding you to compare your thoughts with others' thoughts, your opinions with others' opinions, to discover alternative ways of structuring reality and making a life.

I'm not talking about "just a job" work whose sole satisfaction is a paycheck, but about a career, which implies the kind of in-depth knowledge that can only be accumulated by dedication and focus. It need not be in a field as esoteric as molecular biology; you may decide to be a potter or a farmer, a bus driver or store manager. But you do have to sort through your strengths and interests and commit yourself to tracking a long-term career path with one of them. The key is to become good at something you love, and specialize in it. That kind of dedication requires deep and pinpointed attention and inevitably results in stability and cohesion.

In the most obvious way, of course, work makes you part of a larger whole, an organization bigger than yourself but at the same time dependent on your talents for full functioning. In that way, it is a fundamental connection to your selfhood, feeding back feelings of achievement, usefulness, and camaraderie so important to good mental health and a positive self-image. The economic rewards of work, of course, enable you to increase the number of choices in your life. The prestige of being successful in your field is a conduit to other fields (and the people in them) that in turn lead to possibilities you might never have known had you not attained that high level of achievement. And as you explore those new vistas, you place yourself alongside the rest of the madding crowd and see how you stack up. Career has an *internal* linkage, too, binding together the many dimensions of your life and giving them continuity, a running theme, purpose, and meaning.

Work is not the only mini-world you can build for yourself, but it's so fundamental that when wealthy widows brag to me about their life of leisure (as if that's an accomplishment), I suggest they remove the rose-colored glasses and see the benefits of productivity. Yes, economic security is important (after the preceding chapter you can't doubt my opinion on *that*), but without the ongoing involvement of work, such women are deprived.

EXERCISE 1:
UPDATE YOUR SINGLE FILE

STEP 1-AND-ONLY: This is the perfect time to update your Single File by writing cards for every business and professional contact you've made in the last few months. (Save time; staple each business card to its own Rolodex card.) What's that you say? You're new to the work force and don't *have* any business or professional contacts to add? Then this is the time to realize you're not as alone as you might feel. If you've been busy raising a family or are newly divorced or widowed, make contact with specialists. The local Displaced Homemakers Network chapter can connect you with support and training programs especially for women returning to work after a long hiatus (see Resources). There are also placement and job counselors on campuses; try a university Continuing Education office. (Reread your personal interest inventory from Chapter One to refresh your mind about what you *like* to do.) Research alternative professions by talking to people who are in them, and ask questions, lots of questions. Whatever you decide, make it a point to climb out of your shell and meet people who can help you reach your goals. The next exercise will help.

EXERCISE 2:
DRAW A TIMELINE

STEP 1:   This time you'll be drawing a timeline, a career path—literally. First, make a box indicating where you are now in your work, then draw a line or "path" to where you want to go. (If you'd rather see a bigger picture, start at the beginning of your work life and also plot up to where you are now.) Draw boxes for positions along the line.

STEP 2:   Now that you've sketched the basic timeline, embellish it with "mileage" figures that indicate how long you want each move to take; rumor has it this was Lee Iacocca's technique for getting to the top. Seeing the steps to be taken is a proven help to making them. Visualization is neither kooky nor metaphysical; it is simply mental discipline at work.

STEP 3:   Look at what you've drawn. Your timeline can be horizontal or vertical, straight or curvy. No rule says one way is better; whatever works for you is correct. Is it a straight path? Are there detours for marriage and kids? (If so, make sure they're not *too* long.) Your timeline is full of clues. Study it closely for information about your work style. Are you an "organization woman" or a free spirit? You should determine which applies to you so you can make the appropriate decisions. If your line is full of curves and you're aiming for a seat on the executive committee by age thirty-five, reexamine your timetable. Either your path or your goal has to change.

A timeline also reveals how *close* you are to achieving

your ends and whether a detour has eaten up more time than originally planned. A line that's too rigid—arrow-straight with no room for spontaneity—means that work is gobbling up your life, leading you away from, instead of closer to, other people, new ideas, and growth, another example of a difference in degree being a difference in kind.

WORKAHOLISM

When career becomes life and there are virtually *no* boundaries in between, work is no longer a connection. How can it be? There's nothing it can connect you *to*! In the same way an alcoholic hides behind a bottle, you could be using your job to protect yourself from life beyond the office walls. If so, you may wake up at age sixty with nothing to show for your days except an overflowing Out box. Working too hard for too long drains the impetus to initiate in the other areas of life. And there are strong pulls toward this kind of excess. You already know them in your heart of hearts, but do yourself a favor and take a look at the dubious "benefits" of extended office hours:

- A reason why you aren't married.

- An excuse for avoiding emotional issues like love, friendship, family relationships.

- A setting where normal cravings for human affection and emotional fulfillment are inappropriate and so are kept under tight control.

- Enough pressure (in the form of ringing phones, urgent reports to write, and so on) to keep your mind fully occupied and (temporarily) unaware of the voids in your life.

- An explanation for a pattern of short-lived romances.

- A place to go when the going gets rough in the outside world.

- A focus for your anxieties.

If you believe you may fit the bill but aren't absolutely certain, look for proof positive in your appointment book, calendar, or journal for the last six months. Do you see meetings and seminars, business lunches and breakfasts, but almost no dates with friends? Do you notice lots of cancellations of social events?

A gratifying career is one of the best allies possible in your quest for a full and balanced life. I am well aware that we all have periods of extreme busyness—say, the first months of a new job or salary-review time—when it makes perfect sense to put on blinders and make work top priority. I'm not warning you about that kind of busyness; what's worrisome is the busyness that longs for Sunday to pass so that Monday morning will take its place and all the raw questions that surfaced in quiet times over the weekend can be shoved aside for another week. That is workaholism in its essence, and that's what I'm here to prevent.

First, say out loud: "I am a workaholic. I have been using my work to hide from important questions in my life." That's a beginning. Next, enter these reminders in your appointment book with a red pen:

1. On *every page* of your daily calendar, write the following note: "If it's 7 P.M. and you're still here, GO HOME!" Write the same message on slips of red paper tucked into your purse or wallet, and wherever else you'll see them. Of course, writing the notes is one thing; following through is what takes guts.

2. Carve out time in your daily routine for physical exercise, at the beginning or end of the day. Your company

may even provide membership or discounts in a fitness club; if so, join up now. If not, ask a few receptive colleagues to take out group membership in a gym or join you for aerobics in the conference room at lunch. (Pop a fitness tape into the video cassette recorder.) Exercise at least three times a week and at least once on weekends. Give exercise some of the dedication you've been reserving for work, but don't let it become another hideout.

3. Invite someone to dinner at your house. If that's not practical, make it a Dutch treat at a nice restaurant. Arrange the dinner for an evening when you're pretty sure you won't be knee-deep in work—so you'll have absolutely no excuse to cancel. (Remember your commitment muscles!)

4. Start to look at the rest of your life with the scrutiny usually saved for the office. When you make that honest effort, it's a sure thing that some people and places will appeal and your worklife will begin to assume a more appropriate niche in your perspective.

5. List the issues that are making you uneasy. This is a test, since you'll be forced to relive the queasiness. But running from it solves nothing, and makes the inevitable more awful when it comes. Writing notes and keeping fit are mere Band-Aids; the real way to stop the pain is to face the reasons behind your workaholism. (Funny thing, they won't seem half as bad on paper as they did in your thoughts.) Listing them is a significant step toward making them manageable. And it's your job; I can't do it for you. But I assure you that *Single File* will stand by you in your search for solutions and make finding them easier than you ever imagined. You'll see—the first one will lead to the next and the next. . . .

One final note: The curious thing about workaholics is that they aren't necessarily successful people. Too often, the work they slave over is busyness for its own sake, disorganized and without focus. Hard work is important, yes, but one of the major prerequisites for success is knowing what success means to you.

EXERCISE 3:
HOW DO YOU SPELL SUCCESS?

The following are classic definitions of success. Number them 1 to 10 (1 being the most important), or feel free to add some of your own:

Money	Helping others
Job satisfaction	Prestige
Self-expression	Power
Fame	Comfort
Personal fulfillment	Influence

You'll notice that some of these are quite simple expectations; others are grandiose. Don't be afraid to admit either extreme. This is for your eyes only. I guarantee this exercise will lead you closer to whatever you consider the pinnacle.

CHILDREN AS CONNECTION

Skip this section if you're looking for startling new techniques guaranteed to benefit the children of mateless mothers like you. As much as I feel a special tenderness for young people who grow up with a single parent (my own son, Scott, was only four when he became part of a two-person family), what we're interested in right now is you. Resilient, resourceful, and valued, those children will grow up and leave to follow their own destinies. And the adult they leave behind, you, will be only as self-reliant and contented as the connections you formed while they were still at home. That's the challenge: giving enough to your family while giving it to yourself. And no one is saying that it can be done without inner conflict.

Really, this all boils down to an identity crisis. The identity is yours, and ignoring its need for expression could bring crisis into your life. It probably won't happen now, while the children are keeping you occupied with their needs, but sometime later, when they drift off (as they should and must) to follow their own paths. No, the crisis will come later, around the time you see the first gray hairs and crow's feet and begin to think about middle age and life's short span.

That is when bridges into the world pay off in friendships and interests and self-esteem. They need time to develop, and you need to start developing them. Now.

I know, you have no time. Between your children, your working life, and what you laughingly call a social life, there is a deficit of hours. Besides, you're too tired at the end of the day to do more than creep into bed with a hot cup of tea and a baked potato. You don't have time for the modern dance classes you used to love or the art films you once found intriguing. The Saturdays once spent in leotards and foreign-film houses today consist of morning TV cartoons and hassled afternoon forays to the supermarket. Without a husband around to make some of the decisions and help wipe the runny noses, you've become Super Mom without realizing it. The good side of being on twenty-four-hour child alert, seven days a week, is the bond that develops between you and those small people living with you; that kind of undiluted, one-to-one closeness is, in my opinion, a blessing. But as wonderful as that is, both parent and child must ultimately lead separate lives for the health of the relationship. And so the connection, while a conduit into the future, is not sufficient unto itself.

But astonishingly, it does hold the kernel of the solution to your identity-versus-time dilemma—you can use your children's routine as a basis for your connections!

- At your child's religious school, host a tea for the parents, and participate in other things there: Join a committee (which may lead to meetings at other parents' homes), be part of the services, join the women's auxiliary if there is one. (Put your singles dances on hold for a while; this approach to meeting people is so much more satisfying.) Your kids will be proud of you, and so will I. When Scott was eleven, he'd come with me to services on Friday evenings and holy days. I like to think that those times firmed up the bond between us.

- At nursery school, ask if you could help the teacher for a day or part of a day. (Take a long, early lunch; you'll be out of your office maybe two hours, but what a difference it will make for everyone involved.) If you have the time, volunteer to be teacher's helper on a regular basis, once a month or so. Your child will realize that you care about more than his grades, since you take the time to meet his teacher and friends and see for yourself what he does during the day.

- Make friends with parents of your child's classmates. Invite them over for a casual coffee and dessert. You'll have plenty to talk about, and open up the possibility of becoming friends with people who share your concerns.

- Talk to the principal at your child's school about hosting a tea, brunch, or after-school coffee for the teachers. (He or she can tell you the best way if there is any other contribution you can make to the school.) You'll enjoy getting to know the teachers as human beings.

• Donate some time to the day-care center or after-school groups your child attends; in other words, don't limit your contact to picking up and dropping off your child. Become part of what your children are doing. It's great for them; it's great for you. Become known to the group leaders and owners as a dedicated and interested parent. And if the time comes when they need to call on you for a favor, do it. With a full heart.

• Think about joining Parents Without Partners (PWP) and work to become part of a committee. Spend weekend time with your children in their activities, not only as another member, but as a potential leader and involved parent. Read their magazine *Single Parent* for resources and support services. The big plus of PWP is that parent and child can recreate side by side with their peers, but still together. Contact your local chapter (see Resources) and give this organization a try. It's the granddaddy of all single-parent groups.

• Join a church group for separated, divorced, or widowed parents; this gives a spiritual dimension to your quest for single-parent connections.

• Become an activist mother. When there is a class play or a cookie sale, donate any time you can spare. There is no more worthwhile cause than working for your children. And they will see your activism as an example of adulthood. Kids trust actions, not words.

• Join the PTA, work on a committee at your child's school. These meetings are important. In my widowhood, dates could always wait, but for PTA meetings I would call a sitter. They gave me a chance to talk about Scott's schoolwork and at the same time meet other parents. I usually found the conversations interesting and meaningful, which is more than I could say for the dates I was having!

Hint from a former PTA member: Do your best not to feel second-class and apologetic when you show up at a parent-oriented event without a husband. In a society as fluid as ours, many of the partnered there will be in your shoes at next year's PTA meeting. (Experts say that one of every three households with children—possibly one out of two—will be headed by a single parent by 1990.) Besides, you never know when a lone man at that meeting may turn out to be a single parent, too. Can you imagine a better meeting place? A healthier common interest?

Children connect you with the world around you, and with the life force itself, so it's logical that children-as-connection can help you balance a role that is inherently lopsided. (You've probably been using this method of connecting instinctively.) Now that you've seen it seconded on these pages, I hope you'll feel even freer to use it. Each of these suggestions gives you a chance to be an example of gregariousness to your children. As they are your links to a wider world, you are their primary connection to the adults they will become.

MADONNA MOTHERS

So far I've been talking to mothers who are single by circumstance, widowed or divorced. But for some of you, becoming a single parent is a deliberate decision. Single mothers by choice (I call them "madonna mothers") are usually already in their thirties or early forties when they realize that a husband is not an absolute requirement for motherhood and go on to become single parents. This is still a controversial practice, definitely more acceptable in urban areas than in small towns, but much more common now than before. And it is a major new possibility for single women. But I warn you, the issue is fraught with controversy over questions of morality, sexuality, and legality. I'll lay out the facts, but you must do the research—and the thinking. I suggest plenty of both.

By my count, there are five ways to become a madonna mother:

1. adoption
2. artificial insemination or donor insemination
3. a random sexual encounter with a stranger
4. a planned sexual encounter involving a man you know who is willing to let you bring up a child on your own
5. same as number 4, except the man is ignorant of your plans

Thoughts about that list:

1. You may not know the full background of the child you adopt. Or you may not receive a child who is of the age, race, or ethnic background you prefer. The same concerns hold true in single-parent adoption as in two-parent adoption: The fact that there is no "genetic match" may in time cause problems. There could be opposing personalities and traits which will be difficult for you to understand. (Then again, who says you ever completely understand your biological child?) The child will ask questions about the parents and may not rest until he learns their identity. See your attorney about adoption laws in your state and other legal issues.

2. Artificial insemination from a donor bank means the sperm is well screened. There are fewer emotional overtones in the procedure, which can be (according to how you feel) a plus or a minus. All in all, an antiseptic method, whose anonymity appeals to some.

3. A random sexual encounter is out of the question because of the possibility of AIDS, genetic mishaps, and hereditary diseases. Unthinkable.

4. A planned sexual encounter with a man willing to go along with the arrangement (as in the movie *The Big Chill*) could work, but the man's reaction *after* the fact is a big, scary question mark. He could legally challenge you for child custody and visitation or even claim the child permanently. Consult your attorney now.

5. See number 4, but with higher odds of having legal trouble and court battles if the father of the baby discovers what you've done. Because he wasn't in on your plan to become a single mother, he may (quite understandably) feel exploited, raped. Repercussions can be devastating to him and subsequently to you as a woman with a new child. Definitely visit your attorney now!

Single Mothers by Choice (SMC), the preeminent New York City–based group working with (and for) madonna mothers, says membership is mushrooming as the issue gains media attention (see Resources for details about their brochure and local chapters). They tell me that women fly to New York City from all over the country to attend their "thinkers' sessions," where a small group of single mothers (madonna mothers whom they call "tryers") meet and share thoughts with a dozen or so women ("thinkers") who are considering single motherhood. If you are also weighing the decision, but can't visit New York, Single Mothers by Choice can put you in touch with a member near you. Even if you're in touch with SMC, also bring up the subject in your Old Girls' Network. You'll provoke opinions, debate, shock—and a little envy. Whatever the final decision, it takes courage to even consider madonna motherhood. Wherever you raise the subject, I guarantee fireworks.

You need to think long and hard about the reasons you are considering motherhood—just as any responsible adult should think about parenthood before the time comes. And above all, you need to consider the ramifications of doing this alone. Look around you at families with young children; it takes many hands to raise a child. And so much patience is needed, which is difficult when you're both breadwinner and care-giver.

Think hard about money, because without an economic base, single parenthood is an impossibility. And realize that you'll be pulled in different directions: knowing you need to work hard to support yourself and your baby—but wanting to spend more time at home. Now is the time to think about long-term financial goals again (as you did in the last chapter) with an eye toward a different kind of family planning. One woman I know has been saving for years to have a baby. With every additional dollar in the bank she grows more sure of her decision.

Realize, too, that the eyebrows raised now because you are unmarried are insignificant compared to the disapproval you could face when you have a baby as a single woman. This shouldn't dissuade you if you're serious, but you must also consider your child and how you will answer questions about the situation. This is the type of thing that SMC is good for, because they've heard it all, and their "tryers" have walked in your shoes—and gotten where they wanted.

First and foremost, you owe it to yourself and your child to talk this decision over with your family and closest friends. Formulate a plan of action, and hear the reactions of people who care about you. They will be the ones who will be there for you when you realize that this baby is no longer just an idea, but dirty diapers and 3 A.M. feedings.

Then, if you're really serious about madonna mother-hood:

- Visit your attorney to find out your rights, the laws in your state, and the possibilities inherent in what you are planning. I can't say this often enough.

- Check into the pension plan, stock-purchase plan, and health plan at work to determine your financial solidity, the existence of maternity leave, and whether that leave is paid. Read between the lines to see how supportive your employer will be. Your motherhood needn't be embraced with open arms, but on the other hand, you don't need an office battle every step of the way, either.

- Discuss your economic situation with your banker, accountant—and financial planner, if you have one. Take notes at these meetings. Now that you're really serious, it's time to figure out numbers: what you'll be earning in five years; how much can you put away for a college education. And what about housing? Where will you both live? You must know the economics before assuming this lifelong responsibility.

- Contact an adoption agency if you've decided to go that route. Since you're serious, it's time to get started; adoptions take time. For faster action, you might consider adopting a special-needs or foreign child.

- If you decide you want the child to be biologically yours, contact a sperm bank to discuss costs and procedure. Single Mothers by Choice will supply addresses of such sources; see the Resource section for more specifics.

- Make an appointment with a physician to have a physical examination and to discuss the possibility of motherhood. Your best bet is a physician specializing in obstetrics and gynecology who offers artificial insemination, but that is a second step. Ask your family doctor for the name of such a physician, possibly a woman, knowledgeable and sympathetic to a single woman wanting a baby. They are not plentiful, but they do exist. Of course, the ideal is a referral from a woman who has had a good experience with a particular doctor. (SMC may be able to help there, too.)

- If you decide to approach a friend with the idea of his becoming a nonparticipating (only biologically involved) father, weigh this idea carefully before acting on it. If he's a good friend, keep in mind that he might want some say in rearing the child. Most women work out legal contracts wherein the father waives rights to raise (and/or visit) the child, sometimes forever, or until the child reaches legal majority, age eighteen. Some men would balk at that arrangement. So, again, it's best to work with an attorney every step of the way.

Whatever the method of conception you choose, there are things you need to know before choosing the biological father for your child:

blood type

history of mental health, presence of any emotional instability

history of physical health, genetic background including deformities, weaknesses, etc.

willingness to pay child support (if you want it)

willingness to give time and attention to the child (if you want this)

willingness to allow you total control over the child (if you want this)

propensity for legal battling

family background, place of origin, etc.

presence of any sexually transmitted disease

personality traits that suggest he may try to claim the child

name of his attorney

Because you do need all those facts, it's a good idea to have your attorney contact his attorney and work out an agreement before the fact. This, of course, presupposes a cozy and ongoing relationship with the man, familiarity with his way of life and attitudes, his willingness to allow this to happen, and then, of course, conception.

Of all the suppositions, the latter is significant, because Single Mothers by Choice is finding that many women who have started to think about motherhood are experiencing fertility problems. Many of them didn't start to consider this option until they were thirty-five or thirty-six, and found that they don't become pregnant so fast. So SMC has formed infertility support groups, where women help one another go through the ups and downs of conceiving later in life.

If you are sincerely interested in motherhood, learn from this and begin crystallizing your decision now. It takes a while to think all this through, and in this particular matter you mustn't feel rushed. Even after the decision is made, it will take time to complete the research and arrangements this very special project entails. Remember, you're up against biological deadlines here.

I don't want to leave you on a negative note; nor do I want you to think the "madonna" decision is cold and calculating. I've dwelt on the hard facts because they're so easy to push aside in the excitement of contemplating parenthood. And I've left the very best part, the emotional payoff, for last. That is the way motherhood links you to tomorrow. Bringing a baby into your life connects you, your parents, and their parents with the future. It is, in the most fundamental sense, what life is all about: life perpetuating itself.

COMMUNITY AS CONNECTION

Linking yourself to the community is the next step to widen your circle of connectedness. By joining a voluntary organization or international agency (whichever seems most important to you and seems to need you most), by manning a hotline for a battered-women's shelter or helping to organize an international fast day for world hunger, you're pouring goodwill out into the human community. Who knows how far that goodness will spread? Positive actions radiate far beyond their originator, you know. And the world could certainly use more love. Sharing yours makes you part of the sea of helpfulness around us.

And while you're helping, you're defining yourself in ways that go beyond marital status. Who gives a damn that you're single when you are joined with good people in a common cause? When you're participating in good deeds, what counts is your solidity of character, follow-through, strength of purpose, and loyalty of spirit.

If volunteerism is new to you, be ready for strong surges of self-esteem that come with a sharpened awareness of other people's needs. Be prepared to receive outpourings of sincere love and appreciation across the bridges that carry your love. More than anything else I know, moving beyond personal concerns to work at bettering someone else's life is an unfailing solution to the absorption-with-navel syndrome that can be prevalent among people living on their own. Your altruistic self may have gotten lost in the shuffle; you'll feel good to get it back.

Hold on! I'm not suggesting you give up people possibilities when you seriously enter the world of volunteerism. Far from it. Actually, there is a much richer mix of men, youths, and senior citizens in volunteerism these days, because it's no longer considered "women's work." Many helping organizations recruit through large businesses. (*Hint:* Ask if your office is one of them. If it isn't, consider using your influence to get something going.) The most decent people I know make it a point to give back to their communities some of the energy and concern that has nurtured them. And some of the best friendships and marriages have sprung from the intense closeness that comes with working for a common cause.

By now you're probably convinced to give it a try, but since you've never really done anything like this, you don't know how to begin. Since you're becoming used to the style of self-inquiry before action, let's stay with that pattern. The first step, then, is to ask yourself a series of questions:

1. How much time can I give? (Better to underestimate so you don't overrextend and hurl yourself into demanding commitments that leave a bitter taste in your mouth.) Start slowly with a short-term project. There will be plenty of time for deeper involvement later.

2. What do I want to give to volunteer work? (Here your list of strengths from Chapter One comes in again. Which of them do you want to contribute to your community?)

3. What environment is best for me? An inside or outside job? With people or in research? A local setting where I can see a direct result of my actions, or in a bigger, world-community project? The details are important. You will do your best in a setting where you feel comfortable.

4. Finally, let the suggestions below (a few of the countless possibilities) lead you to an organization that interests you and utilizes you best. Remember, voluntary work is not meant to be drudgery. Don't intentionally choose a job you loathe just to make yourself a martyr. (If you hate the sight of blood, for Pete's sake don't volunteer at a hospital.) You'll get much more out of your volunteer time if you help in an area *you* find meaningful. You'll do more good, too.

If you're interested in local opportunities, consider:

> crisis hotlines for rape victims, battered women, potential suicides
>
> soup kitchens or homeless shelters
>
> Meals on Wheels, food banks
>
> tutoring children or adults who cannot read
>
> working with the mentally impaired or emotionally disturbed
>
> providing transportation for the elderly or disabled
>
> becoming a foster parent or part-time cuddler of needy newborns
>
> recording books for the blind and reading to terminally ill patients
>
> doing secretarial or phone work at a local blood bank
>
> coaching a Little League team
>
> sorting soda cans at a local recycling plant
>
> writing a history of your neighborhood for the local library or historical society
>
> working with your local Big Sisters program

If you'd like to get involved in a national organization, consider:

> Mothers Against Drunk Driving (MADD)
>
> March of Dimes
>
> Sierra Club
>
> handgun control movement
>
> American Cancer Society
>
> Juvenile Diabetes
>
> Save the Whales
>
> the fight against AIDS

American Red Cross

Planned Parenthood

If you'd like to work on an international cause, consider:

Save the Children

a church or other group (such as Oxfam) fighting world hunger

Peace Links, an international peace organization

Amnesty International, to gain release for world political prisoners

Peace Corps, the ultimate in volunteer work

That's only a small sampling; you can get involved in other ways: all sorts of community and civic organizations, attending town meetings or zoning board hearings, running for public office, becoming active in legal aid or crime prevention, lobbying for children's causes, or, best of all, starting an organization yourself. The key here is to feel your personal power so that you will be someone who makes a difference—not someone who feels impotent because she's not married. This old world has gotten pretty crazy, to be sure, but sometimes the most noble actions come from a small number of dedicated people working together. What you do *does* make a difference, potentially a gigantic difference. So take a minute right now to add your own ideas to this list.

Once you find the activities that attract you, develop a direct and continuing relationship with one or two of them. Go down to the local hospital and hold a newborn who may have a drug-addicted mother—or no mother at all. Go to the local orphanage to see if you can donate some sort of ongoing, part-time help. If a larger cause is more appealing, offer to lick envelopes for local mailings of a worldwide environmental group. Go slowly, try different tasks, see which one —they're all needy and all worthwhile—gives you a special thrill. In the final analysis, there will be only one or two and you'll make more of a difference by focusing your energies on them.

I guarantee plenty of stimulation from community work, and less time squandered on The Man Who Isn't There. (I'll bet you haven't been thinking much about him lately, anyway.) Sharing yourself with someone who needs you adds to your womanhood in a way nothing else can—not even a sensitive, loving man. Take Big Sisters, for example, which will match you one-on-one with a young girl who needs attention. You will be her role model and mentor. (Even if these girls have *mothers*, they're sadly lacking in mother*ing*.) You can make such a difference for them. The caring flowing between that needy girl and you can get to be white hot, so hot that lesser issues in your life melt. When soul touches soul, who has time for trivia?

If you're still unsure of how you'd like to give of yourself, confer with your Old Girls' Network or volunteer clearinghouses. The United Way, for example, can direct you to a pressing need in your community. (There's a chapter in virtually every community, each one autonomous and independent. You may want to become active in the one near you. Because each chapter is staffed by volunteers, you can become a factor in the decision-making process for your community.) The same applies to your local Voluntary Action Center (listed in your local telephone directory, often in the "local government" section).

Finding your own niche takes time, but you'll meet wonderful people while you're searching—to say nothing of the friendships that can blossom once you're deeply committed. The camaraderie that comes from joining hands and helping is unique and very special. Volunteers have a potential for intimacy not usually possible in the workplace, because they do not have to overcome the competitive race for the dollar.

Or, you might want to sidestep an agency and find a

way of helping privately, without the bureaucracy demanded by an organization. In that case, go back a few pages and ask yourself that series of questions again. Direct or indirect, your route to a deeper level of personhood is in part through the community that gives so much to you. You might, for example, want to find an older person in your neighborhood who could use company. As our nation grays, more and more older people will need our help, and, heaven knows, we need their wisdom. Offering your friendship to a senior will turn out to be among other things a learning experience.

A reader wrote about her individual involvement in others' lives: "One of the ways to get out of the quagmire of self-pity, when the circumstances in my life are so overwhelming I can't bear them, is to get wholly involved in doing something for someone I love. I don't try to erase the disagreeable, but I allow my positive feelings and care for another person to overwhelm my negative feelings." Being an advice columnist is certainly an education.

Ultimately, extending yourself to others in need will help you focus on what *is*, not what *isn't*, in your life. We've talked about loneliness before, and one of its components—maybe its core—is a lack of connectedness. Every human being needs to touch a world beyond co-worker, partner, parent, child, and feel a part of something larger than self. There can be little satisfaction for the person fixated in an egocentric position. And I don't think you'll decide to give up your outreach after you're partnered, either. Like most other aspects of your "single self," it will remain a permanent dimension of your individuality. Service to others is service to self. Everybody wins.

CHURCH AS CONNECTION

You can commune with God-as-you-perceive-Him while you're walking or riding in a car—any time the need surfaces. Out of the fundamental craving for connection comes a deeper hunger to go beyond known boundaries and reach a level higher than human.

That hunger I call "churchness" draws some people toward one another, and their common pursuit forms a linkage like none other. Go to your house of worship soon to discover those who find their churchness together. I am hoping the visit will be the beginning of a new connection in your life. I suggest your initial foray into shared churchness be a service that is followed by a reception; that way, you could introduce yourself as a newcomer and mingle. (Consider meeting with the spiritual leader beforehand, so that she or he is prepared to make introductions for you.)

Even if formal worship sounds corny to you, go once, for my sake. I wouldn't steer you wrong. Only in a society that worships "coolness" could the benefits of spiritual seeking earn such little respect. Reconsider your first reaction, and try churchness on an evening when you feel at loose ends; it could lead you to some very nice people and positive thinking. It could become the crown jewel in your connection collection, the one that brings out the very best in you. It could be the ultimate connectedness between you and self, you and your God, for all the seasons of your life.

EIGHT

SEX:
STYLE AND
SYNERGY

Author Robertson Davies calls the act of love "a metaphor for spiritual encounter." Sex as communion is certainly a lofty ideal, but for single women that degree of intimacy is practically nonexistent. Since the late sixties, they have been telling me that sexual union for them nearly always turns out to be a prelude to greater frustration and deeper feelings of loneliness than the cravings that drove them to seek it. Frustration was the payoff for them during the sexual revolution, and it has only escalated during this age of AIDS and fear-haunted sex. Nothing has changed, they tell me: The men who are willing to share their bodies turn out to be commitment-shy and emotionally bankrupt, while the truly warm and caring man seems almost impossible to find.

My own sexual experiences (or lack of them) while a widow and single mom led me to the same conclusion. For me, sex was a matter of feast or famine, brief bursts of intense activity interspersed with seemingly endless dry spells, with womanly urges only unwelcome reminders of the palpable lack in my emotional life. Even those milliseconds of ecstasy proved deficient when they finally materialized, because behind them lay the certainty that the man responsible for them would not be around to share my life after they had subsided. I can say with assurance that women without mates have a long way to go to reach the level of intimacy Davies describes. And I can go one step further to prove that statement.

Questionnaires don't lie. A high spot in my ongoing exploration of the single life was my survey on single sexuality, a three-year project that ultimately drew responses from thirty-nine states and became nationally representative of the single community. (For a condensed version of the survey, turn to the end of this chapter.) Its findings were historic, defying every stereotype of the unmarried mentality. For example, although more than half the respondents had lived through the death of a marriage, they told me they would rather have one lifelong love than a different one at each stage of their emotional development. They said that sex was much more satisfying with a committed partner, and they were convinced that monogamy could offer all the sexual satisfaction they required. Some swingers, eh?

But more telling than any single finding was the size of the response. When all the questionnaires had been coded and tallied, 1,900 completed forms had flooded my post office box, nearly one-third of the original mailing of 6,000. Many had additional pages stapled to them, outpourings too lengthy to fit on the original sheet. And more than a few included names, addresses, phone numbers (some private and unlisted) to identify the respondent, specifics that were entirely optional.

There was no doubt about it: The survey had hit a nerve. We had uncovered a wide-ranging need, a ravenous hunger in single people to talk about the side of their lifestyle that brought such confusion because it lacked guidelines ... and precedent. Each individual who entered (or reentered) the single world was forced to make order out of the chaos of their individual sexuality, and trial and error seemed the only route to some semblance of peace of mind.

Since the years of that survey (1979–81), the confusion has only deepened. A mutant virus and a range of other sexually transmitted diseases have complicated the sex life of every thinking person who is neither monogamous nor abstinent.

At the end of these exercises you'll have a chance to try your hand at the questions that made up the survey. The issues raised may pique your interest even further, and the findings should help clarify your own opinions. Lord knows, there are few enough ways single people can compare lives, so this may be your chance to discover how the rest of your community feels about sexuality.

This entire chapter, then, is the place to put matters straight. Here is where you can sort out your tastes, ethics, standards, and priorities. Now, before the underwear starts flying, is the time to take a stand about whom you lie down with.

I promise you a clearer sense of your sexual self and much greater insight into your personal morality. That's a weighty promise, one I don't make lightly. Stay open to its challenge and tackle the subject with optimism. As a sexual being, you have a hefty responsibility for your libido and your emotional well-being. Whether or not you are currently involved, in fact, *regardless of the state of your sex life*, this section is for you.

These days, a single woman has a lot on her mind. Take condoms, for example. You may never have thought much about them, but today they're everywhere, enticingly packaged and practically shouting at you from pharmacy shelves (where they sit next to your favorite shampoo), or pitched by movie stars on televised public service announcements.

One woman I know has been so influenced by the media that she carries a "six-pack" in her purse—and it isn't beer. With all the hype, you probably know by now that condoms are inexpensive and easy to purchase. You may also know (firsthand) that they are not exactly romantic aids, that they can rob you of sensitivity and detract wildly from the eroticism of the moment. (We'll talk about ways to handle the negatives later.) When bedmates don't know each other well enough to share a laugh over this "New Age" form of sex, the event can degenerate into an embarrassing disaster. After one or two of those, small wonder both lovers soon go separate ways, vowing "never again."

Where does the condom conundrum and other modern sexual dilemmas leave you? Where else, dear Reader, but on the threshold of yet another mission—this time to plumb through outdated beliefs and discover the attitudes that influence your current sex style. My hunch is that you haven't examined them for a long time, maybe never, but I feel sure that once exposed, they will be updated. Some—the basics—won't change, because they are the ones that enable you to look in the mirror each morning and feel pretty good about the person looking back. But there are bound to be others, holdovers from childhood, adolescence, or college years, which are out of sync with the woman you are today. They're still hanging around because they've been overlooked in the press of daily living. But it won't take a mighty heave to dump them. They're dry rot, and because you're more sure of who you are these days, you're much stronger and more able to throw them overboard.

All this is not to say that you'll suddenly become a "swinger." After twenty years in the field of single living, measuring the attitudes of single people through those 6,000 questionnaires on sexuality, I still have come across only one of that species—a never-married Indianapolis college graduate in his mid-forties, who signed his questionnaire "Don

Juan" and said he was "pleased to embody that name in all ways." Articulate, self-assured, eager to tell all, DJ's nine typewritten pages make provocative reading, but, believe me, his thinking stood out as stale and pitiable. In that survey, the fiction of the "swinging single" was for all time blown to smithereens.

Yes, even in better times, before the advent of AIDS and its awfulness, the myth of the single swinger was only a myth. The real swingers, when they exist, are much more likely to be in the married world rebelling against its boundaries and propriety. It is the legally partnered who can at times feel oppressed by sexual monotony and the claim of a mate's ownership. Freedom and variety are already built into the single life, and so very few of its proponents are likely to swap and group and engage in hard-core kinkiness. And yet millions of you with sex lives that could barely qualify as active worry about a mythic image. Well, I am here to pass along the news that, even as we speak, a whopping 60 percent of your peers are sexually active once a month or less. That statistic should be the death knell of the swinging stereotype.

But even if your sex life is as fiery as a wet noodle, do not skip this chapter. Use it to sort out thoughts, perhaps find a middle ground between total abstinence and dangerous plurality, and at the same time heighten awareness of your personal sexuality. The straightforward exercises coming up are designed to develop a sexual sophistication repelled by junk sex. But before the exercises, these basics:

1. Trust your instincts. Refuse any part of sex that feels wrong, for any reason. Inner cues will help you resist outside pressure. When you feel unsure, ask the opinions of those close to you, but in the final analysis no one can decide what is right for you. It's your body.

2. Do your homework. *The Joy of Sex*, by Dr. Alex Com-

fort, contains thoughts you might want to incorporate into your own store of sexual facts. And you will profit by contacting the Sex Information Council of the United States, 80 Fifth Avenue, New York, NY 10011, for information about their publication and services (tel: 212-929-2300). Their librarian (tel: 212-673-3850) will direct you to the information you want, such as the truth about sexually transmitted diseases (STDs) and preventative measures. (Much more about all of that in the Resources section in the back of the book.)

3. When you do find a situation that feels right and caring, be a participant. Open up the dialogue. Show your partner the breadth of sensations possible when lovers communicate with all their senses. Your man will follow your lead—or he is wrong for you.

4. Come back to this chapter and exercises at least once a month, as your relationships progress and you learn more about the role sex plays in your life. Finding your individual sex style is a continuing process. Stay with it.

EXERCISE 1:
SITUATIONAL SEX

WHEN TO SAY YES—WHEN TO SAY NO

Imagine the following situations and feelings about sex. Check the boxes "yes" or "no" depending on whether in that case you would pursue or forgo intimacy. (If you're undecided, take more time and answer later.) There is space at the end of this exercise to write in other sexual situations you may think of once you have started to think along these lines.

SITUATION	YES	NO
1. You feel ambivalent and unsure about your feelings toward him and the relationship.	✓	
2. You are just plain curious about his lovemaking, and want to experience it for no other reason.		✓
3. You are physically drawn to him, but underneath it all you don't really like most of his values.		✓
4. You want to express your deepest feelings of love for him.	✓	
5. You want him to keep coming back.		✓
6. You think sex will ease your loneliness.		✓
7. You want to express tenderness for him.	✓	
8. He is threatening to break off the relationship unless you sleep with him.		✓
9. You want to give and receive pleasure.	✓	
10. Sex is your way of making up after the fight.		✓
11. You're just plain tired of sleeping alone.		✓
12. You are terrified that your organs will atrophy, it's been so long since you had sex.		✓

SITUATION	YES	NO

13. There is mutual caring between the two of you.

14. You are out for a kicky "high."

15. You are starved for closeness.

16. You want to get back at your folks, your ex, your religion, and other parts of your life that repress you.

17. You want to give something uniquely valuable to him.

18. You two have become good friends, and this is the next step in your closeness.

19. You need an ego boost.

20. You need to be reminded of your femininity.

21. To find a compatible partner.

22. To reaffirm mutual love.

23. To make each other happy.

24. For a sense of conquest.

25. To share mind, body, soul.

26. For entertainment.

27. As an emotional release, pure and simple, when caring is not part of the emotions.

28. To please him and keep the peace.

29. When you're drunk or drugged and not in control of your responses.

SITUATION	YES	NO

30. To gain a sense of security.

31. To feel desirable.

32. To show the depth of your feelings for him.

33. It's the "thing to do"—to be "with it" and part of the sexual revolution.

34. To get him to like you more.

35. It's an act of love, not sex.

36. He expects it.

37. To thank him for dinner.

38. Sex is the culmination of caring between the two of you.

39. To gain strength from him.

40. You love him so much you want to be a part of him.

41. You are not sure of what you want and need, and a small voice inside advises you to say no.

42. To put yourself in touch with another part of yourself and lose yourself in sensation.

43. To gain a hold over him.

44. You believe that going without sex makes you cranky.

45. You want to feel "grown up."

46. Your lovemaking is a celebration of a perfect union.

*Add other situations and a "yes" or "no" for how you would resolve them.

You might notice that only a yes or no answer is allowed; there's no space for "maybe" or "sometimes." (I'd love to know how many times you wished for one!) You might as well know that I left them out on purpose; I left you no choice but to come down on one side of an issue or another, because your body and sensitivities count too much to waffle on matters that concern them. If you left some blank spaces, try answering the questions again in a few days, and keep on thinking until you reach a yes or no conclusion about every one. Don't be afraid to change your mind; this is the time for second thoughts. Here, on paper, you have all the chances you want to change your mind. There is no second chance the morning after.

Another point: If you were expecting the quiz to have a neat little tally at the bottom ("If you had 20 *yes* answers, you're a nymphomaniac; if you had 30 *no* answers, you're frigid"), you won't find it here. I wouldn't presume to tell you how to express your sexuality—or how to decode your answers. If you study them thoroughly, you, yourself, will be able to pick out meaningful patterns in your beliefs. But I do suggest you memorize this short list:

REASONS THAT YOU'LL REGRET HAVING SEX

To win affection

To appease

To barter

To avoid intimacy

To hide anger

———

Now, let's tackle the broader question of sexual ethics. Again, don't look for a scorecard. I'm not going to *dictate* a moral code here, simply help you discover yours. If you're newly single, you probably went through a brief phase of bed-hopping immediately following the breakup but have returned to the lifelong values that sustained you. If you've never been anything but single, the odds are just as likely that you favor conservative and traditional mores. What's most important here is that your values coincide with what you currently believe. It's easy to get stuck in beliefs you believed yesterday, when the fact is, if you gave the matter some thought you'd discover your thinking has totally changed. For instance, most of the women and men in my survey found that they had become less judgmental, more "live and let live" since their marriages ended. But they didn't realize that growth had occurred until my question provoked them. If you let these questions ignite your thinking, they'll lead to other breakthroughs that will settle conflicts and put your mind at ease.

EXERCISE 2:
PERSONAL INVENTORY

SORTING OUT SEX: QUESTIONS TO ASK YOURSELF

Relax before you begin. It's important you start this section with shoulders loose and mind clear. Don't rush the following questions, because chances are they will lead to still more probing. (Jot down any additional questions that arise on a separate sheet of paper.) The best way to do these justice is to read them through in one sitting, let them "marinate" a while, then reread and give your answers. Some of them may trigger an immediate response; others take more thought. Don't write the pat answer; search deeper for your real belief.

- How do you feel about sex outside of marriage? Does your religion, upbringing, or personal morality make it out of bounds? Would denying those inner controls upset you so much that you wouldn't enjoy yourself even if you became sexually active?

- If you can enjoy sex outside of marriage, how do you feel about sex outside of caring?

- Can you imagine having sex on the first date? If yes, what sort of "ingredients" would have to be present? If no, when do you feel is a reasonable time to begin sexual involvement?

- Would you get involved with someone even if you knew it was to be for a very short time—perhaps only for one night? Under what circumstances?

- Can you imagine having a married lover? Why or why not?

- Would you ever consider having a sexual relationship with more than one person at a time? (This question deals with plural ongoing relationships, not group sex.)

- Ideally, how often would you like to have sex? How long can you go without it?

- Do you enjoy periods of celibacy? For how long? Are you ever concerned about losing your sex drive?

- What do you think about giving yourself pleasure? Masturbation is still a taboo subject, but it's one that should be very clear in your mind because of the episodic nature of single sex.

- If you are sexually active, have you settled on a safe and effective method of contraception? If you answered no or are unsure, are you clear about the range of options open to you and which one is best for you?

- Do you know enough about sexually transmitted diseases—such as AIDS and herpes—to protect yourself? If not, do you know how to get information about them? (See Resources.)

- Do you/would you ask a new partner his history of sexually transmitted disease before becoming intimate, even though it might be embarrassing?

- How do you (plan to) handle pressure from a date or partner to have sex when you'd rather not?

- As a single parent, are you clear about your policy on sleep-over lovers? Do you have a way of separating the fulfillment of your womanly needs from those of your children? How honestly do you talk to your children about your own sexual relationships?

- What do you appreciate most about sex? What makes it wonderful for you?

- Do you feel comfortable telling your partner what you enjoy?

- How strongly do you feel about the answers you have given here?

- What, if anything, would make you change your mind about them?

- Do you have an idea of how you would handle your sex life if you were to be single for a lifetime?

- Do you feel you could adapt your sexual attitudes to make yourself more comfortable as an unmarried person? If yes, how would you accomplish this?

- What other questions do you think you should ask yourself, now that you are thinking along these lines? If you've come up with any additional questions, write them down and answer them. Remember there are no "rights" and "wrongs" here—only clarity, as the philosophy of a lifetime begins to take shape.

You might want to declare the next four weeks your personal "Sexuality Month" and spend your spare time thinking about your sexual ethics. You don't have to announce this to the world at large—I hope you don't—but you might want to talk out some of the questions here with one close friend, especially when a question defies resolution. The attention you give each other will make tough questions easier to resolve.

———

It's odd: You're moving toward full-blown womanhood —setting up an investment plan, talking things over with a banker, building and renewing business and personal networks—but sex stays in the attic, with little girls' dreams of magical moments and irresistible emotions. Somehow, it seems cold and calculating to arrive at "zero hour" (the Erotic Moment) with a decision made beforehand. You'd rather be swept off your feet by emotion than admit you'd planned ahead. In fact, says Carol Cassell, Ph.D., in *Swept Away*, many women use this feeling of being out of control to justify having sex. (Which reminds me of a woman I knew in college. She said she would rather not know the "facts of life" because she wanted them to remain "mysterious.") But it's precisely because sex *does* exert such an emotional tug that it should be thought out and demystified in the light of day, and, yes, through the unimpassioned printed word. I'm sure you'll agree that sex is too dangerous these days to lose your head in a moment of mystery.

EXERCISE 3:
FANTASY ISLAND

Take the title tongue-in-cheek. I'm not proposing you seek sexual salvation in escape, only that you take time to exercise the part of you that thrives on fantasy. Eager to become more interesting in bed and perfect their erotic fantasies, some readers may browse through the exercises and start with this one. To those few let me say it won't work. Imagination takes practice; you can't jump into that old black magic. Those of you who have worked through each exercise, gently prying open mental compartments, have found the next one more rewarding, because it builds on the success of its predecessor. And the payoff? The ability to expand erotic boundaries. After all, sex is a creative act, limited only by the imagination. Tell rationality to take a catnap, because right now we're concentrating on fantasy.

STEP 1: Think exotic. Imagine yourself on a remote island, a sandy beach in front of you, a grass hut ringed with swaying palms behind you. It is early morning; you and your lover have not slept all night.

Or maybe you'd rather be in a rough-hewn cabin on the outskirts of a dense forest. It's winter, a blazing fire is crackling in the fireplace. In front of the stone hearth is an oversized bed heaped with rainbow-hued pillows and soft down comforters.

Or escape to a cool forest glade, where no one can see you and your lover.

Maybe you'd rather be on a mountaintop, in a boat adrift on placid waters, in an airplane, or at a deserted palace in an Eastern land. The setting can be a whitewashed Greek isle, a sultry Mediterranean resort, the Australian Outback, the American West. There are no limitations here.

STEP 2: Once you've established the setting, add the characters. One of them will, of course, be you. But you can appear in another form: an Egyptian princess, Indian maiden, or Lolita the nymphet. If you're a redhead, see whether blondes really do have more fun! If you're tall, try being petite.

STEP 3: Now, for your partner. How about the movie star of your dreams? Imagine Clark Gable or Gary Cooper in their prime, or William Hurt, Gene Wilder (well, someone I know thinks he's sexy), Richard Gere, Tom Hanks, or a younger, thinner Marlon Brando. Or it could be a rock star, Bruce Springsteen, for example; or Olympic diver Greg Louganis. It doesn't matter whether he's single or married; real-life facts are not important in this exercise. Funny thing, you may discover that the things that turn you off in real life are the very things that titillate in fantasy.

Of course, your dream partner could be a real-life partner—past, present, or future—someone you long for. The only condition is that he excite you. (I've been speaking in the singular here, but if the idea of group sex secretly thrills you, assemble as sexy a group as you can imagine.)

STEP 4: Once the setting and the characters are in place, add action. Imagine having sex while a crowd looks on, if that turns you on. Or think about positions you've imagined but never dared try. Anything goes: Have sex standing up, doggie fashion, in a police car. Some women like their fantasies with an air of danger to them. (Remember the scene from *Butch Cassidy and the Sundance Kid* where the outlaw makes his girl friend strip in front of his loaded gun?) Besides expanding your creativity, this exercise is a way to learn about your erotic tastes. What you discover must inevitably spill over into real-life lovemaking and make you a better partner. And when you know your own preferences, you can get in touch with someone else's secret yearnings.

Even the most delicious fantasy must fade when the time comes to leave the island, but you can take significant gains back to mainland reality:

- a sense of fun. Sex should be playtime, a light touch that only enhances the more serious romantic moments.

- a sense of the infinite possibilities of sex. There needn't be limitations to pleasing each other and expressing mutual tenderness.

In other words, imagination is the royal road to your deepest sexual needs. Don't desert your private island until it yields the fruits it promises: a sexier you.

EXERCISE 4:
CELIBATE SEX

You may be "between men" right now, but that's even more reason to fan the flames of the femininity so often smothered by routine busyness. To help you stay in touch with your sensual side, repeat this exercise three times a week (five minutes daily) when you're feeling up; add another session at the end of the day when you're not.

STEP 1: Remember the last time you were feeling particularly sexy. It may not have been with a man at all. Was it when you made an important decision about your life and reveled in self-confidence? Or when you were jogging and reverberating with joyous movement, in harmony with nature?

STEP 2: Conjure up that feeling, whenever or however you remember it. Recapture in your mind's eye every detail of that moment when you felt totally integrated: mind, body, and soul blended into ripe womanliness. Meditate on that feeling of completeness; let it soak into your very being.

STEP 3: Begin each day with this mental stretch to prepare yourself for the day ahead. Concentrate on the feeling again when you go to bed. Remember your morning affirmation? "Each day is mine to make the most of, through my own decisions. I will bring myself happiness"—or whatever words you decided on. Before you say that every morning, visualize an appealing, soft, feminine you.

The glowing face you may soon present to the world will have friends curious about the new man in your life, certain that such radiance must come from love. But deep inside, you will feel secure knowing these good feelings about yourself don't depend on an external source, but spring from within you as part of your wholeness. By staying in touch with your sensuality you stay open to the stimuli in life and keep yourself emotionally accessible. You make yourself fertile ground for the relationship to come.

EXERCISE 5:
SLOWER, SAFER, AND MORE FULFILLING SEX

Just when it seemed that the social upheavals of the 1970s were paying off with a modicum of understanding between men and women, a retrovirus shows up and sends everyone racing to the safety of single beds. Seems unfair. But the awfulness of AIDS has an ironically bright side that shows us a better path to physical closeness: We are being forced into liking our men before loving them.

You ask how on earth we can understand men enough to like them (in a voice quivering with apprehension). The answer? By piercing the macho mirage and discovering the man as he is—not as date, boyfriend, or lover. You've every right to be cautious; this is an even bigger challenge than initiating a sexual relationship. Yes, I'm asking you to take an emotional risk. It's not the last one I'll ask of you, either. (For moral support, I suggest Dr. David Viscott's *Risking*, see Resources.) I'm asking you to open up to a man as a friend. Read on.

PART A:
GO SLOW FOR SAFER SEX

The concept may seem odd if you're accustomed to easy intimacy, but the best way to safer sex with a man now is to begin with a totally nonsexual relationship. We can remove the risks from our sex lives by learning the facts, avoiding sex with strangers, and telling our lovers "no condom, no sex," but knowing a man as a *person* practically guarantees a risk-free experience. For one thing, you'll be confronting your feelings about the man first and will be less likely to act on physical attraction alone. You'll have an inkling of his tastes, patterns, preferences. (You still won't know the lifestyle and antibodies of every person he's ever slept with, but he'll be a lot more trustworthy in your eyes.) And don't fall for the fiction that knowing him destroys the magic. If anything, familiarity intensifies the chemistry.

You may wonder how you can do this exercise unless you're seeing a man romantically. But the steps work equally well in a platonic relationship. To put them into action you may choose a current male friend who (sad to say) might still seem a stranger to you, or you could choose someone you would like to know better, a man you feel you could respect and trust. You could choose parts of this exercise to use with a current lover—if you feel it is appropriate and could work. Obviously, you can't manufacture a man just for this exercise. But know that its payoff can be a prelude to friendship as well as to love.

This is also a good time to think about the kind of man you usually fall for. If you go for the exciting "love 'em and leave 'em" variety, think about why you're attracted to dangerous men. Do they "sweep you off your feet"? Do you need them to reaffirm your femininity? If you look to a lover for the qualities you like in a friend, you may surprise yourself and settle on a kind, gentle man—even if the initial fireworks aren't there. (You'll be surprised how things can suddenly start to sizzle after you know each other well.)

I don't believe there is only one man for each woman, but I do believe there is one best *type* of man. When I say that, I do not mean visual appearance (though each of us has a physical ideal), but rather a personality type. The man right for us could be calm or emotional, serious or lighthearted, steady or capricious. Curiously, the most interesting men often are not "husband material" because the qualities we find intriguing do not blend with a lifetime commitment. At some point (and this may be it) you will have to resolve that dichotomy and pinpoint what you *really* need for the long haul. If you haven't found your type yet, maybe it's because you're looking in the wrong direction. Or in too many directions. While you are thinking about which man to target for your assignment, some rules to keep in mind:

STEP 1: Remember our code words: *Go slowly.* Revealing too much of yourself before the two of you have developed a strong base of friendly feelings could spell the death of the relationship. There's no rush; allow plenty of sizing-up time (preferably months). If this is a man you already know, use the time to get to uncover his hidden sides.

STEP 2: If he's a man you know from work, be scrupulous in keeping his position there totally separate from your friendship. Assume two different ways of relating to him, professional and extracurricular.

STEP 3: Think of him as companion, not savior. In other words, don't lapse back into the old ways. This is a pioneering venture, with no place for yesterday's attitudes. It's also the perfect arena for both of you to work out the old issues that impede man-woman relating. Down with mind games!

STEP 4: If he's a potential lover, don't have sex with him yet. At this stage, that would only change the dynamics and confuse both of you.

STEP 5:   Be yourself. Someone has to dare to open up first. Since it is you who is heavily into growth these days, let that someone be you. Being who you are without pretense will encourage him to drop his posturing and be himself, too.

STEP 6:   As the relationship progresses, you may decide it will be no more (and no less) than a friendship. That's fine. You've triumphed; you've made a true friend of the other sex, an accomplishment these days.

You may find yourself attracted to your "friend" as you go along. Friendship between the sexes has a way of creeping up and changing its colorations. It can be very appealing to be in "deep fond" with a man. You'll see. And I can't imagine anything more perfect than falling in love with a good friend!

You probably won't have to do this exercise again; it will quickly become second nature. In fact, I bet that after just this once you'll feel differently and *insist* on knowing a man well before considering anything else.

There is a lot to be said for taking things slowly. Concentrating on friendship first gives you the right to skip sex entirely or edge toward it slowly. And if you do decide to be sexually intimate, you are better prepared for the next challenge.

PART B: THE STD CHAT

(Wherein the female of the species, responsible and concerned, initiates a frank and open discussion of sexually transmitted diseases with a potential sex partner.)

STEP 1:   Do your homework before the time comes for this discussion. In fact, do it now.

- If you have had or currently have an STD, discuss it with your physician and ask for a written statement describing your current condition.

- Read the Surgeon General's Report on AIDS. (See Resources for address. The report is free.)

• Call appropriate hotlines with questions that have not been answered to your satisfaction. (Again, see Resources.)

STEP 2: You will discover somewhere during your research that a latex condom is the best kind, and, when it's used with spermicidal jelly, is the number one choice for preventing the spread of AIDS and other STDs. *But have no illusion about that combination.* While it makes sex safer, it does not assure total safety. *Only abstinence and monogamy with an uninfected partner are totally risk-free.*

Knowing that, go to your local pharmacy and buy a half-dozen latex condoms and a tube of spermicidal jelly. (It would be a plus if you could talk with your pharmacist about brands, because you might gain some useful information.) Tuck a condom into your purse and carry it at all times.

STEP 3: Now, before doing anything else, take a mini-quiz that could save countless hours and energy. Ask yourself these questions at the start of every new romantic relationship. They will end social clutter by helping you discern the men with potential.

Could this man be someone important in my life?

Does he seem solid, dependable, responsible, grown up?

Is he easy to talk to?

Do we have fun together?

Does he treat me the way I like to be treated?

Is this strictly a lust situation—or something more?

It makes no sense at all to spend time and energy on an STD chat until you've had this session with yourself and are satisfied with all the answers!

STEP 4: Even after you give yourself the green light, talk the situation over with your network group. It could help to have a few phrases rehearsed to use when "zero hour" arrives, and the network is the perfect place to piece together the right phrases and then practice saying them.

When you've done this and feel ready to meet the moment, you are ready for the STD chat.

STEP 5: Find a time and place where you and he will be relaxed enough to give full attention to the exchange. Do not have this talk as you are walking into the bedroom. *This is sex education on the most personal level, and the time for it is very early in the relationship.*

Use no drugs or alcohol during the talk or before. They only distort judgment and alter the atmosphere.

Talk in a way that shows concern for the other person, as well as for yourself. Don't come on as an inquisitor. Show sensitivity; act as a person who respects herself and her partner.

STEP 6: It's a sure thing that both of you will be nervous, uncomfortable, ill at ease. You don't know each other very well and here you are talking about a very intimate subject. In a way, sharing sexual histories is even more intimate than getting into bed. But it needn't be gloom and doom if you approach the subject in a practical, caring, and light manner. By "light" I don't mean using off-color jokes or wisecracks, but a sense of irreverence will make the moment much more bearable and help the relationship survive beyond this talk.

Again, *this bears repeating*: If you are a carrier of an STD, learn as much as you can about your disease before the chat and bring printed information to share. If that sounds like a lot to ask of yourself, ask your physician which facts you should discuss. Your part in the STD chat is not only to initiate, but to mention any high-risk sexual behavior in your past (intravenous drug use, bisexual or homosexual lovers). You can also discuss birth control at the same time you are arranging safer sex.

STEP 7:   Core questions to ask:

- How many partners have you had in recent years?

- Were any of them drug users, bisexuals, homosexuals?

- To your knowledge, have they had any sexually transmitted diseases?

- Have you had any sexually transmitted diseases in the past? Do you have any now?

Ask anything else about this person that is on your mind. Don't hold back. If you make the right approach, you can ask anything. Just remember to keep your tone of voice sensitive, warm, and caring.

STEP 8:   A reasonable amount of tension comes with this conversation, but anyone with a healthy attitude toward sex and their own sexuality will go along with the spirit of the talk and acknowledge its necessity. You will come across as a clear-headed and responsible person—a most attractive woman to get to know better. But if the man you are speaking with refuses to look you in the eyes or is inappropriately ill at ease, he's not for you. Show him the door, console yourself with milk and cookies, and consider yourself a lucky woman.

STEP 9:   Have this talk with yourself and a man before every new sexual encounter. No one said it's easy, but it's about time people in this puritanical society became comfortable talking about sex with the other sex. Without forfeiting romance.

PART C: THE CONDOM QUESTION

STEP 1:   If the talk about sexual histories has met your standards, you are ready to tackle the subject of condoms—wearing them, that is. You may have mentioned them to your partner earlier, when you broached the subject of birth control, but it was probably glossed over in the intensity of the STD chat. Perfectly understandable. But here it is again, a question to be asked directly, without fidgeting or apology.

STEP 2:   Raise the topic by referring to something you saw on the Oprah Winfrey Show or read in a magazine, and segue into "I have sex only with a man who wears a condom." Say it your way, but say it—and don't make it too subtle or he won't get the message. (Ignore your fluttering heart or his possible rejection; this is a matter of life or death.)

STEP 3:   Okay, you've asked him, and now the moment is here. While you're in bed, waiting for *him* to slip into something that makes *you* more comfortable, remind yourself that no matter what is said at this critical juncture, wearing a condom is not a debatable point. (By the way, one should be worn during oral sex, too.)

STEP 4:   Some men have been known to come up with some pretty fancy resistance at the last moment:

"These things make me impotent."

"I'm too big for those."

"I'm too small for them."

"They make me feel like I'm taking a shower with my raincoat on."

"These things never work. They're old-fashioned."

"Just this once without it." (The all-time favorite and the biggest turnoff of all, indicating a brainless and reckless male in your bed.) If he isn't scrupulous and protective, tell him to put on his pants and leave. No *if*s, *and*s, or *but*s. Your final line as he is being led to the door? *"If you say no, I say no."*

STEP 5:   As a responsible woman meeting all kinds of men, it is imperative that you live by these rules:

• Limit your number of sexual partners; three or four in a period of one year is a reasonable number.

- Know your partner well—very well—*before* having sex. Have an STD chat as soon as you think the situation warrants it.

- Always use a condom, in addition to any other form of birth control either of you might already be using.

STEP 6:   Even if all goes according to plan, there are still awkward moments; removal and disposal of a condom are not romantic sights. This is a time to make your partner feel as comfortable as possible. Again, your good attitude will make all the difference, and a laugh shared by the two of you can bring you closer to each other than the gymnastics of sex ever could.

PART D: FULFILLMENT

Once you've tackled the safety issue, you're balancing practical needs with romantic expectations and are ready to move into the many-pleasured realm of fulfillment. You've already begun by understanding your own sexual needs; a good lover knows her own pockets of pleasure. If you're sensitive to your own stirrings, it's easier to be sensitive to your lover's. But sexual self-knowledge is a beginning, not an end in itself, to be extended into better understanding of a partner. Until it is, you won't achieve the spiritual union that love can deliver. The "mini-exercise" below will help. Again, you can make good use of it without a lover. Its techniques are as crucial to friendship as they are to love.

HOW TO BECOME A MORE SENSITIVE LOVER

STEP 1:   Communication. I don't mean discussing your "relationship" and analyzing it to little pieces (this can actually erode feelings), but genuine openness and talk, without shame or fear of censure.

STEP 2:   Concentration. Your mind must be on the moment and nowhere else. There is no past and future; just you and your friend, enveloped in the present. Focus only on what is being done and said.

STEP 3:   Caring. Sounds obvious, but you would (or maybe you wouldn't) be surprised how many times this ingredient is missing. You've got to care honestly, otherwise sex is meaningless. Ask yourself how you can give him pleasure. What does he like?

STEP 4:   Patience. It takes time and motivation to get to know someone's needs, with room for many false starts. For that kind of relating, good sex needs that solid base of friendship.

STEP 5:   Flexibility. You must be able to suspend your own needs while tending to his. (The beauty of mutual friendship, of course, is that he does the same for you.) As you trust each other more, you'll be freer to move out of role-playing and even trade positions. You'll be able to be the aggressor, allowing him the passivity men secretly fantasize. Lovemaking will gain the exciting fluidity it was meant to have.

Beyond this, becoming a more sensitive lover implies the *inter*dependence, physical and emotional, that creates a working partnership. The sexual side of you, like any other, is not a fixed entity. Respected and cultivated, it can develop and change along with the rest of your psyche. Of course, some women are secretly relieved when their childbearing years come to a close, so that they can consider sexual activity finished too. That's okay for them. But I think they're missing out on a good thing—sexual union with absolutely no risk of pregnancy. Still, that's only my opinion; they're certainly entitled to theirs. If you're one of them, I hope you will consider my view, but don't be swayed unless it feels right in your life.

If you're like most women, you'll make a conscious effort to retain your womanly appeal—for your own esteem and for the men in your life. You'll stay a sexual being and remain in touch with your sexuality throughout the years. The details may change: The number of orgasmic pulsations will decrease with age, as will their intensity. The childbearing years will come to a close. The physical body will thicken. But your womanliness need not be diminished through the years, nor your potential to spark magic with a man. After all, sex is not only what you do, but what you're thinking and feeling, the condition of your body and skin. That's sensuality, and it can be lifelong. If the ego is nourished, how can any of that good stuff wither or die?

Sure, you'll have periods of charged sexuality, when the nerve endings are supersensitive and orgasm becomes superimportant—but there will be other times when the drive is sublimated into projects and goals. Learn to accept these swings and allow yourself to go with their natural rhythms. Go with the ebb and flow of your body's chemistry and learn to recognize the influence of outside pressures on inner drives. Diseases will be controlled, prevented, cured. Your life situations will change. But in matters sexual, your peace of mind is the constant. Don't worry about keeping your sex style "current"; stay tuned to that voice within. Be faithful to yourself.

That inner loyalty strengthens your contribution to the love and joy and intimacy you create with your partner. The two of you can make shared sex a creative venture. But at the same time you can shape something even more wonderful, a whole greater than the sum of its parts. Because it requires the harmony of caring and consideration, it cannot occur until friendship has grown up between you. But when that prerequisite has been met, each sexual act becomes another step in the co-construction of a very special type of sex, on a different plane than the usual. Self-knowledge plus mutual liking will lead to sexual synergy, a combination that produces the real fireworks!

I propose the following guidelines for a healthy sexuality ... to be reread as needed.

SEXUAL BILL OF RIGHTS

1. Realizing that it is an integral dimension of human health and well-being, I will incorporate sexual fulfillment into my singleness in ways that mesh with my personal morality.

2. Being of adult age and having a reasonable amount of life experience, I will aim toward being both sexual and autonomous, assuming full responsibility for my behavior.

3. I will adopt a consistent "live and let live" attitude regarding the sexual choices of others. I will be deliberately slow to condemn.

4. I will shape a code of sexual conduct from my special needs and ethics, with the purpose of attaining peace of mind, sexual fulfillment, and general ease.

5. I will not allow myself to be coerced insofar as sexual behavior is concerned, nor will I influence others unduly in that aspect of their lives, since sexuality is a highly personal and private issue.

6. I will assume total responsibility for my own sexual gratification and for the communication thereof to my partner, bearing in mind that sexual independence enhances erotic pleasure and intimacy.

7. I will reserve the right to remain sexually virgin or chaste, realizing that neither state can harm. Rather, abstinence can produce periods of peak productivity and creativity.

I will avoid those who attempt to dissuade me from either choice.

8. I will not be enslaved by useless and destructive stereotypes that view the male role as sexually aggressive and the female role as passive.

9. If I so choose, I will bring to masturbation a guilt-free attitude, aware that it is a natural and legitimate source of pleasure. It does not do harm and can serve as preparation for coupled sex and a source of insight into my own sexuality.

10. I will bear in mind as I age that sexual needs are an appropriate and healthy aspect of later years and ought not to cause shame or embarrassment. Rather than denying them, I will find expression for them through wholesome, appropriate outlets.

11. I will respect the fact that all persons, including the mentally and physically impaired, are entitled to full-dimensioned relationships. Sexual expression and fulfillment are among their dimensions.

12. I will be aware and responsible in respect to the disease AIDS (and all sexually transmitted diseases), and will do my utmost to encourage intelligent, responsible conduct in others. Rather than shun or condemn people afflicted with such diseases, I will make real efforts to help them in every way possible and enlighten those who may be burdened by ignorance of the facts.

13. I will be prudent to the nth degree in my sexual dealings, preferring abstinence to mindless risk. I will bear in mind that the person I sleep with is bringing with her/him the sexual history of every previous sex partner. That truth will be in the forefront of all my sexual decisions. As much as I may desire to express my sexuality, I am not willing to die for it.

—Susan Deitz

INTRODUCTION TO THE
SEXUALITY SURVEY

When I began asking single people about their sex lives, survey mavens told me this was the first study ever to define single people's sexual patterns. Whether that's true, I cannot say for sure, but I do know my research covers the emotional issues that can make or break sexual union—the feelings seldom put on paper.

Deciding what to ask wasn't easy. I grudgingly whittled my original 450 questions down to a less intimidating number; the core that you are about to read (and answer, if you'd like) represents what I believed was uppermost in the minds of single men and women.

My research began in late 1979, a relatively quiet time in the history of our national psyche, when the major upheavals of the Seventies had settled down to the dull roar of the very early Eighties. It seemed the right time to assess the sexual revolution, the women's movement, and men's response to the shifting dynamics between the sexes.

At the time I could not have predicted that the AIDS virus (which was "discovered" in 1981) would change everything, or that other sexually transmitted diseases ("venereal diseases") would become a major factor for the sexually active. So this survey does not deal with them. If it did, the question about sex on the first date would be the first to go, since no prudent person rushes into sex these days (a step forward for all of us, in my opinion), and the queries about one-night stands, plural lovers, and group sex would also become relics of the past. If I were to rewrite the questions now, they would be stated in a totally different way. But since that's not possible, I've kept them in their original version. If they bother you or are not relevant in your life, skip them. (I've included only a sampling, the more provocative questions from the original survey.)

You'll notice that the rest deal with issues that are still very much a part of being single. In fact, the most significant finding of the survey—the conservative attitude toward sex —has only been intensified by the AIDS issue. There was hardly a seasoned swinger in the bunch even then, before that disease shook the single community.

For the record: The 1,900 men and women who took part in this survey represented thirty-nine states, which gives the findings a wide national base projectable to 85 percent of the unmarried population in this country. Respondents in the research include a widow of eighty-eight who still loves to reminisce about a dear husband gone for twenty-three years, a woman married four times and now happily single, a spirited teacher of a Sunday school class of single adults who remarried during the research, a sixty-year-old virgin who was participating in the study to learn more about his attitudes. The results do not speak for the homosexual community, since that segment has a sexuality all its own and very few of its members took part in this research.

For me, the survey's most exciting discovery was how much the single world wanted to talk about sexuality. I went into this project with high hopes and a hunch that the questions would be well received. But the 32-percent rate of response (1,900 of 6,000 questionnaires) told me more than that. Many questionnaires came back with typewritten supplements attached to the original forms, outpourings that could not be contained on the original questionnaire. (Some included unlisted phone numbers and other personal data that had certainly not been requested.) There was such a high degree of trust and such a thirst for communication that my head spun when the mailsacks came from the post office and I began to read the feelings behind the responses.

For you, this survey's main benefit is a chance to compare your thoughts with those of other single women. You'll enjoy thinking about the issues too, of course, but at this point you're probably accustomed to self-questioning. The real kick will come when you put your answers next to the majority view. But enough about my research; jump in and do some digging on your own.

SURVEY

CORE QUESTIONS

These are basic questions given to all who participated in the sexuality survey:

Have you experienced close friendships with people who could have been sex partners, that did not involve sexual intercourse?

_____YES   _____NO   _____N/A

85.1 percent said yes.

Did you become closer or more distant because of not having intercourse?

_____BOTH   _____NEITHER   _____FELT OKAY

_____N/A   _____CLOSER   _____MORE DISTANT

48.7 percent of women said closer; 38.4 percent of men said closer; 31.4 percent said more distant.

Do you prefer the continuity of married sex life or the stop-and-start character of single sex?

_____MARRIED   _____SINGLE

67.1 percent said married.

While single, have you gone for longer periods of time without sexual continuity? How long?

_____NO   _____WEEKS   _____MONTHS

45.2 percent said months; 37 percent said years.

Do you feel "rejected" or "less of a person" during these chaste periods?

_____NO   _____YES   _____REJECTED

_____LESS WOMAN

65.5 percent of women said no.

Are you living (or have you lived) with a lover on a long-term basis without marriage?

_____NEVER   _____NEVER BUT MIGHT

_____AM NOW   _____ONCE OR TWICE

_____MORE THAN TWICE

44.9 percent said never but might; 26.9 percent never; 21.3 percent once or twice; 1 percent more than twice.

When you began to live together, did you view the arrangement as a "test marriage"?

_____YES   _____NO   _____UNSURE

18.1 percent said no; 9.4 percent said yes.

If your answer was yes: Do you envision your future as a series of living-together arrangements or do you intend to marry?

_____SERIES   _____MARRY   _____UNSURE

51.8 percent said marry.

Were there children living at home at the time?

_____YES   _____NO

15.7 percent said no; 7.2 percent said yes.

Do you plan to have children outside of marriage?

_____YES   _____NO   _____UNSURE

6.4 percent said yes; 44.1 percent said no.

As a single person, do you choose married people for sex partners?

_____YES   _____NO

_____HAVE DONE SO, BUT NOT AGAIN

24.9 percent said yes.

Is this your preference?

_____YES   _____NO

47 percent said no.

Are your sexual responses more inhibited or less inhibited with a married partner?

_____MORE   _____LESS   _____SAME

19 percent said less; 13.2 percent said more.

Would you date a married person if their mate had no objections?

_____YES   _____NO

_____N/A OR DON'T KNOW

42.3 percent said no.

Do you expect to have sex on the first date?

_____YES   _____NO   _____SOMETIMES

_____N/A

Women: 76.4 percent said no; 6.7 percent yes; 13.8 percent sometimes. Men: 15.1 percent said yes; 75.6 percent no; 9.3 percent sometimes.

Do you think people of the other sex expect you to?

_____YES   _____NO   _____SOMETIMES

_____N/A

Women: 25.2 percent said yes; 27.7 percent sometimes; 20.8 percent no. Men: 10.5 percent said yes; 33.7 percent no; 26.7 percent sometimes.

How often have you picked up someone for the express purpose of a one-night sexual encounter?

_____NEVER   _____ONCE OR TWICE

_____SEVERAL TIMES   _____OFTEN

_____N/A

61.5 percent of women and 36 percent of men said never; 24.3 percent of women and 33.7 percent of men said once or twice.

Do you feel more lonely or less lonely after casual sex?

_____MORE LONELY   _____LESS LONELY

42 percent said more lonely.

Would you rather go without sexual activity (except perhaps for masturbation) than be part of casual or noncaring sex?

_____PREFER GOING WITHOUT

_____PREFER CASUAL SEX

82.5 percent said prefer going without.

Are you now (or have you ever been) sexually active with different partners within the same day or week?

_____YES   _____NO   _____N/A

48 percent said no; 47.6 percent yes.

Did your partners know you were involved with others at the same time?

_____YES/PROBABLY   _____NO

_____SOME (BUT NOT OTHERS)   _____N/A

23.5 percent said no; 14.9 percent said yes/probably.

If you have had several partners at the same time, were you emotionally close to two or more of them?

_____YES   _____NO   _____N/A

26.3 percent said yes.

Do you need more than one sex partner to fill all your sexual needs?

_____YES   _____NO

62.4 percent said no.

Or do you think you could meet someone who could fill all of your sexual needs?

_____YES   _____NO

60.1 percent of women said yes; 77.9 percent of men said yes.

How often have you engaged in group sex?

_____NEVER   _____1–3 TIMES

_____4–10 TIMES   _____MORE THAN 10 TIMES

89 percent of women said never; 79.1 percent of men said never.

On double or multiple dates, have you ever exchanged partners for sexual purposes?

_____YES   _____NO   _____N/A

90.7 percent said no.

How often do you masturbate?

_____NEVER   _____ALMOST DAILY

_____2–3 TIMES WEEKLY   _____ONCE A WEEK

_____TWICE A MONTH   _____ONCE MONTHLY OR LESS

23.3 percent of women said never; 8.1 percent of men said never.

Do you believe there is a certain age at which a person should stop masturbating?

_____YES   _____NO   _____N/A

86.7 percent of women said no; 93 percent of men said no.

Do you have other outlets (besides masturbation and other aspects of your sexuality) through which you express your need to love and be loved?

friends and co-workers (14.7 percent)
children (7.9 percent)

work (6.6 percent)
family (5.8 percent)
physical contact (4.5 percent)
helping others (6.8 percent)
animals (3.9 percent)
music (.5 percent)
creativity (2.8 percent)
dreams (.8 percent)
church (2.3 percent)
talk (5.0 percent)
activity (5.2 percent)
kindness/compassion (7.4 percent)
other (6.5 percent)
none (10 percent)

Which would you prefer, ideally: one love for a lifetime, or one at each stage of your emotional development?

_____ONE LOVE   _____EACH STAGE

_____OTHER

73.6 percent of women and 69.8 percent of men said one love.

How well prepared were you to handle your sex life as a single adult?

_____WELL PREPARED   _____POORLY PREPARED

_____FAIRLY WELL PREPARED

_____TOTALLY UNPREPARED

35.2 percent said fairly; 30.1 percent said poorly.

Are you or do you plan to be sexually faithful to your current partner?

　　　　　YES　　　　　　NO

38.9 percent said yes.

Future sexual partners?

　　　　　YES　　　　　　NO　　　　　　UNCERTAIN

44.5 percent said yes.

Which places have brought you the most success in meeting suitable partners?

friends (33.6)
clubs/parties (11.7)
work (15.9)
bars (5.6)
church (4.7)
random (5.8)
school (6.3)
housing (.8)
other (7.7)

Please indicate your current frequency of intercourse:

several times a week (20.9)
once a week (12.5)
once every two weeks (9.8)
once a month (7.2)
less than once a month (34.9)
don't—or none (13.7)

At approximately what age did you first have sexual intercourse?

> under 16 (8.7)
> 16–18 (31.3)
> 19–21 (33.8)
> 22–25 (14.2)
> 26–30 (3.4)
> over 30 (2.1)
> never (6.2)

Do you date (or have you dated) significantly younger men?

_____YES   _____NO

45.4 percent said yes; 51 percent said no.

Would you marry him?

_____YES   _____NO

24.7 percent said yes; 26.6 percent said no.

Is the attraction mainly sexual?

_____YES   _____NO

36.4 percent said no.

Do you plan to (re)marry, or do you simply want a companion?

_____MARRY   _____COMPANION ONLY

_____NEITHER   _____UNSURE

54.9 percent said marry; 20.4 percent companion only;
18.7 unsure.

How large is the town or city where you live?

> under 5,000
> 6,000–25,000
> 26,000–100,000
> 100,000–500,000
> 500,000–1,000,000
> over one million
> 27.7 percent said 26,000 to 100,000; 15.3 percent over
> one million.

Which of these factors do you believe have contributed to
changes in your sexual satisfaction?

> greater self-knowledge, understanding, and acceptance
> (27.4)
> fewer responsibilities (3.8)
> more self-confidence (22.9)
> other (specify) (4.5)
> greater self-respect (17.6)
> variety of sex partners (8.8)
> success in life (8.6)
> therapy (3.5)

Do you feel your sexual relationships have changed since
your early youth?

> _____YES   _____NO/SAME
> 83.9 percent said yes.

Have you become more sexually assertive as you develop?

> _____YES   _____NO   _____N/A
> 65.5 percent said yes.

More imaginative in your lovemaking?

_____YES _____NO _____N/A

57.4 percent said yes.

More honest?

_____YES _____NO _____N/A

62.9 percent said yes.

Does the forbidden aspect of sex outside of marriage make your sex life more exciting?

not a factor (43.3)
more exciting (13.9)
less exciting (inhibiting) (27.8)
both (at different times) (2.4)

Does commitment to your sexual partner increase or decrease your sexual pleasure?

_____INCREASE _____DECREASE

_____NEITHER _____N/A

70.9 said increase.

Has your sex life as a single person lived up to your expectations?

_____YES _____NO _____SOMETIMES

_____NO EXPECTATIONS _____N/A

35.8 percent said no.

What do you consider to be the positive aspects of your singleness?

> freedom, independence (42.8)
> money (5.1)
> less responsibility (9.8)
> growth (14.8)
> privacy (5.0)
> mobility (4.4)
> variety (2.8)
> free time (4.6)
> other (7.1)

Have you ever developed a meaningful relationship with someone you met at a singles bar or disco?

> 72.9 percent said no.

Do you want to have children?

> 30.2 percent of men said yes; 24.3 percent of women said yes.

LIFESTYLE QUESTIONS

The respondents could also choose from three sets of questions: never-married; single again with children; and single again with no children. Now you can answer the set of questions appropriate for you.

Answer if you're single again with no children living at home:

Has your sex life in general become freer, less inhibited, less routine?
　　55.2 percent said yes.
Why are you single—again?
　　78.9 percent divorced; 16.5 percent widowed; 4.1 percent separated.
How long were you married?
　　59.9 percent said over 10 years.
Have you revised your definition of promiscuity since you've been single?
　　50.6 percent said yes.
Have you adopted more of a live-and-let-live attitude since your own life has changed?
　　55.2 percent said yes.
For how long have you been single (again)?
　　75.6 percent said over 10 years.

Answer if you've never been married:

Have you chosen not to marry because you want to grow as a person?
　　57.5 percent said no.
Is it possible to grow as an individual within marriage?
　　78 percent said yes.
Does planning for the future (if you intend to marry) include a marriage contract or other type of contract?
　　37.9 percent said no; 31.7 percent said yes.

Have you not married because you do not want the responsibility of coordinating your sexual needs with those of another person on a long-term basis (not having sex whenever you want; feeling pressured to have sex when you don't want to)?

89.5 percent said no.

If you were to marry, do you think your sex life (in terms of frequency and satisfaction) would change? In which ways?

64.7 percent said would change in frequency; 61.6 percent said would change in satisfaction; 14.6 percent said no change.

Answer if you're single again with children living at home:

Are you more sexually responsive when your children are away from home?

72.8 percent said yes.

Would the frequency of sexual intercourse change if your children did not live at home?

56 percent said yes.

Do your sex partners sleep over in your home?

23.4 percent said yes; 60.7 percent said no.

Do you respond to your children's questions about your sexual activity and relationships?

52.9 percent said yes.

Do your children resent your dating?

66 percent said no.

Do you tell your children about masturbation?

63.9 percent do not tell.

How soon after your marriage ended did you resume some degree of shared sexual activity?

41.4 percent said months; 21.5 percent said years.

Have your sexual fantasies changed since you became single?

20.4 percent said they're freer.

How do you intend to prepare your children to handle their sex lives as single adults?

49.3 percent said I will talk to them; 33.8 percent said I will be honest with them.

Do you feel that the way you conduct your sex life and the way you are rearing your children are consistent with each other?

81.7 percent said yes.

Were you sexually faithful to your spouse during marriage?

73.3 percent said yes.

Was your spouse faithful to you?

43.8 percent said no; 29.9 percent said yes.

What effects (if any) do you think your fidelity or lack thereof had on your marriage?

26.7 percent said positive; 19.4 percent said negative.

Do you intend to be faithful if you choose to remarry?

88.4 percent said yes.

Would you be a different kind of sex partner in a new marriage?

67 percent said yes.

INTERMEZZO

Think of this as sorbet between courses, intermezzo before the final movement. Use this pause to consider carefully what you really need in love—and where you'll compromise to achieve it.

EXERCISE:
FRIENDS AND LOVERS

This exercise has several parts, meant to be done in order. You'll need several sheets of paper.

PART A:
DETERMINING WHAT YOU REALLY
NEED IN A MAN

STEP 1: List the qualities you need in a lover.

STEP 2: Now, on the same sheet of paper, in another column, list what you value in a male *friend* who is *not* your sexual partner.

STEP 3: Read the lists carefully and underline any needs that show up on both "lover" and "friend" lists. They are the ones that form the basis for solid love between you and a man. (The rest are details that probably have little influence on your long-term happiness.)

STEP 4: Write those overlapping needs on another piece of paper, so that you can see that group as a separate entity. Take a good look at the list because it describes the qualities in the kind of man who is right for you. But this is not the final version; there is more to be done. Set this list aside for the moment and go on to Part B.

PART B:
DETERMINING WHAT YOU REALLY NEED
IN A RELATIONSHIP

STEP 1: Carrying the same thinking one step further, make a list of your expectations from an unmarried relationship.

STEP 2: On the same paper, in another column, write down what you expect from marriage.

STEP 3: For fun, and to measure your growth, refer back to the "Single and Expecting" exercise in Chapter Two.

STEP 4: As in the first part of this exercise, underline the overlapping qualities and then write them on a separate sheet of paper and put it together with your Part A list.

PART C:
WHERE ARE YOU WILLING
TO COMPROMISE?

STEP 1:   Look again at those two lists, in a new way. This time, find areas where you are willing to bend a little, make substitutions, or take less. Mark them with an asterisk.

STEP 2:   On separate sheets, list those asterisked items and the nonasterisked ones. The goal here is to develop flexibility in less important requirements, while strengthening your resolve to stick with the more major ones. Maybe you don't care much about a man's height, age, or the amount of hair on his head—but you feel you *do* want a man of the same religion. Whether or not that seems crucial to someone else, your unbending needs are important to *you*.

STEP 3:   At this point you have in front of you:

a) two lists describing your right man, with areas for possible compromise on one list and inflexible needs on the other;

b) two lists describing the kind of relationship right for you, one with possible areas for compromise and the other with necessities.

Staple each set, so you end up with both "man" lists and both "relationship" lists joined.

STEP 4:   Memorize the four sheets. (There can't be that many entries on each list.) Give the asterisked items a little more importance than the nonasterisked ones, because there are probably more of them and they give you room to move about and make changes. They'll be fun to work with, challenging your creativity. Keep the lists in the drawer of a desk or your night table, somewhere out of view but easily accessible for a quick refresher course.

———

Clearing up the picture is probably long overdue, but it feels good to get rid of clutter whenever it happens. Seeing your demands on paper will make you realize the gap between the superficialities and the essentials. Compromising on less important factors clears the way for you to focus better on gut issues such as compassion, warmth, integrity. It's a quick lesson in growing up, too. When I was twenty, a man had to sweep me away with a Grecian profile and a sexy sports car. Now I'm impressed by good judgment, tenderness, consideration. Lightning bolts have lost their appeal; in fact, I don't even trust them anymore. In my experience, relationships that start with instant attraction fizzle just as quickly. The real thing for me has a slow takeoff that steadily grows into what I call love.

And indeed, it is our expectations that get us in the end. To a large degree, what we expect is what we make happen, one way or the other. A woman who expects to fail in marriage will marry a man for all the wrong reasons—usually rosy, romantic reasons—and then wind up divorced and more convinced than ever of her own inability to make a go of marriage. Unreal expectations can hide a great deal of pessimism and a will to fail. Look back over the lists you've just made and pluck out the fantasies, substituting realistic, sensible, practical hopes. (Yes, there *are* such things as practical hopes.) I'm not suggesting that you pare down dreams to a bare-bones minimum. Quite the opposite: Dream hard and go for the best. No one believes that more than I do. But take time to see the *big* picture of your needs and come to an understanding of what it takes to bring you contentment. Seeing a realistic listing of the ingredients will give you something to aim for—and increase the chances of getting it. In other words, turn your dreams into goals. That way, you have a better chance to reach their happiness.

And before moving on, consider The Word According to Scott:

My own mother tried for months to dissuade me from using the word *relationship*, arguing that it has lost meaning. But my son Scott, a wise man in his twenties, sees beauty in that lack of specificity. It allows a relationship to be like an empty vessel, he says, a container that in itself places no judgment on what it holds, but obediently waits to be filled with the magic of love as each couple creates it. So, dear Reader, as we move into the loving room, bring with you the concept of love as adaptable and personalized.

MUTUALISM: BEYOND GENDER

Not to worry. This is no blazing finale about finding a man in thirty days. After all our concentration on building independence I wouldn't abandon you to a gothic-novel ending or put you in a vine-covered cottage with Mr. Right. Not that we're against your meeting him and sharing some healthy interdependence in a nest for two; far from it. Come to think of it, the path you're on will probably lead to some very nice people—and logically some very nice men will be among them. But catching a man is not the point of this book.

On the other hand, we're not going to leave you wondering whether your newly developed strength will put you under a bell jar, you and your self-sufficiency distanced from men and even further from love. The journey inward is enabling you to find your center, and you are living truer than ever to that core, while your expansion into the world is bringing you a planned and resourceful approach to your life.

That duality is good preparation for the mutually enriching relationships that can be the big payoff of your efforts.

A stronger sense of self is giving you the confidence to know what you need—and to ask for it from the relationships you enter. Knowing and liking yourself is the beginning of satisfying dealings with the people in your world. Once you see this in action, you'll realize that the same principles work with everyone, in all kinds of relationships. All through this book you've been developing "people" skills while working on your own life. Curious, isn't it, that self-interest leads not to self-absorption, as you might expect, but to the ability to reach out and connect beneficially with other people? Curious—and thrilling, I'd say.

You probably have not worked through every one of the exercises up to this point, and you're certainly nowhere near your peak of growth, but my hunch is that you're well on your way to achieving mutualism with the people around you. If not this month, soon.

What is mutualism? Think about the relationships you're in now; let your mind roam among friends, relatives, co-workers, male friends. Does this or that relationship benefit both of you, giving each person what he or she needs? Honestly ask yourself whether it is based on partnership, mutual contribution, or the dependency that plagues our gender. Begin thinking this way, and I guarantee you'll start to alter— or leave—many of the relationships in your life today. After a while, you'll ask three things of the people you meet— reciprocity, enrichment, and equality—the components of mutualism. The fact that they are not oriented toward gender is their strength—and consequently your strength. Approaching people on those terms wipes out the superficial boundaries between you and them and gives you a broad, rich, and varied spectrum from which to make your selections. Unnecessary limitations such as age, sex, height, and income fade into oblivion, as they should, while the fundamentals become more important than ever.

Not that mutualism is a guarantee of lifelong bliss. Any relationship is at root speculative, a jointly ventured stab in the dark of indeterminate duration. But a mutualistic relationship has the best chance for survival because its lovers are helpmates, a perspective that releases gender-tied expectations and ends the playing of roles. Whether it's making love or taking out the garbage, the issue of who does what becomes irrelevant.

Don't expect to wake up one day and stage a one-woman uprising against the old ways of relating; progress will be more evolution than revolution. But the end of one-way arrangements has been coming since you opened this book, and this chapter is their death knell. And, because, as we said before, the only person you can change is yourself, you will be challenged here to open your mind to new ways of looking at relationships. While this chapter's exercises will not necessarily deliver a man to your doorstep next Tuesday, they will make most of your relationships with the other sex more satisfying and meaningful.

I can promise you this because you will be making changes that improve your dialogues with most people, and common sense dictates that some of them will be with men.

Most of the techniques here revolve around men. That is because, while the elements of male-oriented mutualism are the same as in other kinds of mutualism, the mix is changed by the addition of sexuality. (Fact, not complaint.) That tension changes the relatedness of lovers because it affects everything they do and think. And while it offers a pleasurable resolution to conflicts, it also adds complexities that result in more conflicts.

That's the basic difference in man-woman dealings, but it is not the only one. A misinterpreted form of feminism that feeds on anger is causing both sexes to cluster into same-sex groups, significantly diminishing the possibility of friendly feelings between the two. And the possibility of AIDS is still another reason for wariness in both camps. That dread disease has totally changed the context of male-female relationships in a way that nothing else could. There is fear now in the single world, and it is a sovereign power.

Yet in the crisis I see an opportunity. Because a prolonged period of courtship is virtually dogma now, the woman who can relate to a man on a more human level, and not as a sex goddess, will reap success in her relationship. The one who regards men as alien creatures, and thus is totally baffled in their company when she cannot use her body as bait, will be a loser. Again and again. Yes, this seems to be a good time to become friends with men. And that's what we're going to talk about next.

YOUR SHARE

The basis of mutualism is partnership—shared effort—a far cry from the classic feminine posture of "owing" a man because he "chose" you. It's good to know, going into a relationship of mutuality, just what you can bring to it, what assets you can share.

EXERCISE 1:
CONTRIBUTING

STEP 1:   List what you can bring to love: a sense of humor, an even disposition, $300 a week. All sorts of things have value: a bedroom suite, a collection of compact discs, a VCR, a diploma in cooking, a backpack in good condition, a rich fantasy life. Write it all down.

STEP 2:   Next to each contribution, write ways you can make it more meaningful.

STEP 3:   Think about this list all week while you're doing other things, expanding and upgrading the kinds of contributions. And don't be afraid of giving too much. You know a relationship is not 50/50 all the time; sometimes it's 80/20 —with you giving 80 percent—and then again, it shifts the other way. There will be times when you are the passive beloved and give less, other times when you are the active lover and give more. The shifts don't matter. What is important is that you think in terms of carrying your own baggage—even with a man alongside.

EXERCISE 2:
TREAT MEN MORE LIKE WOMEN!

One of the most important early steps you can take in achieving mutualism is treating the men in your life more like women. Sound strange? Give it a minute to sink in. The truth is, men are rarely offered the straightforward, sisterly gestures of friendship we give spontaneously to other women. A few examples:

- Send a man flowers; any excuse will do. You'll knock his socks off!

- Ask a man out to a casual dinner; make the event part of your weekly routine, nothing special, just relaxed and easy.

- Ask a man you like to volunteer some time with you at the Humane Society.

- If you have an extra ticket to a subscription concert or lecture, ask a male friend to come with you.

- The next time you need a shoulder to lean on, go to a man you've been befriending, instead of running to the same tried-and-true female buddies. Give a man a chance!

- After a man helps you out, send him a thank-you note or gift. It doesn't have to be expensive, just "one from the heart" in sincere appreciation.

- Take a man out for a candlelit dinner. It's okay to woo a man, you know! In fact, being pursued is a favorite male fantasy; men are weary of chasing.

I'm sure you'll come up with many more ideas; do your best to make each one an honest effort to treat men as friends. And then, once you've begun to adjust your mindset, work on putting the dating game on the back burner for a while and looking at your social life in a new way.

EXERCISE 3:
I DARE YOU

I DARE YOU ... to plan your free time without leaving spaces for possible "dates."

I DARE YOU ... to regard Saturday night—that holy of holies—as merely one-seventh of the week.

I DARE YOU ... to plan the week ahead as a unit. Pencil in at least two nights a week at home to build bookshelves and pay bills and paint your toenails. And save a couple of nights for friends, maybe a night for work if you're involved in a big project.

I DARE YOU ... to call friends, male and female, and plan weekend brunches and suppers with the same equanimity as weeknight dinners.

I DARE YOU ... to invite your mother for Saturday night dinner (gasp). Make it just you two at the best restaurant you can afford. (Yes, you're going to reach for the check and insist on paying.) Or, cook at home. If you go out, I can see the two of you, dressed to the teeth and flaunting your companionship in front of the coupled geese who will envy your poise, your company, and most definitely your courage to be soaring eagles, unafraid to be different.

These challenges do not mean you stop seeing men. If anything, you'll see them more. But this does put a damper on mindless dating. Most important, it is the end of attitudes that blind you to the pleasures of the single life. It makes no sense for a woman who struggles for liberation during the week to shackle herself willingly to only "date"-related activities on the weekend. You need to consider your nonworking hours as usable in other ways. My hunch is that for some time now, you've felt more than a little silly while you were sitting and waiting for a man to remember your phone number and call. And when you stop to realize that that man usually means next to nothing to you, the waiting goes from being ridiculous to absurd.

Once you dare to see dating differently, a whole new world opens up:

- Time expands. Suddenly you realize that weekends have six segments: two mornings, two afternoons, and two evenings, all of them equally important and all yours to fill as you see fit. Each of these stands on its own—which means no Saturday afternoons spent getting ready for Saturday night, no "getting through" a Sunday morning because of a sour Saturday night. Every hour is at your disposal.

- The number of men increases. Care to read that again? It's true. Restricting your sights to the superficially eligible narrows the number of men in your life, while looking beyond romantic potential widens the field of possibilities. (And you know how I feel about that.) As you work on friendship with the other sex, you'll see new prospects come out of the woodwork. (Prospects for friendship, that is.) Married men, older men, younger men, less attractive types, friends of friends, former lovers, and former husbands (if you've been especially clever at handling the finale) will suddenly become emotionally available because you're sending out signals that you're approachable. And who knows? With your new openness and their new eligibility, something quite new could develop.

But that's not the object of the exercise: Your goal is to stretch your mind as an actor stretches himself for a new role. This will become a long-term philosophy. Once you insist on being friends first, you won't go back to the old guidelines.

THE DATING GAME

Okay, that's all fine, but what to do if you're already in a relationship? If that's the case, and you are unsure about continuing in it, ask yourself:

- When do you call him if he doesn't call you—after an hour, a day, a week?

- How many times can he not call or show up late and still find you willing to see him?

- Are you being too tolerant, too flexible, too forgiving? Too grateful for small favors?

- Do you feel diminished by his treatment of you?

• Are your needs being met in the relationship?

• As far as you can tell, are his?

I can't answer these; that is up to you. But if your heart skips even one small beat before answering any question, or if you come up with two or more "undecided" answers, you need to think about what's going on.

After all, you are a rather independent type these days, and if you're involved in a less-than-satisfactory romance, you can get out; you're not locked into anything by need. And with your new financial game plan, the next relationship will involve a woman (you) who will be able to:

• consider a man eligible even if he has a lesser income

• love for reasons that have nothing to do with funding or security

• liberate a man from a job that is all-consuming, enabling him to work in a field that might pay less but allow more time and energy for the rest of his life, you included (a perfect example of role-swapping for mutual benefit)

MALE BASHING: HOW TO RECOGNIZE IT AND AVOID IT

One day soon, in the middle of male-bashing with your friends, you're going to discover that you're not participating as enthusiastically as the rest. When that happens, pat yourself on the back and think of me. It was through these exercises of self-exploration that you strengthened yourself and became more able to give yourself fulfillment, a giant leap forward taking you away from man-dependency (one area where I sanction maximum distance). And as you move away from needing men as saviors, they look more and more like good guys—which most of them are. The resentment caused by your dependency diminishes, and you can see men as friends.

Your evolution is causing a shower of benefits, preeminent among them the whittling down of gratuitous anger toward men. Yes, I know. Men are pretty angry at us, too, for real—and unreal—reasons. But as we agreed before, you can change only yourself, because the call to change must come from inside. My sense is that men take their cue from women, and if we soften, they will follow. As long as you and I have worked to reach this point, let's remove *all* the stumbling blocks. Gratuitous anger is certainly a superblock.

Maybe a man ran out on you years ago, and you're still smarting. Or maybe you haven't recovered from being forced to stand by and watch a man being promoted to a career spot you deserved. Whatever its source, anger is nothing to ignore; like the hiccups, it keeps coming back until you confront and resolve it. But before we get to that, an overview.

FUSION FEMINISM

Gloria Steinem's softly curled tresses (noticed in a recent photograph) marked an important but largely unnoticed change from the determinedly rigid hairstyle that seemed so fitting for the leader of a revolution. Seeing the figurehead of feminism "out of uniform," fashionably dressed and obviously coiffed, made me do a double-take. Again and again, my head spun back to her image while my mind raced to the disillusioned letters I've been receiving from women who are discouraged and frustrated in their relationships with men. In a flash, the connection between her picture and their words jelled in my brain: In a visual message, the chief exponent of female equality was urging her flock forward to a more fulfilling phase of its upward climb—an appreciation of the female qualities that many women renounced when the fervor for "women's lib" was at its height.

Anyone familiar with history knows that the softened flourishes of womanhood have been powerful tools for women, winning them results that direct action could not. Manipulating the male through her wiles was a woman's game, and it usually achieved its ends. But when Friedan and Steinem offered women their own personhood as a direct route to potency, those flourishes were tossed aside. Our instinctive knack for compromise and cooperation, the diplomacy and tact we had transformed into art, were suddenly regarded as relics of the past and signs of weakness.

Well, it's time to reclaim those "soft" touches, as a progression toward a more complete expression of womanhood. We're second-generation feminists now; we don't have to spout our message at the drop of a hat. We've been *nouveaux riches* with our new wealth of power, squandering energies. And, like the newly arrived, our wasteful spending of anger has alienated potential friends in the male camp and made it nearly impossible to make new ones. Is this why we've come so far, to escalate hostilities between the sexes? I think not. It's time to be creative and discriminating when we assert ourselves.

The Fusion Feminist, the new breed of feminist I am proposing, will move forward with her selfhood well defined but with her womanliness undiminished. (Even, perhaps, with some irreverence blithely tossed into the mix.) This new kind of woman can practically assume that a man will understand her right to partnership. She is a primary person, defined by her own achievements and no longer dependent on a husband for status. She does not feel pressured to deliver her message of independence, because she *is* the message with her confident bearing and her strong sense of self. Her strong presence speaks louder than any words.

The Maenads, who tore Pentheus to bloody scraps and devoured him because he was male, still exist in some women, urging them to see all men as foes. But not the Fusion Feminist. She has not forgotten past oppression, but she has conquered irrationality because she knows it to be self-defeating. Male-bashing is not for her because she is too much of a humanist to condemn according to gender and too aware that oppressors, those who would return women to second-class status, exist in both camps.

When this expanded woman enters a coupled phase, she retains her sense of individuality but will mold that independence to suit both of the individuals involved, in the spirit of shared living. She can graciously suspend the sovereignty she has earned, certain she is not surrendering one drop of her identity in the process. Willing and able to lead, she can also assume the role of copilot when the situation calls for it.

She is able to disagree without being disagreeable. Because she voices her needs and insists on reciprocity at every step of the way, she does not hoard anger, which can lead only to overreaction. When she does take exception, her voice is modulated, steady, and firm. She knows that blatant confrontation alienates, so whenever possible she approaches in another way. And even when direct contradiction is indicated, her manner is less confrontational than purposeful because she is sure of her ground. She is a formidable opponent, eloquent in her own defense.

The Fusion Feminist is optimistic about sharing her life, since a loving man is for her the finishing touch. Now that she has brought into harmony the opposing factions within herself, she is better able to be his friend. Inner security makes her an amiable companion. She has built a life that is whole and fulfilling, and now she can turn to a man for the very best motives. She wants him for emotional fulfillment, and, recognizing his need for female groundedness, she extends her hand to him in authentic friendship. An expanded mixture of independence and classicism, the Fusion Feminist is too much of a person to do anything less.

To begin your journey toward genuine friendship with men:

EXERCISE 4:
ARE YOU ANGRY AT MEN?

Ask yourself the following questions, as the first part of a seek-and-destroy mission:

1. Do you find yourself using the cause of feminism or independence or equality or women's rights (or anything else, for that matter) as a cover-up for your resentment toward the male of the species?

2. Was your father reluctant to show you his love or approval?

3. Did your older brother leave you out of things? Did your folks show him preferential treatment because he was male?

4. Were you badly burned by a teenage crush?

5. Have men wanted you only as a sex object most of the time? Did they make you feel worthless in other roles?

6. Do men promise to phone and not deliver on their promise? Do they promise other things and not follow through?

7. Did your father hurt your mother in some important ways?

8. Did she complain to you about him and men in general?

9. Has a man abused you physically or emotionally?

10. Was your father an abusive man? An alcoholic?

11. Are you afraid in your heart of hearts that a nice man will reject you and so you reject all men first?

12. Are you overweight to keep men away and to be sure that you'll be left alone?

13. Did your mother have bad experiences with men when she was young?

14. Does your anger toward men scare you? Are you afraid that if released, you will drown in its torrent?

15. Do you think you are friendly toward men?

16. Do you want a good friendship with a man? Have you ever had one?

17. What can you learn from your answers here that will help you get closer to men?

18. Will you talk about these questions with your network group? Soon?

GETTING RID OF YOUR ANGER

Okay, let's assume you've asked yourself these questions and have discovered some residual anger. (Most women have at least a low-level amount.) Whether you think all men are insensitive brutes or whether your psyche is simply raw from a recent isolated incident, you would be wise to vent the anger soon. Pent-up resentment can only delay your agenda. These are times of liberation, brimming with opportunities to get to know the other gender as fellow humans. It helps to realize that men have their issues, too. It helps to know that men:

• are confused and tentative about what women really want.

• are fearful of offending us and setting off a time bomb.

• are, like us, often stuck in routine jobs with no fulfillment, but unlike women, can seldom opt to stay home and be a full-time parent.

• are not as linked to their feelings as women are, and so often don't really know how to proceed in their emotional lives.

- are reluctant to admit fears, insecurity, confusion as signs of weakness.

- have difficulty talking about their problems with other men.

- still feel burdened with 100 percent of the responsibilities—in marriage and relationships. Yes, despite everything that's happened in society, men still perceive themselves as Atlas holding up the world. A major part of being an effective woman is carrying your own weight. If you'd like to explore this subject further, I recommend Warren Farrell's *Why Men Are the Way They Are* (see Resources).

WHY YOU DON'T HAVE TO BE ANGRY AT MEN ANYMORE

You've begun to see that men don't have such a great deal, so maybe now is the time to start bending your swords into plowshares. You should let go of your anger because:

- You don't have the time or the energy.

- You have more important things to do.

- Some of your best friends are men.

- You work with men every day and see too many of their human facets to condemn them as a group.

- Seething doesn't do much for your blood pressure, and frowning doesn't exactly help wrinkles.

- You're getting your own life together, and anger only gets in the way.

- You see that some of the problems you've had with men in the past have been at least partially your responsibility.

• You realize that a bad attitude about men will keep
you from ever getting close to them.

In short, you really have too much going for you now
to let an undigested lump of ill-feeling stand between you
and progress. So get busy and . . .

TURN YOUR ANGER INTO POSITIVES

1. The next time you start to blame all men because one
of them doesn't call, think again. Settle down and think
the matter through. Then call him.

2. If you work mostly with women, get involved in a community project or church group where you'll meet some
men. They can be any age or stage. The purpose isn't
to get a date, but to get you in the same room with men
where you'll see their humanness.

3. The next time you find yourself at a gathering where
men are being ridiculed, speak up in their defense or
leave. The first choice is definitely better, but if you're
not feeling up to supporting the male of the species, at
least don't waste your energy in putting them down.

4. Look through your address book (and your heart) for
men you used to be involved with, people who used to
be special to you. Isn't at least one of them worth res-
urrecting as a friend? Getting things started again may
not be easy at first, but in the end former lovers can
make very good friends. Make an overture by sending a
funny card, or phone to say hello. Then test the waters
by asking him to dinner or lunch. Make it clear you
aren't trying to reignite a romance, simply reinstate a
friendship. One word of caution: Unless it's been a while,
don't call a man who suffered because you broke off
with him. Be sensitive to his healing process. It may be
too soon for him to be anything but a lover to you. It
takes time to move from love to friendship, and not every

man can make the shift. But it is crucial that you continue to grow in your knowledge of men, and that takes practice.

EXERCISE 5:
MAKING A FRIEND

STEP 1: Invite a male co-worker to lunch. No setting could be less romantic or threatening than a workday meal in broad daylight. Both of you will feel (and appreciate) the lack of sexual overtones and man-woman expectations. (*Tip:* Avoid sexist remarks, angry quips about male oppression, flirtatious actions.) Treat him like your sister—not to diminish his maleness, but to eliminate the defensiveness common in the "dating" frame of mind.

STEP 2: Talk about your biggest common interest—work—and build the friendliness from that point. If you pay attention, you'll learn a lot about your companion—and I don't mean office gossip. You'll hear clues to his slant on life, whether he likes women, whether he's an optimist or pessimist. (*Tip:* When you're with him, be part of the moment. Do your heavy analysis later alone in the tub, a better place to mentally replay the lunch.)

STEP 3: Sooner or later, the talk will turn to dating, women, and love. I guarantee you'll learn a lot about the male mind, even if this man is married. So make it a point to pay attention. Forget everything else for the moment and soak up one man's view of the social scene. It may change you forever.

STEP 4: Make this kind of invitation on a regular basis, to men you'd like to know better. Being the one to ask will feel awkward at first, but that only means you're moving out of your comfort zone—and growing.

STEP 5:   Somewhere along the way, you may find one man you like better than the others. He may not look like Tom Selleck, but there will be something about his sense of humor or the way he sees life that hits home. This is when the real challenge presents itself: to continue treating a man like your best buddy even when you care about him romantically. Ironically, pretending he's a *female* friend is the way to make sure he'll become your best *male* friend. If he gets promoted or has a birthday coming up, send him a card or telegram. Make it very clear that you are befriending, not pursuing. (If you're naturally a flirt, that means keeping the lid on more tightly than ever.) Yes, there is a chance this will lead to something more than platonic friendship, and you may be hoping it does, but your mission at this point is to keep in mind that anything more is strictly a plus and not the object of this exercise. I know that's a lot to ask, but there's a lot at stake here. So bear with me.

STEP 6:   In fact, even if this man does eventually become special in your heart, your goal is still ahead of you: Continue asking other men to casual events, "practice sessions" in your plan. The more often you are around men in low-stress settings, the sooner you'll be able to show grace under higher tension, as in romance. Naturally, some men you will like more than others, just as with women. But the main payoff is you'll no longer see the male as alien and the enemy. In fact, after you walk in their size-10s for a while, you'll probably feel greater compassion for the gender that is expected to always make the first moves. And you'll be more of a woman because you do. This exercise has the potential for triggering some pretty exciting growth on your part.

Your confidence in initiating will grow as you keep practicing. Prod yourself out of lethargy at group meetings, on your child's school committee, in your house of worship's committee, in your family clan. Naturally, you probably will not become a mover and shaker overnight (you are, after all, the product of long-term conditioning), but in time you *will* develop into a more effective woman. Be patient with yourself, but be careful not to accept too many excuses from yourself. Being tired or headachy can stop you once or twice, but the third time, your superego *must* play taskmaster and insist. Funny thing, after a while you'll relish being effective; you'll actually feel exhilarated making things happen!

Note: So many readers complain that romance is dead. I don't agree. It's not moribund, but simply overstressed from too many years of one-sidedness. And it's my sense that women are ready to breathe new life into the situation, ready to assume the responsibility that comes with being an equal in an enormously important relationship. The safety net you are weaving into your life as a single woman will prove to be the linchpin of your transition into that loving partnership. You'll see.

PARTNERSHIP IN LOVE

Like walking off a moving escalator, you won't miss a step as you leave singleness. If you spent this phase building self-reliance and self-acceptance, and if you keep in mind the principles you learned in this book (and live by them), you will make the transition to partnered living quite smoothly. Becoming half of a couple can be an extension of the lessons learned during this single phase—with one joyful addition: romantic love.

REASONS TO TAKE A PARTNER—FLIMSY AND SOLID

Of course, when love is in the picture, marriage could be in the wings. But whether or not you choose to take the next step, it's important to be clear about motives. There *are* flimsy reasons for becoming half of a couple, and they need to be exposed before going further.

The most common is to banish loneliness. Many people enter (and stay) in relationships primarily to avoid being alone. When that's the underlying motive, it's not possible to achieve the kind of emotional communion you're after, so you will ultimately feel alone in the relationship anyway. It's a sad irony, and if you think it's happening in your life, ask yourself why you don't want to be alone. Do you want to avoid knowing yourself? And if you're unhappy alone, consider whether you're able to nurture yourself. Maybe you're looking for someone to love you because you can't love yourself. The experience of aloneness is really a chance to establish a loving communion with ourselves. When you love and trust yourself, you can love and trust another person. Approached that way, being in your own company can be preparation for all kinds of relatedness.

More flimsy reasons:

2. To make the future secure.

3. To prove to yourself (and others) that you're desirable.

4. To gain life experience.

5. To fit into the social world.

6. To make yourself forget a loss or rejection.

7. To make others envious.

8. To feel okay about yourself.

9. To have a baby.

10. To please your family.

11. To win society's Seal of Approval.

12. To get the material possessions you crave.

13. To solve your problems.

14. To give your child a father.

15. To please your parents.

16. To show your parents your independence.

But let's not be negative. There *are* solid reasons, of course, for entering couplehood, and though they are fewer in number, their potency overshadows the negatives. Any one of them can support a lifetime love.

1. To share your dreams.
2. To demonstrate your love.
3. To make a sacred commitment to this man.
4. To show that you want him above all others.
5. To share the future.
6. To add a special kind of fulfillment to an already fulfilling life.

If we are indeed living through a relationship revolution, as Warren Farrell says (and I believe we are), then you as an unmarried woman are on its leading edge. Your chances for a successful love partnership are better than good because you have what it takes:

- You know who you are.

- You know what you need.

- You are building your own life.

- You live in the present moment.

- You look to yourself and your own goals as a reference point.

- You are striving for flexibility and compromise in your life.

- You respect yourself and you elicit respect.

As you build on these assets and the self-esteem they bring, it is almost inevitable that you will eventually form a loving relationship. (And remember, a "relationship," in the purest sense of that overused word, can take whatever form you both decide.) The key is to keep your eye on the ball and not become so involved with self-improvement that you forget to notice the people you meet along the way—which is, after all, one of the primary motivations behind your effort.

My brother long ago told me an incident that says it all. He was on the beach watching a group of women tanning and close enough to hear them talking about the men they hoped to attract with their healthy glow. Another man had also noticed them and approached, but they were deeply engrossed in the conversation and didn't immediately see him standing beside their blanket. When they did speak to him, it was to deliver an angry scolding about blocking their sunshine. The women were so wrapped up in getting what they wanted they lost sight of why they wanted it! I'm not suggesting that you are strengthening yourself to meet men—we've gone over all of that. But as you develop yourself, bear in mind that relationships (of all kinds) are the expression of that selfhood. It would be a hollow victory if after all your work to reach the living room you found there was room in it only for one. The whole spirit of the living room is to gather in it the warmth and love of many people.

LAST HURDLE
TO LOVE: FEAR

Conscious or not, fear can be a decisive barrier between you and successful loving. Of course, every fear has its own issue—rejection, intimacy, independence—but any one of them can reach proportions that eventually block the flow of trust so crucial to mutualism.

FEAR OF STRANGERS (MEN)

Most women, even wives and mothers of sons, know very little about the male mentality. I'll leave it to the sociologists to explore whether that is because men don't know themselves. (One of the oppressions men cite is being perpetual breadwinner, a role that leaves them little time for self-inquiry.) Could be. But whatever the cause, the best solution is practical education—in the form of befriending a wide variety of men. Once you get to know the male species on a more casual and real basis and the realization seeps into your psyche that men are not the *opposite* sex but simply the *other* one, this fear will slip away. Familiarity and fear cannot co-exist under the same roof.

FEAR OF REJECTION

There is no way to obliterate the hurt of loving-and-losing, except by living a life totally devoid of risk-taking—and how cramped and empty that would be!

There is a way to mitigate the pain, though: being scrupulous not to wrap your very being around your man. While there is a romance in progress, maintain your own friendships, your work, your interests. Holding fast to your wholeness in the heat of togetherness is the only way to avoid emotional meltdown if and when the relationship ends.

FEAR OF LOSING INDEPENDENCE

This is the Big Whopper of fears, because at its heart is the loss of selfhood, and as a woman you've fought hard for yours. In fact, we've been fighting for independence for so long that the merest possibility of that loss terrorizes us. And yet we want a man in our life! I read about this dilemma almost daily, in letters from women caught between wanting love and dreading its price.

"Can I love a man and keep my independence?" is the number-one dilemma of the postfeminist woman, because its conflict keeps her from a gratifying partnership with a man.

In an odd twist, we women are being enslaved by the

prize we've won. Independence is becoming a tyranny for women—and both sexes are suffering. Not knowing how to handle it, we've contorted its essence into a driving force that blocks us from getting what we want. So, rather than freeing us to experience the full range of human relationships, a corrupted form of independence is alienating some very choice specimens of the male species.

We bristle at his compliments, we bridle when he opens a door for us, we insist on having our own way and saying whatever we think (whenever we want)—all the time believing that we are expressing independence.

Nonsense. That sort of overreaction merely shows us to be newcomers in the world of whole people. Frankly, I never thought I'd be saying this; I'm as surprised as you are. But the movement that brought us ownership of our lives neglected to supply an owner's manual. Because I see signs of dangerous misuse of that selfhood, some guidelines are in order.

The point of women's liberation is to use our freedom masterfully, with subtlety and diplomacy, as one of the assortment of tools that get us what we want for ourselves. The trouble is, we have been squandering our hard-earned assertiveness, not realizing that judicious use increases its potency. You see, what we've been calling the hallmarks of independence are, in fact, pent-up aggression and resentment. The woman who sees and asserts her independence clearly is capable of friendship with her male counterpart because she is dealing from a position of equal strength. She doesn't hide from romantic love, because she knows that—without her consent—no one can take away what she has built into herself.

So, the answer to the big question is a resounding "yes." An independent woman can *indeed* have it all—love, romance, emotional interdependence. The precondition, however, is achieving true independence. Handled with grace and dignity, it serves love exquisitely well.

RECIPROCITY

Once you are involved with a man who values your identity, it is imperative that you insist on reciprocity in the relationship. Because unless you ask for it, you may ultimately find yourself swamped by his needs. And if you ignore the need to ask (because you are afraid of the confrontation), the omission will surely come back to haunt you. This advice goes to the essence, because it concerns women's need for personhood and the hold it has over us. (You might want to clip this section and reread it when you feel weak-kneed with love.) In a firm, gentle voice, speak your piece. He must recognize and try to fill your needs as you do his. Reciprocity is the password, and it opens the door to an intimacy where two people retain their individuality while at the same time are being joined emotionally, intellectually, spiritually, and ultimately physically.

Once you've made inroads on your fears, you've minimized the last major stumbling block to mutualism. The remaining task, of course, is the continuing challenge to remain whole. The following explanation may help.

LOVE AS CATALYST

Once we fall in love, we tend to think that it's the other person, our lover, who makes us feel complete, filling in the missing element of our emotional neediness. Unfortunately, the same thing is true when women are hungering for love. We tend to look for the man who makes us feel like a "real woman," totally fulfilled. Let's clear up this misconception right now. What actually happens in love is that the act of loving puts you in touch with your ability to love, and *that ability* is the missing part you've craved. By inspiring you to express love, your beloved connects you with the missing element of *you*. It isn't that he fills you up and makes you whole and you're all jagged edges without him. The man you love is a catalyst, not a missing piece. No person outside yourself can make you whole.

Remembering that, you won't be so quick to look to love (or a man) as your salvation. You'll build a life filled with other sources of satisfaction—friends, family, work, interests—and save yourself. And at the same time, in a mutual benefit, you'll be freeing some man from having to be all things to you.

EXERCISE 6:
HEALTHY BRAINWASHING

STEP 1: Set aside ten minutes a day to "brainwash" yourself (in a positive, natural way) about new beliefs.

STEP 2: Each day select one belief ("I am a capable woman" or "I am building a full life") and repeat it aloud or think it to yourself, over and over until it resonates in your mind.

STEP 3: Breathe slowly and form the words as you exhale. (Remember to keep your phone off the hook and close the windows. This is quiet time.) Eventually, you will be feeling the words in your body.

STEP 4: Repeat the phrases as you drift off to sleep, on your way to work, as you walk the supermarket aisles. (They're especially valuable when you're feeling blue.) Learn them as you would learn a language, and with repetition your thoughts will mimic the words and you will feel more self-assured, energized, and unburdened. People will notice these new attitudes; their reaction will reinforce your new behavior—and *they* may even be changed! You can begin a cycle of transformation while you are becoming . . .

- clearer about who you are and what you need

- readier to express your clearheadedness

- surer of the decisions you make

- more compatible with yourself and others

- less self-conscious about being unmarried

- less timid about taking the initiative

- less anxious about the future

- more content with your life

- more honest with men

- better able to be a friend

During this metamorphosis, while you are assimilating these changes (and growing comfortable with them), I suggest you avoid making a major love commitment. Now, while you are growing into wholeness, is the time to be looking around at relationships of all kinds for examples of working mutualism. Make your romantic goal an equal partnership with a man, with mutual dependence and reciprocal responsibility.

WALKING SINGLE FILE

Single or not, each of us walks single file through life's landscape, because each of us carries a single part of ourselves, our own individuality, separate and apart from the human crowd. From time to time, we will walk two by two, when someone we like comes near to walk alongside. Drawn by love's force, this person may stay with us a lifetime or not.

Lifelong partnership in a world so full of options and random events is rare, and so most women, even in a long marriage, will again walk single file as survivor. Divorce and widowhood are practically scripted into the female experience. And even without wifehood, a woman can still experience loving relatedness with several men and yet have more uncoupled phases within her lifetime.

More and more of us are electing to postpone or bypass the marriage decision, not as a choice made early in life but more often as a result of circumstances that simply occur and evolve into lifelong singleness. New to the world of equality, we are focusing heavily on achievement and are on the vanguard of a future where women are primary people from birth, achievers and creators in their own right, less and less dependent on a husband for status.

Dread disease has jockeyed us into a new dynamic with men and forced upon us the wisdom of putting friendship before sex. The possibility of death from the AIDS virus has made impulsive intimacy an outdated option. Holding hands can feel more intimate than casual sex ever did; our generation of women is richer for achieving this sophistication.

Relating to men in friendship is enabling us to realize that a true friend would not ask us to surrender selfhood in the name of love. A man who really regards us as a person rather than a sex object will actually invite our individuality to bloom—and that is the new criterion that is beginning to replace the chemical reaction we exalted for so long. Physical attraction as a guide to a soulmate has been a disappointment. So now, stronger in our independence and surer of our womanly potency, we are tuning in to the enormous payoff of a love partnership based on mutual enrichment.

The metamorphosis we women have engendered is bringing both sexes, happily, toward reciprocal spiritual development. There is always room in our lives for that sort of love from a man, because we can trust it to enhance our own self-development, even as we tend to our partner's nurturance.

In your odyssey, marriage may come (and go) or it may not appear. Whether it does is up to you for the most part, because the flexibility and compromise needed to make the choice are steadily coming under your mastery. The things you discover about yourself through the exercises in this book will help you make that choice with more assurance. But marry or not, relating to men sometimes as friend/lover, sometimes as platonic buddy, will most assuredly be among your future challenges. And so you will at different times in your lifespan be asked to juggle your individuality with shared togetherness—not an easy task. But again, incorporating the principles in this book into your way of living, and making them habitual through practice, will over time see you embody them and grow into your own hero. You will become your own guide.

Now that you are out of the waiting room, chances are you will not return. There is abundant space in your life for a man who will enrich you in your expanded way of life. But never become distanced from your single core.

The uniqueness that is yours alone can be a lifelong ally throughout all of life's seasons. A life lived true to that selfhood will be constantly unfolding and expanding. And while you are moving into that larger self, challenge yourself to remain eager about life and firmly connected to your spirituality. Lived that way, life will have few boundaries: Work and relationships will be natural outgrowths of a daily communion with your inner and outer worlds. That integration will better you and every person you meet along your journey, whether you are traveling as part of a couple or single file. I wish it for all of us.

> *Who has not found the heavens below*
> *Will fail of it above.*
> *God's residence is next to mine,*
> *His furniture is love.*

—EMILY DICKENSON

EPILOGUE

It is quite unusual for the son of an author to write the epilogue for a book, especially this kind of a book, but when that author (my mother) and I were talking recently, it became clear that I was in a unique position to offer comments, and that my epilogue might be a good way to cap this work. I've known her as mother and columnist, as single woman, single parent, and as friend, and I've seen the many stages that led to the completion of this book.

From my close vantage point I see how she has lived this material before setting it down in print, how she has brought herself from feelings of helplessness and self-pity to the pride and self-affirmation that come from an inspired creative process. I've watched her grow as a person and as a parent, taking control of her life and developing self-determination while building a marriage. All of this enables her to be a much better mother, and our relationship has strengthened. I can affirm the value of the ideas embodied in this book because I've seen them put to the test and provide sure guidance to a life.

But more than express admiration and appreciation for my mother's determination and faith in herself, and for the practical value of these exercises, I want to share some of my perceptions of the chapters you have read.

Essentially, this is a book of empowerment. At every step the goal has been to offer those ideas and techniques that can bring greater understanding and self-fulfillment, so that single women in transition can take advantage of their singleness and exert greater control over their lives—with growing confidence in the fullness of their inner resources.

This book can be a valuable catalyst and support system, pointing the way toward a more satisfying life. I know better than anyone else that it was written with the conviction that each one of us can fulfill our dreams and our unique potential, as I know that my mother is striving to fulfill hers.

SCOTT DEITZ
San Francisco

THE DECLARATION OF UNDEPENDENCE

More than seventy million strong, let the unmarried community resolve to affirm the undependent life.

I RESOLVE to think for myself in all situations rather than allow an "expert" to decide the course of my life. While I will remain open to wise counsel, I alone will make the final decision in all matters that affect me. I will make myself heard when there are shared decisions to be made.

I RESOLVE to remain aware of my identity and my wholeness at all times, particularly when in a coupled relationship. I will exercise my need for personal space without impinging on that of others.

I RESOLVE to be a loving friend and to nurture worthwhile friendships, realizing that self-sufficiency is in no way the same as isolation. I will cultivate relationships with all generations and people from every conceivable background—provided they derive the same benefit as I from the friendship.

I RESOLVE to become acquainted with the other gender burdened with a minimum of bias, aware that they are neither alien nor enemy. I will focus on the similarities we share and strive to develop real closeness with them, aimed at establishing authentic intimacy that goes beyond mere sexual sharing.

I RESOLVE to plan my own life for myself insofar as possible: career goals, family future, personal growth.

I RESOLVE to make my single status only an incidental fact. I will remember that above everything else I am a distinct and unique individual who merely happens to be without a mate at this moment. I will also remember that there are times when being single is an advantage and others when it is not. Yet when I consider myself in the big picture, marital status will not be a major consideration. Involvement will.

I RESOLVE to go with occasional loneliness, being cautious not to flee from it nor wallow in it or make impulsive decisions in the midst of it. I will bear in mind that every one of us, married and single, feels momentary twinges of loneliness; it may well be an inevitable dimension of being human. But I will note the difference between aloneness and loneliness, and not confuse the two. Most importantly, I will appreciate the fact that my own company can at times be the best.

I RESOLVE to maximize the possibilities for growth and freedom within my single status. I will make it a point to keep my eye riveted on the positive aspects of singleness.

—Susan Deitz

RESOURCES

CHAPTER ONE

> **TIP**
>
> These Resources are designed to help you delve further into subjects that pique your curiosity. Enjoy.

CELEBRATE YOUR SINGLENESS:

- Eric Berne, *What Do You Say After You Say Hello?* (New York: Harper & Row, 1985).
- Dr. Esther Harding, *The Way of All Women* (New York: Harper & Row, 1975).
- Jean S. Bolen, *The Goddesses in Every Woman* (New York: Harper & Row, 1985).

— M. Scott Peck, *The Road Less Traveled* (New York: Simon & Schuster, 1978).
— Carl Rogers, *On Becoming a Person* (Boston: Houghton Mifflin, 1961).

TRAVEL RESOURCES:

For a free catalog of travel books that will help you plan a vacation:
> Forsyth Travel Library
> P.O. Box 2975
> Shawnee Mission, KS 66201
> (800) FORSYTH

Other Recommendations:
Paul Grimes, *The New York Times Practical Traveler* (New York: Times Books, 1985).
Rosalind Massow, *Travel Easy—The Practical Guide for People Over 50* (Glenview, IL: Scott, Foresman, 1985).

To Find a Travel Partner:
> Partners-in-Travel
> P.O. Box 491145
> Los Angeles, CA 90049
> (213) 476-4889
> Six-month membership: $20

> Singleworld
> (800) 223-6490 or (212) 758-2433

> Travel Companion Exchange
> P.O. Box 833
> Amityville, NY 11701
> Att.: Jens Jurgen
> (516) 454-0880, 0674

> World Travel Club
> Colpitt's Travel Center
> Westgate Mall
> Brockton, MA 02401
> (800) GO-TOURS or (617) 588-5600

For Educational Travel Worldwide:
  Elderhostel
  80 Boylston Street, Suite 400
  Boston, MA 02116
  (617) 426-7788 or 426-8056 for registration on their thousand-school network

Personal Endowment:
Heilbrun, *Reinventing Womanhood* (New York: W. W. Norton, 1979).
Mildred Newman and Bernard Berkowitz, *Be Your Own Best Friend* (New York: Random House, 1973).
Penelope Russianoff, Ph.D., *Why Do I Think I'm Nothing Without a Man?* (New York: Bantam, 1983).

GENERAL RESOURCES:

  Consumer Information Center-C
  P.O. Box 100
  Pueblo, CO 81002
  Write for free consumer information catalog of government publications, including "Plain Talk About Mutual Health Groups," "The Mortgage Money Guide," "Tips for an Energy-Efficient Apartment," "Buying and Borrowing: Cash in on the Facts," "What Every Investor Should Know," "Financial Management: How to Make a Go of Your Business," "Where to Write for Vital Records," "The Job Outlook in Brief," "Higher Education Opportunities for Minorities and Women," and "A Woman's Guide to Social Security." Many titles are free; others cost from 50 cents to $4.
Encyclopedia of Associations, a library reference book listing thousands of associations.
Dr. David Viscott, *Risking* (New York: Simon & Schuster, 1977).

Time-Management Books:
— Alan Lakein, *How to Get Control of Your Time and Your Life* (New York: McKay, 1974).
Alec Mackenzie and Kay Cronkite Waldo, *About Time! A Woman's Guide to Time Management* (New York: McGraw-Hill, 1981).
— Stephanie Winston, *Getting Organized* (New York: W. W. Norton, 1978).

Stephanie Winston, *The Organized Executive* (New York: W. W. Norton, 1983).

Time-Management:
"Working Smarter," 60-minute audiocassette by Michael LeBoeuf, Nightingale-Conant Corp., 3730 West Devon Avenue, Chicago, Illinois 60659

National Association of Professional Organizers. Has listings of one hundred time-management and organization consultants. For the name of a member in your area, send a stamped, self-addressed envelope to:
NAPO
5350 Wilshire Boulevard
P.O. Box 36EO2
Los Angeles, CA 90036

Other Books:
Susan Crain Bakos, *This Wasn't Supposed to Happen* (New York: Continuum, 1985).
Rebecca E. Greer, *Why Isn't a Girl Like You Married?* (New York: Macmillan, 1969).
— Ari Kiev, M.D., *A Strategy for Daily Living* (New York: Free Press, 1973).
Sheldon Kopp, *If You Meet Buddha on the Road, Kill Him* (New York: Bantam, 1973).
Jane Baker Miller, M.D., *Toward a New Psychology of Women* (New York: Beacon Press, 1986).
William Novak, *The Great American Man Shortage* (New York: Rawson Associates, 1983).
Carl Rogers, Ph.D., *Carl Rogers on Personal Power* (New York: Delacorte Press, 1976).
— Dorothy Sarnoff, *Make the Most of Your Best* (New York: H. Holt & Co., 1983).

Also:
The Rights of Single People
Order this handbook from:
Literary Department
American Civil Liberties Union
132 West 43rd Street
New York, NY 10036

CHAPTER TWO

FINANCIAL PLANNING:

Annette Lieberman and Vicki Lindner, *Unbalanced Accounts: Why Women Are Still Afraid of Money* (New York: Atlantic Monthly Press, 1987).

Perkins and Rhoades, *The Women's Financial Survival Handbook* (New York: New American Library, 1980).

National Association of Investors Corporation
1515 East Eleven Mile Road
Royal Oak, MI 48067
Investment education for individuals and clubs.

SINGLE MOTHERHOOD:

Los Angeles County Department of Children's Services,
  Adoption Division
2550 West Olympic Boulevard
Los Angeles, CA 90006
Att.: Community Affairs
(213) 738-4577
Ask for free brochure, "Single Parent Adoption."

New York Council on Adoptable Children
666 Broadway
New York, NY 10012
Att.: Christine Jacobs
(212) 475-0222
Information on adoption and contacts for specifics on state adoption laws.

Parents Without Partners
8807 Colesville Road
Silver Spring, MD 20910
(800) 638-8078

Single Mothers by Choice
P.O. Box 1642
Gracie Square Station
New York, NY 10028
(212) 988-0993

Ask for free brochure and ordering information for back issues of newsletter; they'll put you in touch with members in your area and also with artificial insemination/donor insemination sources.

HOUSING:

National Shared Housing Resource Center
6344 Greene Street
Philadelphia, PA 19144
(215) 848-1220

Jack Cummings, *Successful Real Estate Investing for the Single Person* (Chicago: Playboy Press, 1980).
Ruth Reginis, *Her Home: A Woman's Guide to Buying Real Estate* (New York: Anchor Press/Doubleday, 1980).

NETWORKING:

Jessica Lipnack and Jeffrey Stamps, *Networking, the First Report and Directory* (New York: Doubleday, 1982).
Jessica Lipnack and Jeffrey Stamps, *The Networking Book* (New York: Rutledge & Kegan Paul, 1986).
Mary Scott Welch, *Networking: The Great New Way for Women to Get Ahead* (New York: Harcourt, Brace, Jovanovich, 1980).

CAREER:

Richard N. Bolles, *Three Boxes of Life* (Berkeley, CA: Ten Speed Press, 1978).
Richard N. Bolles, *What Color Is Your Parachute?* (Berkeley, CA: Ten Speed Press, 1979).
David Campbell, Ph.D., *If You Don't Know Where You're Going, You'll Probably End Up Somewhere Else* (Valencia, CA: Tabor Publishing, 1974).
Order from:
National Computer Systems, Inc.
4401 West 76th Street
Minneapolis, MN 55435

Directory of Occupational Titles
(Washington, D.C.: U.S. Government Printing Office)

Lists over 20,000 job descriptions, also found in libraries and counseling offices.

Susan Schenkel, Ph.D., *Giving Away Success* (New York: McGraw-Hill, 1984).

Occupational Outlook Handbook
(Washington, D.C.: U. S. Government Printing Office)
Major source of vocational information and employment opportunity trends, also found in libraries and counseling offices.

Also:
American Women's Economic Development Corp.
60 East 42nd Street
New York, NY 10165
In New York state: (800) 422-AWED
Out-of-state: (800) 222-AWED
Write for free brochure or call for telephone counseling appointments.

CHAPTER THREE

FAMILY INFORMATION:

P. William Filby, *American and British Genealogy and Heraldry, Third Edition* (New England Historical Society, 1983).
To order, write:
101 Newbury Street
Boston, MA 02116
William P. Fletcher, *Recording Your Family History* (New York: Dodd, Mead, 1986).

The National Genealogical Society—Education Division
4527 North Seventeenth Street
Arlington, VA 22207-2363
(703) 525-0050
Inquire about home study course.

NOVELS ABOUT SEVERAL GENERATIONS OF A FAMILY:

Colleen McCullough, *The Thornbirds* (New York: Harper & Row, 1977).
Howard Fast, *The Immigrants* (New York: Houghton Mifflin, 1958).
Boris Pasternak, *Doctor Zhivago* (New York: Pantheon Books, 1958).
Taylor Caldwell, *Answer as a Man* (New York: Aeonian Press, 1984).

MEDITATION:

Mary Ellen Penny Baker, *Meditation: A Step Beyond Edgar Cayce* (New York: Doubleday, 1973).
Herbert Benson, M.D., and Miriam Z. Klipper, *The Relaxation Response* (New York: Avon, 1976).
Patricia Carrington, *Freedom in Meditation* (New York: Anchor Press/Doubleday, 1978).
Simon Court, *A Meditator's Manual* (Northants, England: Aquarian Press, 1985).
J. Krishnamurti (Mary Lutyens, ed.), *The Only Revolution* (London: Gollanz, 1972).
Eric Lerner, *Journey of Insight Meditation* (New York: Schocken Books, 1972).
Anthony Starr, *Solitude: A Return to the Self* (New York: Free Press, 1988).

CHAPTER FOUR

LEARNING TO SAY NO:

Herbert Festerheim and Jean Baer, *Don't Say Yes When You Want to Say No* (New York: Dell Publishing, 1975).
Manual J. Smith, *When I Say No I Feel Guilty* (New York: Bantam, 1985).

FOOD:

Consumer Cooperative Center of Truman College
1145 West Wilson Avenue
Chicago, IL 60640
Ask for free publication, "How to Form a Food Cooperative."

Center for Science in the Public Interest
1501 16th Street, N.W.
Washington, D.C. 20036
(202) 332-9110
Ask for free list of publications and posters, and about membership in their organization, Americans for Safe Food.

Kim Chernin, *The Obsession: Reflections on the Tyranny of Slenderness* (New York: Harper & Row, 1981).

Adele Davis, *Let's Eat Right to Keep Right* (New York: Harcourt, Brace, 1954).

Adele Davis, *Let's Eat Well* (New York: Harcourt, Brace, 1965).

Adele Davis, *Let's Stay Healthy* (New York: Harcourt, Brace, 1981).

Tony Vellela, *Food Corps for Small Groups* (New York: Workman Publishing, 1980).

ASSERTIVENESS:

Jean Baer, *How to Be an Assertive Woman* (New York: Signet, 1976).

L. Bloom, K. Coburn, and J. Pearlman, *The New Assertive Woman* (New York: Delacorte Press, 1976).

Merna Galassi and John Galassi, *Assert Yourself: How to Be Your Own Person* (New York: Human Sciences Press, 1977).

Stanley Phelps and Nancy Austin, *The Assertive Woman* (San Luis Obispo, CA: Impact Publishers, 1975).

Byrna Taubman, *How to Become an Assertive Woman* (New York: Pocket Books, 1976).

ORGANIZATIONS:

Center for Science in the Public Interest
1501 Sixteenth Street, N.W.
Washington, D.C. 20036
(202) 332-9110
A nonprofit consumer-oriented nutritional organization
seeking to improve the public's health.

CHAPTER FIVE

— David D. Burns, *Intimate Connections* (New York: Morrow, 1985).

Leo Buscaglia, any and all books.

DeRosis and Pellegrini, *The Book of Hope: How Women Can Cure Depression* (New York: Macmillan, 1976).

Max Ehrmann, *Desiderata* (Boston: Bruce Humphries Publishing Co., 1948).

Ari Kiev, M.D., *A Strategy for Daily Living* (New York: Free Press, 1973).

Jean Baker Miller, M.D., *Toward a New Psychology of Women* (Boston: Beacon Press, 1973).

M. Scott Peck, M.D., *People of the Lie* (New York: Simon & Schuster, 1983).

Maggie Scarf, *Unfinished Business* (New York: Doubleday, 1980).

— Robert Harold Schuller, *The Be (Happy) Attitudes* (Waco, TX: Word Books, 1985).

Dr. Bernard Siegel, *Love, Medicine and Miracles* (New York: Harper & Row, 1986).

Ira J. Tanner, *Loneliness: The Fear of Love* (New York: Harper & Row, 1973).

Philip Zimbardo, *The Shy Child* (New York: Doubleday, 1981).

Philip Zimbardo, *Shyness* (New York: Addison-Wesley, 1977).

CHAPTER SIX

FOR YOUR INVESTMENT CLUB:

American Association of Individual Investors
625 North Michigan Avenue
Chicago, IL 60611
(312) 280-0170

An independent, nonprofit corporation to help people become effective managers of their own assets.

National Association of Investors Corp.
1515 East Eleven Mile Road
Royal Oak, MI 48067

For small investors—investment education for individuals and investment clubs.

BUDGETING:

Mary Bowen Hall, *More for Your Money* (Boston, MA: Houghton Mifflin, 1981).

NEGOTIATING:

G. I. Nierenberg, *The Art of Negotiating* (New York: Simon & Schuster, 1968).

John Wright, *American Almanac of Jobs and Salaries* (New York: Avon Books, 1982).

FOR INFORMATION ON GROWTH MUTUAL FUNDS:

Investment Company Institute
1600 M Street, N.W., Suite 600
Washington, D.C. 20036
Write for a free list.

MONEY BOOKS:

Sylvia Aurbach, *A Woman's Guide to Money: A Guide to Financial Independence* (New York: Dolphin/Doubleday, 1976).

Helen Breuning, *Nest Egg Investing: How to Build a Secure Financial Foundation* (Homewood, IL: Dow Jones/Irwin, 1986).

Judith Briles, *Money Phases: The Six Financial Stages of a Woman's Life* (New York: Simon & Schuster, 1984).

Judith Briles, *The Woman's Guide to Financial Savvy* (New York: St. Martin's Press, 1981).

Carol Colman, *Love and Money: What Your Finances Say About Your Personal Relationships* (New York: Coward, McCann and Geoghegan, 1983).

Annette Lieberman and Vicki Lindner, *Unbalanced Accounts: Why Women Are Still Afraid of Money* (New York: Atlantic Monthly Press, 1987).

Paula Nelson, *Paula Nelson's Guide to Getting Rich* (New York: G. P. Putnam's Sons, 1985).

Carole Phillips, *The New Money Workbook for Women* (Andover, MA: Brickhouse, 1987).
Available by writing:
Women's Financial Center
340 South 16th Street
Philadelphia, PA 19102

Also:
American Association of Retired Persons (AARP) has a free kit called Money Matters. Write for it:
AARP
1909 K Street, N.W.
Washington, D.C. 20049
(202) 728-4370

IF YOU'RE CONSIDERING DIVORCE/SEPARATION:

Alan Zipp, *Handbook of Tax and Financial Planning for Divorce and Separation* (Englewood Cliffs, NJ: Prentice-Hall, 1985).

FOR SINGLE PARENTS:

Darcie Bundy, *The Affordable Baby* (New York: Harper & Row, 1985).

Consumer Financial Institute, a financial-planning service in Massachusetts, has worked out a computer-generated savings program for parents.
51 Sawyer Road
Waltham, MA 02154
(617) 899-6500

FOR THE JOB SEARCH:

Richard Bolles, *What Color Is Your Parachute?* (Berkeley, CA: Ten-Speed Press, 1979). See page 143 (p. 105 in 1977 edition) for budget help, and the section on "Putting a Pricetag on Your Lifestyle."

MAGAZINE:

Financial Planning
Nielsen Clearing House
P.O. Box 2911
Clinton, IA 52735-22911

ASSOCIATIONS:

Financial Planners:

Financial Planner (for lower-priced financial planning)
700 Brisbane Building
403 Main Street
Buffalo, NY 14203
(716) 842-6860
They offer low yearly rates for consumers or small businesses.

Institute of Certified Financial Planners
3443 South Galena, Suite 190
Denver, CO 80231

International Association for Financial Planning (IAFP)
Two Concourse Parkway
Suite 800
Atlanta, GA 30328
(404) 395-1605
This is the oldest and largest organization representing financial planners (24,000 members, 128 chapters). Write for free brochures, "Building a Capital Base," "Consumer Guide to Financial Independence," and "Financial Planning Consumer Bill of Rights." They also offer a directory and referral system. Contact them to receive the names of qualified financial planners in your area.

The Registry of Financial Planning Practitioners
(same address as above for IAFP)
This organization is the standard-setting program for the financial planning industry, setting even more rigorous standards for membership than IAFP. Write for their directory—a state-by-state listing of all individuals who have met these standards and have been admitted to this program. Available to consumers at $2.50 for postage and handling.

For Self-Study:

College of Financial Planning
9725 E. Hampden Avenue
Denver, CO 80231
(303) 755-7101
Self-study via mail, or study at an affiliated school nearby.
When graduated, you receive a CFP degree.

Consumer Videos:

"Planning Your Financial Future"
($39.95 plus $3 shipping and handling)
To order, call the Foundation for Financial Planning,
(800) 241-2148.

CHAPTER SEVEN

CAREER:

Richard Bolles, *What Color Is Your Parachute?* (Berkeley, CA: Ten Speed Press, 1979).

David Campbell, Ph.D., *If You Don't Know Where You're Going, You'll Probably End Up Somewhere Else* (Valencia, CA: Tabor Publishing, 1974).
Available from:
National Computer Systems, Inc.
4401 West 76th Street
Minneapolis, MN 55435

Catalyst Staff, *What to Do With the Rest of Your Life: A Career Guide* (New York: Simon & Schuster, 1980).

Directory of Occupational Titles, a listing of over 20,000 job descriptions (Washington, D.C.: U.S. Government Printing Office).

Don Dillon, *Toward Matching Personal and Job Characteristics* (Occupational Outlook Quarterly, Vol. 19, No. 1, Spring 1975, pp. 3–18); see also U.S. Government Printing Office, Washington, D.C., for reprints.

Betty Lehan Harragan, *Games Mother Never Taught You: Corporate Gamesmanship for Women* (New York: Warner Books, 1977).

Margaret Hennig and Anne Jardim, *Managerial Woman* (New York: Doubleday/Anchor Press, 1977).

Richard K. Irish, *Go Hire Yourself an Employer* (New York: Doubleday, 1973).

Jobs for Which Apprenticeships Are Available
   Available from U.S. Department of Labor
   Bureau of Labor Statistics
   1515 Broadway, Suite 3400
   New York, NY 10036

Marilyn Moats Kennedy, *Office Warfare: Strategies in Getting Ahead in the Aggressive 80's* (New York: Macmillan, 1985).

Ted Engstrom and Alec MacKenzie, *Managing Your Time*, revised edition (New York: Zondervan, 1988).

Richard Lathrop, *Who's Hiring Who?* (Berkeley, CA: Ten Speed Press, 1977).

Occupational Outlook Handbook (Washington, D.C.: U.S. Government Printing Office).

Anthony Medley, *Sweaty Palms: The Neglected Art of Being Interviewed* (New York: Van Nostrand Reinhold, 1978).

ASSOCIATIONS:

   American Women's Economic Development Corporation
   60 East 42nd Street
   New York, NY 10165
   In New York state: (800) 442-AWED
   Out-of-state: (800) 222-AWED

The group encourages women to develop new businesses by offering technical assistance and information. Write for a brochure of general information. Call hotline numbers (above) for advice and guidance and bank referrals. There is a $10 charge for a five- to ten-minute call (pay by credit card or check), and a $35 charge for a lengthy conversation (one hour or more).

   Displaced Homemakers Network
   1010 Vermont Avenue, N.W., Suite 817
   Washington, D.C. 20005
   (202) 628-6767

CHILDREN:

Books:

Jane Adams, *Sex and the Single Parent* (New York: Coward, McCann, Geoghegan, 1978).

Carol Vejvoda Murdock, *Single Parents Are People Too! How to Achieve a Positive Self-Image and Personal Satisfaction* (New York: Butterick Publishing, 1980).

Susan Robinson, M.D., and H. Pizer, *Having a Baby Without a Man* (New York: Simon & Schuster, 1985).

Judith Wallerstein and Joan Berlin Kelly, *Surviving the Breakup: How Children and Parents Cope With Divorce* (New York: Basic Books, 1980).

Robert S. Weiss, *Going it Alone: The Family Life and Social Situation of the Single Parent* (New York: Basic Books, 1979).

Associations:

Family Resource Coalition
2300 Green Bay Road
Evanston, IL 60201
(312) 869-1500

Los Angeles County Department of Children's Services,
    Adoption Division
2550 West Olympic Boulevard
Los Angeles, CA 90006
Att.: Community Affairs
(213) 738-4577
Write for free brochure, "Single Parent Adoption."

"Network," the Paper for Parents (newsletter)
The National for Citizens in Education
410 East Wilde Lake Village Green
Columbia, MD 21044
(800) NETWORK

New York Council on Adoptable Children
666 Broadway
New York, NY 10012

Att.: Christine Jacobs
(212) 475-0222 (for general information)
Write for information on laws (which vary state-by-state) and
contacts in your area.

Parents Without Partners
8807 Colesville Road
Silver Spring, MD 20910
(301) 588-9354 or (800) 638-8078

Single Parent Resource Center
1164 Broadway
New York, NY 10001
Suzanne Jones, Director
(212) 213-0047
Will help establish single-parent support groups.

COMMUNITY:

Books:

Susan Ellis and Katherine H. Noyes, *By the People* (Philadelphia,
    PA: Energize Publishing, 1981).
Wendy Kaminer, *Women Volunteering* (New York: Doubleday, 1984).

Associations:

Big Sisters of America
230 North 13th Street
Philadelphia, PA 19107
(215) 567-7900 or (800) 852-5000

Girl Scouts of America
335 chapters. Contact the local Girl Scout Council in your
area.

United Way. Its 2,300 local chapters act as clearinghouses for
volunteer projects. Each chapter is a "volunteer action center."
Contact your local United Way. See phone book for local listing.

Consult your local phone book's white pages for the Voluntary Action Center in your town. There are 343 across the country;
each one can connect you to the cause you want to help.

CHAPTER EIGHT

FOR INFORMATION ABOUT AIDS AND OTHER STDS:

AIDS hotline:
(800) 342-2437 for four-minute toll-free recorded message. Then, if you have any questions, call for live answers 24 hours a day: (800) 342-7514

Write for Surgeon General's Report on AIDS (free):
AIDS
Box 14252
Washington, D.C. 20044
(202) 245-6867

Herpes Resource Center
For $20 a year, you support herpes research and receive a quarterly newsletter:
HRC
Box 100
Palo Alto, CA 94302
(415) 328-7710

National Sexually Transmitted Disease hotline:
(800) 227-8922
In California: (800) 982-5883

Sex Information Education Council of the U.S. (SIECUS)
80 Fifth Avenue, Suite 801
New York, NY 10011
(212) 929-2300

VD national newsletter: "Hotline" (quarterly) published by:
American Social Health Association
260 Sheridan Avenue
Palo Alto, CA 94306
(415) 327-6465

Brochures:

Leaflets coproduced by the Public Health Service and the American Red Cross:

"AIDS and Children—Information for Parents of School-Age
   Children"
"AIDS and Children—Information for Teachers and School
   Officials"
"AIDS and Your Job—Are There Risks?"
"AIDS, Sex, and You"
"Caring for the AIDS Patient at Home"
"Facts About AIDS and Drug Abuse"
"Gay and Bisexual Men and AIDS"
"If Your Test for Antibody to the AIDS Virus Is Positive . . ."

Order free copies of these brochures from:
   InterAmerica Research
   1200 E. North Henry Street
   Alexandria, VA 22314
   Att.: Clint Jones

   National AIDS Network
   729 8th Street, S.E., Suite 300
   Washington, D.C. 20003
   (202) 546-2424

   National Association of People With AIDS
   P.O. Box 65472
   Washington, D.C. 20035
   (202) 483-7979

   The Women's Health Research Foundation
   700 Arizona
   Santa Monica, CA 90401
   (213) 459-6567

Books:

Eric Berne, *Sex in Human Loving* (New York: Simon & Schuster,
   1970).
Boston Women's Health Book Collective, *The New Our Bodies, Our-
   selves* (New York: Simon & Schuster, 1984).
Rudolph Brasch, *How Did Sex Begin?* (New York: D. McKay and
   Co., 1973).

Carol Cassell, Ph.D., *Swept Away: Why Women Confuse Love and Sex . . . and How They Can Have Both* (New York: Bantam, 1985).

David Viscott, *Risking* (New York: Simon & Schuster, 1977).

John Langone, *AIDS: The Facts* (New York: Little, Brown & Co., 1988).

Dagmar O'Connor, *How to Make Love to the Same Person For the Rest of Your Life* (New York: Doubleday, 1985).

Dr. Marie Robinson, *The Power of Sexual Surrender* (New York: Doubleday, 1959).

George Whitmore, *Someone Was Here* (New York: New American Library, 1988).

CHAPTER NINE

Anthony Astrachan, *How Men Feel* (New York: Anchor Press/Doubleday, 1986).

Frances Baumli, ed., *Men Freeing Men* (Jersey City, NJ: New Atlantis Press, 1985).

Dr. Nathaniel Brandon, *The Psychology of Romantic Love* (New York: Bantam, 1981).

Wayne Dyer, *Your Erroneous Zones* (New York: Funk & Wagnalls, 1976).

Warren Farrell, Ph.D., *Why Men Are the Way They Are* (New York: McGraw-Hill, 1986).

Eric Fromm, *The Art of Loving* (New York: Harper & Row, 1956).

Eric Fromm, *The Heart of Man* (New York: Harper & Row, 1980).

Kahlil Gibran, *The Prophet* (New York: Knopf, 1923).

Harville Hendrix, Ph.D., *Getting the Love You Want* (New York: Henry Holt and Company, 1988).

Ari Kiev, M.D., *Active Loving* (New York: Crowell, 1979).

Ari Kiev, M.D., *How to Keep Love Alive* (New York: Barnes & Noble Books, 1982).

Madonna Kolbenschlag, *Kiss Sleeping Beauty Goodbye* (New York: Harper and Row, 1979).

Sheldon B. Kopp, *If You Meet Buddha on the Road, Kill Him* (New York: Bantam, 1973).

Law and Marriage: Your Legal Guide (Chicago: American Bar Association Press, 1983).

Linda Leonard, *The Wounded Woman: Healing the Father–Daughter Relationship* (Athens, OH: Ohio University Press, 1982).

Robert Masello, *What Do Men Want From Women?* (New York: Ballantine Books, 1983).

Rollo May, *Love and Will* (New York: Dell Publishing, 1969).

Milton Mayeroff, *On Caring* (New York: Harper & Row, 1971).

Carl Pearson, Ph.D., *The Hero Within* (New York: Harper and Row, 1986).

Stanton Peele with Archie Brodsky, *Love and Addiction* (New York: New American Library, 1975).

Carl D. Rogers, Ph.D., *Becoming Partners: Marriage and Its Alternative* (New York: Dell Publishing, 1972).

Carl D. Rogers, Ph.D., *On Personal Power* (New York: Delacorte Press, 1976).

Susan Schenkel, Ph.D., *Giving Away Success: Why Women Get Stuck and What To Do About It* (New York: McGraw-Hill, 1984).

Merle Shain, *Some Men Are More Perfect Than Others* (New York: Charterhouse, 1973).

Merle Shain, *When Lovers Are Friends* (New York: Lippincott Co., 1978).

"The Psalms of David," in the Old Testament of the Bible.

ORGANIZATIONS:

Miscellaneous Groups:

Battered Women's Hotline
(800) 333-SAFE

Big Beautiful Women
5535 Balboa Boulevard, Suite 214
Encino, CA 91316
Magazine for ample women.

FOCUS
550 Old Country Road
Hicksville, NY 11801
Specializing in child-support issues.

The Institute for the Study of Women in Transition
5 Market Street
Portsmouth, NH 03801
(603) 436-0981

International Pen Pals (IPF)
Box 65
Brooklyn, NY 11229
Att.: Leslie Fox, regional representative
(718) 934-5479

The Letter Exchange
P.O. Box 6218
Albany, CA 94706
Att.: Steve Sikora, Editor
A correspondence club.

Mothers Without Custody
P.O. Box 56762
Houston, TX 77256-6762
(301) 552-2319
Support groups for women living apart from their children.

National Organization for Women (NOW)
425 13th Street, N.W.
Washington, D.C. 20036
(202) 347-2279

Organization for the Enforcement of Child Support (OECS)
119 Nicodemus Road
Reisterstown, MD 21136
Att.: Elaine Fromm
(301) 833-2458

Personal Ads
Friendship Express
19611 Ventura Boulevard
Tarzana, CA 91356

Single Booklovers
Box AE
Swarthmore, PA 19081
Pen-pal group that connects people according to literary
    taste.

Tall Clubs International
c/o John Young, Secretary

825 North Hayden-C108
Scottsdale, AZ 85257
In Arizona: (602) 326-5373
Out-of-state: (800) 521-2512

Women's Equity Action League
12550 I Street, N.W., Suite 305
Washington, D.C. 20005
Specialists in women's economic issues.

Groups for Widows:

Theos Foundation Inc.
306 Penn Hills Mall
Pittsburgh, PA 15235
(412) 243-4299
Does work similar to the AARP's Widowed Persons Service.

Widowed Information and Consultation Services
15407 First Avenue South, Suite E
Seattle, WA 98148
Att.: Sharon Hale, program assistant
Will help others start a support group.

Widowed Persons Service
c/o AARP
1909 K Street, N.W.
Washington, D.C. 20049
(202) 728-4370, 71
A nationwide network of support groups for the widowed.

Sinai Hospital
Baltimore, MD
Att.: Adele Rice Nudel
(301) 578-5018
Will help locate or establish groups for *younger* widows.

Groups for Older Single Women:

American Association of Retired Persons (AARP)
1909 K Street, N.W.

Washington, D.C. 20049
(202) 728-4370, 71
Umbrella group for anyone over the age of 50, offering
group rates on insurance, travel, etc.; publishes *Modern
Maturity* magazine.

National Senior Sports Association, Inc.
10560 Main Street, Suite 205
Fairfax, VA 22030
Att.: Lloyd Wright, Director
(703) 385-7540

Older Women's League (OWL)
1325 "Y" Street, N.W., Lower-level B
Washington, D.C. 20005
(202) 783-6686

The Over-40 Club of America
Box 8502
Albuquerque, NM 87198
(505) 268-2827

Groups for the Disabled:

ACCESS (non-profit agency for disabled travelers)
(718) 263-3835

Independent Living Program for the Disabled
3601 Hempstead Turnpike
Levittown, NY 11756
(516) 796-0144

Mainstream Magazine
8861 Sixth Avenue, Suite 610
San Diego, CA 92101
Carries personal ads.

Peoplenet
257 Center Lane
Levittown, NY 11756
National newsletter that runs personal ads for people with
disabilities. Write for free brochure.

Greyhound buses and Amtrak trains have special services for the disabled who wish to travel.

Canwee Travel
553 Broadway
Massapequa, NY 11758
(516) 798-7171
Travel agency for the disabled.

Dating for the Disabled
P.O. Box 452
Katonah, NY 10536
(914) 232-8881
Serves New York City and its suburbs and also offers a national pen-pal service.

Handicapped Introductions (National Dating Service)
P.O. Box 232
Coopersburg, PA 18036
(215) 282-1577